About the author

Dominic Frisby writes an investment column for *MoneyWeek* and has written and produced numerous short films and videos. His script-writing ranges from episodes of the kids' show *Roary the Racing Car* to the feature documentary *The Four Horsemen*, about the global financial crisis. He is a frequent speaker on gold and money on television, radio and at conferences.

Frisby is also a comedian and actor, described as 'viciously funny and inventive' by the *Guardian*; 'masterful' by the *Evening Standard*; and 'great comedy talent' by Chortle.co.uk.

Day-to-day he is found trotting about the sound studios of London, voicing everything from BBC nature documentaries to zombies in Hollywood blockbusters.

He has also worked as a TV presenter, a boxing-ring announcer, a florist, a removal man, an extremely camp theatrical agent's PA, a sports commentator and a busker.

Life After the State is his first book.

The debasement of money has become a damaging but everyday feature of our lives. Its consequences are everywhere, yet, somehow, it goes unseen. The implications to all in society and on future generations are profound.

So I am delighted to be supporting Dominic with his book; he is a great communicator, and the issues he raises deserve a wide audience. Let us hope that his words inspire an optimistic debate leading to real and positive change.

ROBERT POCOCK

FOUNDER, FYI BUSINESS ECONOMICS LTD

Life After the State

Dominic Frisby

unbound

This edition first published in 2013

Unbound
4–7 Manchester Street, Marylebone, London, W1U 2AE
www.unbound.co.uk

The author and publisher would like to thank the following for allowing or
not raising objections to the use of copyright material: *English History 1914–
1945* by A. J. P. Taylor (Oxford University Press, 1965) © Oxford University
Press; *The Rational Optimist: How Prosperity Evolves* by Matt Ridley (Fourth
Estate, 2011) © Matt Ridley; *The End of Politics and the Birth of iDemocracy*
by Douglas Carswell (Biteback Publishing, 2012) © Douglas Carswell;
Capitalism and Freedom by Milton Friedman (University of Chicago Press,
2002) © The University of Chicago; *Liberty Versus the Tyranny of Socialism* by
Walter E. Williams (Hoover Institution Press, 2008) © Walter E. Williams.

Typeset by Palindrome
Cover design by Mecob

A CIP record for this book is available from the British Library

ISBN 978-1-908717-89-4 (Trade)
ISBN 978-1-908717-88-7 (Ebook)
ISBN 978-1-908717-90-0 (Limited edition)

Printed in England by Clays Ltd, Bungay, Suffolk

Contents

Part IV
Towards Life After the State

To Samuel, Eliza, Lola and Ferdie,
who I love more than life itself

I hope you get to experience life after the state

With special thanks to Brian Cartmell

The more laws and restrictions there are,
The poorer people become . . .
The more rules and regulations,
The more thieves and robbers.

Therefore the sage says:
I take no action and people are reformed.
I enjoy peace and people become honest.
I do nothing and people become rich.
I have no desires and people return to the good and simple life.

Lao Tsu, *Tao Te Ching*

Prologue:
Why Every Cuban Father Wanted His Daughter
To Be a Hooker

In the 1990s, when I was in my twenties, I was mad about Latin America. I loved the people, the tropical weather, the forests, the mountains, the beaches, the language, the ancient history – and I was nuts about the music. All I wanted to do was go there and have adventures. Every year I would catch a cheap Boxing Day flight and come back at the beginning of February. I went to all sorts of wonderful places: Colombia, Bolivia, Brazil, Chile, Guatemala, Peru, Honduras and, in 1996, Cuba.

This wasn't at the height of Cuban repression. Fidel Castro was still president and the very worst of the poverty that followed the collapse of the Soviet Union was now behind it. But the country was still desperately poor.

Havana was an amazing place, full of contrasts. The only cars were either huge American classics – symbols of booming 1950s USA that looked like something off the set of *Back to the Future* – or dour and bleak Ladas that had been imported from the Soviet Union in the 1970s and 80s, symbolic of the Cold War and communism. There were magnificent Art Deco or Art Nouveau buildings, yet there'd be a hole in the roof, or part of it had fallen down. There were pro-Castro symbols and slogans everywhere you looked, but the walls on which they were painted would be crumbling. The entire city looked like it needed re-rendering.

After one obligatory, over-priced night in a government hotel, I found a room in a Havana apartment belonging to a well-educated

Cuban family. Luis was a political economist and a professor, no less; Celia was a doctor. They had three young children: two girls and a boy.

I had gone to Cuba with preconceived notions about what an amazing place it was. Any problems it had were entirely due to sanctions and other American punishments, I thought. It had the best health service in the world, the best education in the world and was a shining example to the greedy West on how things could be run. I don't know where I got those ideas from – conversations at university, probably – but Luis quickly put me right.

'What is the point of a great hospital, if there is no medicine?' he would whisper to me. 'What is the point of great schools when you have no paper?' I didn't have an answer.

I say whisper. Criticism, even indoors, was always whispered. Many Cubans would loudly declare how wonderful the regime was, surreptitiously look about to check no potential informant was in earshot, then come up close and whisper, 'I hate Castro' – or something along those lines. So oppressive was the regime that paranoia, secrets, denial and deception permeated every area of life. People didn't dare to be honest. They were too scared of what the repercussions might be.

Some Cuban friends of mine in London had told me before I left, 'You need dollars. You can't buy anything with pesos.' I was a pretty intrepid explorer in those days and dismissed this advice. I thought I'd be able to get off the beaten track into the real Cuba, where I could use pesos like real Cubans. But my friends were right. You couldn't. There was, simply, nothing available to buy with pesos. There were no shops or businesses that accepted pesos, except the odd street stall that sold ice cream or bits of cooked dough, loosely described as pizza. Cubans got their bread and other essentials with ration books and a lot of queuing.

Western goods did exist. Clothing, electrical and hardware goods, and food and drink – Havana Club rum, beer, cheese and cured meats, for example – were sold in grey, colourless supermarkets. The supermarkets were not at all cheap and, despite the fact that they were state-run, would only accept US dollars – one of the many hypocrisies I would encounter.

So the only way anyone could buy anything was with US dollars at a state-run store. However, most people were employed by the government in some way or other, and paid in Cuban pesos. So how did they get dollars?

The answer was: from tourists.

Luis and Celia got their dollars renting out a room to people like me. Most Cubans didn't have the option of an apartment with three bedrooms. (Luis's parents had somehow managed to avoid it being expropriated.) Some were lucky enough to have the use of a car and could be taxi drivers. But this was another option that was only available to a tiny few – there was no manufacture of cars and no import trade. You, or more likely your parents, would have somehow had to have acquired a car way back when, and kept hold of it. There were a few restaurants and bars scattered about, and a tiny, well-connected elite could become waiters. Where did that leave everyone else?

As an economist and a doctor, you'd expect Luis and Celia to be a fairly wealthy couple. And by Cuban standards they earned good salaries – about 500 pesos a month each. The official exchange rate was one peso to the dollar, thus they earned the equivalent of $500. The unofficial rate, however – the real market rate – was 20:1, so Luis and Celia's 500 pesos amounted to about $25. A pair of jeans in the supermarket cost twice that. But, remember, you couldn't actually buy anything with pesos.

One night's rent from me was more money than Luis, with a PhD, would earn in an entire month. A taxi driver might land that figure in two or three fares. On a good night, a waiter might earn that in tips. But the big money was in selling sex. If she found a generous boyfriend, a prostitute – a 'jinetera', as they were called – could earn many times that in one night.

More than any of the other European nations, it was Italy that seemed to have caught the Cuba bug. My flight out was full of Italians. All over Havana there were Italians. They loved Cuba. I naively thought it might have to do with the historical links between

Italy and communism, but wandering around Havana I soon saw another reason. The Italian men loved the black Cuban women – and vice versa, it seemed. Everywhere you looked you'd see stylish Italian men arm in arm with young Cuban black girls, their paid girlfriends for the two weeks they spent there.

Cuban men were selling their bodies too. A rather plump Greek-English woman I knew in her late forties married a beautiful (yes, beautiful) man – a 'jinetero' – at least 25 years her junior. I had to deliver some money to him for her. I was amazed when I met him. He looked like a young Sidney Poitier. She looked like a chubby, middle-aged Bette Midler. A most unlikely couple.

In some cases, I've no doubt, couples fell in love. Marriages and families may have resulted. Cuba is a famously sexual country. I expect that many of the jineteras derived some occasional pleasure from their work. But, in most cases, the reality was rather more dark and sinister. Their economic circumstances meant that these people felt they had no other option but prostitution, if they wanted to improve their lot.

It's hard to believe just how widespread 'jineterismo' was, and probably still is. There has been no formal study, but anecdotally it appears that more than 50% of Cuban women below 50 have practised prostitution at some stage – if not with a tourist, then with another Cuban.

*

'Everyone is jinetera,' said Luis. 'Look around. Everyone. Jinetero, jinetera. Look what Fidel has done to our country. Look what he has done to our people'.

We were sitting on the Malecón – the wall which runs along the Havana sea front – watching good-looking jineteros and jineteras attempting to snare a tourist. Of all the Latin American countries I visited, I found I had the most intense conversations in Cuba. This was one of them. I transcribed it into my diary later that night. 'I don't want my children to be a doctor like their mother, or a political economist like me. What is the point? MD, PhD, a month's work and I cannot buy a pair of shoes.' Luis continued: 'Useless life. A much better life for my son is if he is a taxi driver or a waiter. Then he can get dollars. Maybe he can get a tourist to fall in love with him. And my daughters? I tell you a secret. I pray my daughters will be beautiful. Every father does. So they can have tourist boyfriends, have money, maybe marry a tourist, and get out of here. That is why every Cuban father wants his daughter to be a jinetera. Jinetera – that is the best life you can have here, that is how you survive, that is how you escape. Thank you, Fidel!'

The Four Lessons I Took from Cuba and How they Apply to Us

I don't know what the motivation behind Castro's great revolution was or why he and his cohorts made the economic and political choices they did – lust for power, political idealism, or, maybe, just to get rid of Batista. It seems his decision to ally himself with the Soviet Union was, at least initially, more of a reaction to US aggression and sanctions than any deep Marxist sentiment. I very much doubt their intention was the eventual consequence: a society so imbalanced and distorted that taxi drivers and uneducated young people could earn, in one night, many times more than a professor, a doctor, a lawyer or an engineer might earn in a month; where the large majority of young girls in Havana were selling their bodies for dollars, and where every Cuban father wanted his daughter to be a jinetera.

Cuba was probably my first lesson in the Law of Unintended Consequences. And my story illustrates many of the themes of this book: the power of the state; how the state interferes in people's lives; how political decisions, often made out of expediency, even if benevolent, can have such grave and unexpected repercussions; why the freedom to trade and exchange is so important; and how, if you limit that freedom, you limit people's possibilities.

The useless peso, moreover, was my first experience of how essential a properly functioning system of money is to a society, and what can happen when politicians start to use money as a political tool.

So what?

I think those lessons could be applied to us here in the West in 2013. Of course, we're not at the stage where we want our daughters to be jineteras. But I believe – and I don't think I'm alone in this – that we've gone badly wrong in the developed world.

I'd like to ask you to remember where you were a decade or so ago, in the year 2000. I'm going to list some of the things that have happened since then. Did it cross your mind that we would see . . .

- Two stock market crashes of 1929 proportions and a financial crisis that almost brought down the entire global banking system.
- Youth unemployment in Greece at 62.5%, Spain at 57%, Portugal at 43%, Italy at 40% and an EU average of 24.4%.[1] With the Greeks calling Germans Nazis.
- Interest rates at almost zero for years on end, runs on banks as people discover their money isn't safe and the Bank of England actually *printing* money.
- The average age of the first-time house buyer at almost 40, with an entire generation of people in the UK believing they will never own a home.
- Obesity rates of 25% in the developed world, yet almost a billion people suffering from chronic undernourishment.[2]
- 36 million people across the globe taking part in 3,000 protests against a war in the Middle East – and UK and US government ignoring them and going ahead with it anyway.[3]
- UK health-care spending more than doubling from £68 billion to £143 billion[4] in the 11 years to 2011, yet 'basic clinical failings' being commonplace across the NHS – with one NHS trust found liable for 1,200 people dying while in its care and a further five facing investigation.[5]
- Spending on schools in the UK rising by over 86%,[6] yet the government's own inspector declaring 'standards have stalled'.[7]
- And debt. Oh, my goodness. The UK currently owes, excluding bank bail-out costs, just under £1.2 trillion.[8] That's

almost £40,000 per working person. In just five years the coalition government, on a so-called austerity drive, will add £700 billion to the national debt. That's more than the combined total of every British government of the past 100 years. For all the talk of 'fiscal cliffs' and 'debt ceilings' in the US, President Barack Obama has overseen an administration that, in its first term, increased the national debt by 60%, adding $6 trillion, on top of the $5 trillion Bush added in his two terms. The first 41 presidents only managed $2 trillion combined.[9]

Many of these things were unthinkable, yet they are now part of our daily experience. So much seems to be going wrong. Is this just an inevitable fact of life, or is it something else? I happen to think it's something else. And that's what this book is about. Many of our most fundamental institutions, social arrangements, economic policies and political ideas seem to be breaking down. They are either in acute crisis, or close to it. Things that we have taken for granted for decades – that a bank is a safe place to put money, that the NHS looks after its patients, or that European countries have left the conflicts of the Second World War behind them, for example – are now in doubt. If we are coming to some sort of boiling point, it's essential to understand what the fundamental problems actually are and how they came about, otherwise there is the real danger that, misguidedly, we replace what we have with something worse – as happened with Fidel Castro's great Cuban revolution, Communist Russia and Nazi Germany. 'Only a crisis – actual or perceived,' said economist Milton Friedman, 'produces real change. When that crisis occurs, the actions that are taken depend on the ideas that are lying around. That, I believe, is our basic function: to develop alternatives to existing policies, to keep them alive and available until the politically impossible becomes the politically inevitable.'[10]

I subscribe to George Orwell's view that, 'on the whole human beings want to be good, but not too good, and not quite all the time.'[11] The problem, as I see it, is not so much individuals but systems.

Accidentally or otherwise, our systems of government, finance and economics have been modified and manipulated and now no longer have the effects their originators intended; they have become entrenched, out of anyone's control, and seemingly impossible to change or remove. It feels like the West is an unstoppable train, hurtling down the tracks; but we are on the *wrong* tracks, going to the wrong place. Nothing seems to slow this train, let alone reverse it. It's too big; it's going too fast. But in this book I'm going to show you a simple method whereby the points on the railway – what Americans call 'the railroad switch' – can be changed and the train re-routed.

Not So Funny: How a Stand-up Comedian Came To Write About Money

People never stop thinking about ways to make money, but barely a soul questions what money actually is. Children do, but adults seem to forget. What is money? Who invents it? Who controls it? And, most important, what are the consequences?

In this book I discuss our system of money in depth, as I believe that reforming it is the only way we can surreptitiously re-route the unstoppable train. All those people agitating for change should forget marches or demonstrations, or calling for this or that regulation or ruling; if they all just concentrated on one thing – reforming our system of money – then, as I hope to show, freedom, justice, equality of opportunity and everything else they want can follow. We have to separate money and state.

There are many very intelligent and well-intentioned people who think the government needs to 'take more action to tackle the crisis'. Perhaps you are one of these. Perhaps you think more needs to be spent clamping down on benefit fraud, immigration or tax evasion; on better facilities in schools, better health care or environmental initiatives; on better policing, house-building, increased regulation of the banks or higher taxes for the rich. Different people have different ideas on what needs to be done.

But let me warn you now: the central tenet of this book is that the one big change governments need to make, aside from money reform, is that they do *less*. Not just a little bit less, but a lot less: almost nothing at all. Government inaction is key. Most of the problems we have are *because* of governments.

What I am agitating for is a society that is free and fair and content, a society with 'equality of opportunity'. But I don't believe the solutions lie in state action. The left wing might have the right goals, but the route is wrong. I believe, you could say, in socialism without the state.

I don't want to oppress anyone, to kill anyone, to leave anyone starving or without the basic necessities. When I talk about getting rid of state education for all, I don't want illiteracy to increase; I want it to decrease. When I talk about getting rid of the NHS, I don't want anybody to go without good medical attention; I want better and cheaper health care for all. When I talk about getting rid of welfare, I don't want people to be penniless or homeless; I want them to be prosperous – and happy. I don't want the rich and powerful lording it over us, nor tyranny, nor mind control, nor even censorship. But all of these things now flourish.

One final thing: I'm not an economist. I am a comedian.

As soon as you say that, people immediately want to know how funny you are. You can look me up on YouTube and make your own mind up.

I was never taught economics at school, at university or anywhere else. I don't have the 'right qualifications' to be writing a book like this. But in 2005 I became infatuated with the subject. I read insatiably. It was clear to me that 'something big' was coming, but mainstream economists, journalists, broadcasters – they all seemed oblivious. I started a podcast as an excuse to meet and talk to some of the minds that had so impressed me in my reading. Then I was asked to write a column for *MoneyWeek* magazine. Comedy became a second priority.

As a comedian you quickly learn that if they don't understand, they don't laugh. This enforces the discipline of clarity. There is no such discipline in the worlds of finance and economics. Frequently, the language used is unreadable – often deliberately, I suspect – using 'long words and exhausted idioms, like a cuttlefish squirting out ink', as George Orwell famously said.[12] The consequence is that many people feel alienated rather than fascinated by these worlds. You won't find that here, I hope. I am writing about matters that can be complicated, but I have tried to make them simple and accessible to all.

My dad argues that many of the ideas in this book will never happen. They're too unrealistic. He may be right but, as an anonymous internet poster who goes by the alias 'Injin' says: 'Find the right answer, realise you'll never see it in your lifetime, and then advocate it anyway, because it's the right answer.'[13]

If the state is now crumbling under the pressure of its debt and its spending obligations, it may have no future. Should you be afraid? No. A better world awaits, a world that is more just, free, progressive, peaceful and prosperous. It really isn't so impossible – if we can just re-route that train. It's time to try something else.

Life After the State.

Part I

The Rise of the Monster

1   How the Most Entrepreneurial City in Europe Became Its Sickest

The cause of waves of unemployment is not capitalism, but governments . . .
Friedrich Hayek, economist and philosopher[14]

In the 18th and 19th centuries, the city of Glasgow in Scotland became enormously, stupendously rich. It happened quite organically, without planning. An entrepreneurial people reacted to their circumstances and, over time, turned Glasgow into an industrial and economic centre of such might that, by the turn of the 20th century, Glasgow was producing half the tonnage of Britain's ships and a quarter of all locomotives in the world. It was regarded as the best-governed city in Europe and popular histories compared it to the great imperial cities of Venice and Rome. It became known as the 'Second City of the British Empire'.

Barely 100 years later, it is the heroin capital of the UK, the murder capital of the UK and its East End, once home to Europe's largest steelworks, has been dubbed 'the benefits capital of the UK'. Glasgow is Britain's fattest city: its men have Britain's lowest life expectancy – on a par with Palestine and Albania – and its unemployment rate is 50% higher than the rest of the UK.

How did Glasgow manage all that?

The growth in Glasgow's economic fortunes began in the latter part of the 17th century and the early 18th century. First, the city's location in the west of Scotland at the mouth of the river Clyde meant that it lay in the path of the trade winds and at least 100 nautical miles closer to America's east coast than other British ports – 200 miles closer than London. In the days before fossil fuels (which only found widespread use in shipping in the second half of the 19th century) the journey to Virginia was some two weeks shorter than the same journey from London or many of the other ports in Britain and Europe. Even modern sailors describe how easy the port of Glasgow is to navigate. Second, when England was at war with France – as it was repeatedly between 1688 and 1815 – ships travelling to Glasgow were less vulnerable than those travelling to ports further south.[15] Glasgow's merchants exploited these advantages and, by the early 18th century, the city had begun to assert itself as a trading hub. Manufactured goods were carried from Britain and Europe to North America and the Caribbean, where they were traded for increasingly popular commodities such as tobacco, cotton and sugar.

Through the 18th century, the Glasgow merchants' business networks spread, and they took steps to further accelerate trade. New ships were introduced, bigger than those of rival ports, with fore and aft sails that enabled them to sail closer to the wind and reduce journey times. Trading posts were built to ensure that cargo was gathered and stored for collection, so that ships wouldn't swing idly at anchor. By the 1760s Glasgow had a 50% share of the tobacco trade – as much as the rest of Britain's ports combined.[16] While the English merchants simply sold American tobacco in Europe at a profit, the Glaswegians actually extended credit to American farmers against future production (a bit like a crop future today, where a crop to be grown at a later date is sold now). The Virginia farmers could then use this credit to buy European goods, which the Glaswegians were only too happy to supply. This brought about the rise of financial institutions such as the Glasgow Ship Bank and the Glasgow Thistle Bank, which would later become part of the now-bailed-out, taxpayer-owned Royal Bank of Scotland (RBS).

Their practices paid rewards. Glasgow's merchants earned a great deal of money. They built glamorous homes and large churches and, it seems, took on aristocratic airs – hence they became known as the 'Tobacco Lords'. Numbering among them were Buchanan, Dunlop, Ingram, Wilson, Oswald, Cochrane and Glassford, all of whom had streets in the Merchant City district of Glasgow named after them (other streets, such as Virginia Street and Jamaica Street, refer to their trade destinations). In 1771, over 47 million pounds of tobacco were imported.[17]

However, the credit the Glaswegians extended to American tobacco farmers would backfire. The debts incurred by the tobacco farmers – which included future presidents George Washington and Thomas Jefferson (who almost lost his farm as a result) – grew, and were among the biggest grievances when the American War of Independence came in 1775. That war destroyed the tobacco trade for the Glaswegians. Much of the money that was owed to them was never repaid. Many of their plantations were lost. But the Glaswegians were entrepreneurial and they adapted. They moved on to other businesses, particularly cotton.

By the 19th century, all sorts of local industry had emerged around the goods traded in the city. It was producing and exporting textiles, chemicals, engineered goods and steel. River engineering projects to dredge and deepen the Clyde (with a view to forming a deep-water port) had begun in 1768 and they would enable shipbuilding to become a major industry on the upper reaches of the river, pioneered by industrialists such as Robert Napier and John Elder. The final stretch of the Monkland Canal, linking the Forth and Clyde Canal at Port Dundas, was opened in 1795, facilitating access to the iron-ore and coal mines of Lanarkshire.

The move to fossil-fuelled shipping in the latter 19th century destroyed the advantages that the trade winds had given Glasgow. But it didn't matter. Again, the people adapted. By the turn of the 20th century the Second City of the British Empire had become a world centre of industry and heavy engineering. It has been estimated that, between 1870 and 1914, it produced as much as one-fifth of the world's ships, and half of Britain's tonnage.[18] Among the 25,000 ships it produced were some of the greatest ever built: the *Cutty Sark*, the *Queen Mary*, HMS *Hood*, the *Lusitania*, the *Glenlee* tall ship and even the iconic Mississippi paddle steamer, the *Delta Queen*. It had also become a centre for locomotive manufacture and, shortly after the turn of the 20th century, could boast the largest concentration of locomotive building works in Europe.[19]

It was not just Glasgow's industry and wealth that was so gargantuan. The city's contribution to mankind – made possible by the innovation and progress that comes with booming economies – would also have an international impact. Many great inventors either hailed from Glasgow or moved there to study or work. There's James Watt, for example, whose improvements to the steam engine were fundamental to the Industrial Revolution. One of Watt's employees, William Murdoch, has been dubbed 'the Scot who lit the world' – he invented gas lighting, a new kind of steam cannon and waterproof paint. Charles MacIntosh gave us the raincoat. James Young, the chemist dubbed as 'the father of the oil industry', gave us paraffin. William Thomson, known as Lord Kelvin, developed the science of thermodynamics, formulating the Kelvin scale of absolute temperature; he also managed the laying of the first transatlantic telegraph cable.

The turning point in the economic fortunes of Glasgow – indeed, of industrial Britain – was WWI. Both have been in decline ever since. By the end of it, the British were drained, both emotionally and in terms of capital and manpower; the workers, the entrepreneurs, the ideas men, too many of them were dead or incapacitated. There was insufficient money and no appetite to invest. The post-war recession, and later the Great Depression, did little to help. The trend of the city was now one of inexorable economic decline.

If Glasgow was the home of shipping and industry in 19th-century Britain, it became the home of socialism in the 20th century. Known by some as the 'Red Clydeside' movement, the socialist tide in Scotland actually pre-dated the First World War. In 1906 came the city's first Labour Member of Parliament (MP), George Barnes – prior to that its seven MPs were all Conservatives or Liberal Unionists. In the spring of 1911, 11,000 workers at the Singer sewing-machine factory (run by an American corporation in Clydebank) went on strike to support 12 women who were protesting about new work practices. Singer sacked 400 workers, but the movement was growing – as was labour unrest. In the four years between 1910 and 1914 Clydebank workers spent four times as many days on strike than in the whole of the previous decade. The Scottish Trades Union

Congress and its affiliations saw membership rise from 129,000 in 1909 to 230,000 in 1914.[20]

The rise in discontent had much to do with Glasgow's housing. Conditions were bad, there was overcrowding, bad sanitation, housing was close to dirty, noxious and deafening industry. Unions grew quite organically to protect the interests of their members.

Then came WWI, and inflation. In 1915 many landlords responded by attempting to increase rent, but with their young men on the Western front, those left behind didn't have the means to pay these higher costs. If they couldn't, eviction soon followed. In Govan, an area of Glasgow where shipbuilding was the main occupation, women – now in the majority with so many men gone – organized opposition to the rent increases. There are photographs showing women blocking the entrance to tenements; officers who *did* get inside to evict tenants are said to have had their trousers pulled down.

The landlords were attacked for being unpatriotic. Placards read: 'While our men are fighting on the front line, the landlord is attacking us at home.' The strikes spread to other cities throughout the UK, and on 27 November 1915 the government introduced legislation to restrict rents to the pre-war level. The strikers were placated. They had won. The government was happy; it had dealt with the problem. The landlords lost out.

In the aftermath of the Russian Revolution of 1917, more frequent strikes crippled the city. In 1919 the 'Bloody Friday' uprising prompted the prime minister, David Lloyd George, to deploy 10,000 troops and tanks onto the city's streets. By the 1930s Glasgow had become the main base of the Independent Labour Party, so when Labour finally came to power alone after WWII, its influence was strong. Glasgow has always remained a socialist stronghold. Labour dominates the city council, and the city has not had a Conservative MP for 30 years.

By the late 1950s, Glasgow was losing out to the more competitive industries of Japan, Germany and elsewhere. There was a lack of investment. Union demands for workers, enforced by government legislation, made costs uneconomic and entrepreneurial activity arduous. With lack of investment came lack of innovation.

Rapid de-industrialization followed, and by the 1960s and 70s most employment lay not in manufacturing, but in the service industries.

Which brings us to today. On the plus side, Glasgow is still ranked as one of Europe's top 20 financial centres and is home to some leading Scottish businesses. But there is considerable downside.

Recent studies have suggested that nearly 30% of Glasgow's working age population is unemployed.[21] That's 50% higher than that of the rest of Scotland or the UK. Eighteen per cent of 16- to 19-year-olds are neither in school nor employed. More than one in five working-age Glaswegians have no sort of education that might qualify them for a job.

In the city centre, the Merchant City, 50% of children are growing up in homes where nobody works. In the poorer neighbourhoods, such as Ruchill, Possilpark, or Dalmarnock, about 65% of children live in homes where nobody works – more than three times the national average.[22] Figures from the Department of Work and Pensions show that 85% of working age adults from the district of Bridgeton claim some kind of welfare payment.

Across the city, almost a third of the population regularly receives sickness or incapacity benefit, the highest rate of all UK cities. A 2008 World Health Organization report noted that in Glasgow's Calton, Bridgeton and Queenslie neighbourhoods, the average life expectancy for males is only 54. In contrast, residents of Glasgow's more affluent West End live to be 80 and virtually none of them are on the dole.

Glasgow has the highest crime rate in Scotland. A recent report by the Centre for Social Justice noted that there are 170 teenage gangs in Glasgow. That's the same number as in London, which has over six times the population of Glasgow.

It also has the dubious record of being Britain's murder capital. In fact, Glasgow had the highest homicide rate in Western Europe until it was overtaken in 2012 by Amsterdam, with more violent crime per head of population than even New York.[23] What's more, its suicide rate is the highest in the UK.

Then there are the drug and alcohol problems. The residents of the poorer neighbourhoods are an astounding six times more likely to die of a drugs overdose than the national average. Drug-related mortality has increased by 95% since 1997.[24] There are 20,000 registered drug users – that's just *registered* – and the situation is not going to get any better: children who grow up in households where family members use drugs are seven times more likely to end up using drugs themselves than children who live in drug-free families.

Glasgow has the highest incidence of liver diseases from alcohol abuse in all of Scotland. In the East End district of Dennistoun, these illnesses kill more people than heart attacks and lung cancer combined.[25] Men and women are more likely to die of alcohol-related deaths in Glasgow than anywhere else in the UK. Time and time again Glasgow is proud winner of the title 'Fattest City in Britain'. Around 40% of the population are obese – 5% morbidly so – and it also boasts the most smokers per capita.[26]

I have taken these statistics from an array of different sources. It might be in some cases that they're overstated. I know that I've accentuated both the 18th- and 19th-century positives, as well as the 20th- and 21st-century negatives to make my point. Of course, there are lots of healthy, happy people in Glasgow – I've done many gigs there and I loved it. Despite the stories you hear about intimidating Glasgow audiences, the ones I encountered were as good as any I've ever performed in front of. But none of this changes the broad-brush strokes: Glasgow was a once mighty city that now has grave social problems. It is a city that is not fulfilling its potential in the way that it once did. All in all, it's quite a transformation. How has it happened?

Every few years a report comes out that highlights Glasgow's various problems. Comments are then sought from across the political spectrum. Usually, those asked to comment agree that the city has grave, 'long-standing and deep-rooted social problems' (the words of Stephen Purcell, former leader of Glasgow City Council); they agree that something needs to be done, though they don't always agree on what that something is.

There's the view from the right: Bill Aitken of the Scottish Conservatives, quoted in *The Sunday Times* in 2008, said, 'We simply don't have the jobs for people who are not academically inclined. Another factor is that some people are simply disinclined to work. We have got to find something for these people to do, to give them a reason to get up in the morning and give them some self-respect.'[27] There's the supposedly apolitical view of anti-poverty groups: Peter Kelly, director of the Glasgow-based Poverty Alliance, responded, 'We need real, intensive support for people if we are going to tackle poverty. It's not about a lack of aspiration, often people who are unemployed or on low incomes are stymied by a lack of money and support from local and central government.' And there's the view from the left. In the same article, Patricia Ferguson, the Labour Member of the Scottish Parliament (MSP) for Maryhill, also declared a belief in government regeneration of the area. 'It's about better housing, more jobs, better education and these things take years to make an impact. I believe that the huge regeneration in the area is fostering a lot more community involvement and cohesion. My real hope is that these figures will take a knock in the next five or ten years.' At the time of writing in 2013, five years later, the figures have worsened.

All three points of view agree on one thing: the government must do something.

In 2008 the £435 million *Fairer Scotland Fund* – established to tackle poverty – was unveiled, aiming to allocate cash to the country's most deprived communities. Its targets included increasing average income among lower wage-earners and narrowing the poverty gap between Scotland's best- and worst-performing regions by 2017. So far, it hasn't met those targets.

In 2008 a report entitled 'Power for The Public' examined the provision of health, education and justice in Scotland. It said the budgets for these three areas had grown by 55%, 87% and 44% respectively over the last decade, but added that this had produced 'mixed results'.[28] 'Mixed results' means it didn't work. More money was spent and the figures got worse.

After the Centre for Social Justice report on Glasgow in 2008, Iain Duncan Smith (who set up this think tank, and is now the Secretary of State for Work and Pensions) said, 'Policy must deal with the pathways to breakdown – high levels of family breakdown, high levels of failed education, debt and unemployment.'

So what are 'pathways to breakdown'? If you were to look at a chart of Glasgow's prosperity relative to the rest of the world, its peak would have come somewhere around 1910. With the onset of WWI in 1914 its decline accelerated, and since then the falls have been relentless and inexorable. It's not just Glasgow that would have this chart pattern, but the whole of industrial Britain. What changed the trend? Yes, empires rise and fall, but was British decline all a consequence of WWI? Or was there something else?

A seismic shift came with that war – a change which is very rarely spoken or written about. Actually, the change was gradual and it pre-dated 1914. It was a change that was sweeping through the West: that of government or state involvement in our lives. In the UK it began with the reforms of the Liberal government of 1906–14, championed by David Lloyd George and Winston Churchill, known as the 'terrible twins' by contemporaries. The Pensions Act of 1908, the People's Budget of 1909–10 (to 'wage implacable warfare against poverty', declared Lloyd George) and the National Insurance Act of 1911 saw the Liberal government moving away from its tradition of laissez-faire systems – from classical liberalism and Gladstonian principles of self-help and self-reliance – towards larger, more active government by which taxes were collected from the wealthy and the proceeds redistributed. Afraid of losing votes to the emerging Labour party and the increasingly popular ideology of socialism, modern liberals betrayed their classical principles. In his *War Memoirs*, Lloyd George said 'the partisan warfare that raged around these topics was so fierce that by 1913, this country was brought to the verge of civil war'.[29] But these were small steps. The Pensions Act, for example, meant that men aged 70 and above could claim between two and five shillings per week from the government. But average male life-expectancy then was 47. Today it's 77. Using the same ratio, and, yes, I'm manipulating statistics here, that's akin to only awarding pensions to people above the age 117 today. Back then it was workable.

To go back to my analogy of the prologue, this period was when the 'train' was set in motion across the West. In 1914 it went up a gear.

Here are the opening paragraphs of historian A. J. P. Taylor's most celebrated book, *English History 1914–1945*, published in 1965. I quote this long passage in full, because it is so telling.

> Until August 1914 a sensible, law-abiding Englishman could pass through life and hardly notice the existence of the state, beyond the post office and the policeman. He could live where he liked and as he liked. He had no official number or identity card. He could travel abroad or leave his country forever without a passport or any sort of official permission. He could exchange his money for any other currency without restriction or limit. He could buy goods from any country in the world on the same terms as he bought goods at home. For that matter, a foreigner could spend his life in this country without permit and without informing the police. Unlike the countries of the European continent, the state did not require its citizens to perform military service. An Englishman could enlist, if he chose, in the regular army, the navy, or the territorials. He could also ignore, if he chose, the demands of national defence. Substantial householders were occasionally called on for jury service. Otherwise, only those helped the state, who wished to do so. The Englishman paid taxes on a modest scale: nearly £200 million in 1913–14, or rather less than 8% of the national income. The state intervened to prevent the citizen from eating adulterated food or contracting certain infectious diseases. It imposed safety rules in factories, and prevented women, and adult males in some industries, from working excessive hours. The state saw to it that children received education up to the age of 13. Since 1 January 1909, it provided a meagre pension for the needy over the age of 70. Since 1911, it helped to insure certain classes of workers against sickness and unemployment. This tendency towards more state action was increasing. Expenditure on the social services had roughly doubled since the Liberals took office in 1905. Still, broadly speaking, the state acted only to help those who could not help themselves. It left the adult citizen alone.

All this was changed by the impact of the Great War. The mass of the people became, for the first time, active citizens. Their lives were shaped by orders from above; they were required to serve the state instead of pursuing exclusively their own affairs. Five million men entered the armed forces, many of them (though a minority) under compulsion. The Englishman's food was limited, and its quality changed, by government order. His freedom of movement was restricted; his conditions of work prescribed. Some industries were reduced or closed, others artificially fostered. The publication of news was fettered. Street lights were dimmed. The sacred freedom of drinking was tampered with: licensed hours were cut down, and the beer watered by order. The very time on the clocks was changed. From 1916 onwards, every Englishman got up an hour earlier in summer than he would otherwise have done, thanks to an act of parliament. The state established a hold over its citizens which, though relaxed in peacetime, was never to be removed and which the Second World war was again to increase. The history of the English state and of the English people merged for the first time.[30]

Since the beginning of WWI , the role that the state has played in our lives has not stopped growing. This has been especially so in the case of Glasgow. The state has spent more and more, provided more and more services, more subsidy, more education, more health care, more infrastructure, more accommodation, more benefits, more regulations, more laws, more protection. The more it has provided, the worse Glasgow has fared. Is this correlation a coincidence? I don't think so.

The story of the rise and fall of Glasgow is a distilled version of the story of the rise and fall of industrial Britain – indeed the entire industrial West. In the next chapter I'm going to show you a simple mistake that goes on being made; a dynamic by which the state, whose very aim was to help Glasgow, has actually been its 'pathway to breakdown' . . .

2   Mr Loss, Mr Gain and Miss Doubt

Stop there! Your theory is confined to that which is seen;
it takes no account of that which is not seen.
Frédéric Bastiat, liberal theorist and economist[31]

Meet Mr Loss. Someone's just thrown a brick through his window.
And that's actually good for the economy, say some, because Mr Loss
has to hire a glazier to repair the window. That involves spending
money with the glazier – we'll call him Mr Gain. His business benefits
and he now has capital to spend on something else: thus money now
flows through the system. Perhaps, then, we should all go round
throwing bricks through people's windows to help the economy.
What I'm describing is Frédéric Bastiat's theory of economics known
as 'broken window fallacy'.

The problem, as Bastiat argues, is that only money spent on the
glazier is tracked. Losses elsewhere are ignored. Had that money not
been spent on repairing his broken window, Mr Loss might have spent
it on something else – perhaps something that would have improved
his own productivity. This might have involved a purchase from someone else – who we'll call Miss Doubt. So, although our glazier Mr
Gain is the cost of a broken window better off, Mr Loss is the cost of
a window down; he is less productive than he might otherwise have
been; and Miss Doubt has – you guessed it – 'missed out' on a trade.
'It is not seen,' says Bastiat, 'that as the shopkeeper has spent six francs
upon one thing, he cannot spend them upon another. It is not seen
that if he had not had a window to replace, he would, perhaps, have replaced his old shoes, or added another book to his library. In short, he
would have employed his six francs in some way, which this accident
has prevented.'[32]

By the time the window is repaired, the greater economy is not even back at square one. We have a functioning window, but Mr Loss is the cost of a window worse off, as is, in effect, Miss Doubt. Mr Loss has also lost time.

To take this idea further, there is a common notion that war is good for the economy. War does boost government spending, yes. There are some parties, such as weapons manufacturers – the glazier, Mr Gain – who benefit from that spending, but this is all money that cannot now be spent elsewhere. The stimulus brought to one part of the economy comes at a direct, but unseen, cost to another sector of the economy (Mr Loss and Miss Doubt).

Who pays for war? The taxpayer pays for a large chunk of it. In most cases, I am sure the taxpayer would rather spend his money on something that benefits him, rather than the agenda of a politician. The next generation pays as well. Governments run up debts and deficits during war, which is left for the future to pay off. Those who have cash – savers – pay. Inflation always strikes during wars and, as prices rise, the purchasing power of money is eroded. Wealth is transferred from savers to debtors.

The time, resources and capital that go into the war are time, resources and capital that could have gone into other, more productive areas. So not only are people paying for the war through taxes, they are also paying for it through loss of business. And the cost is not just financial. War destroys property, lives – entire families.

The rebuilding effort that follows a war can produce booms, particularly in the construction sector, but these are often just restoring pre-war conditions. Instead of a rebuilt city, those resources could have gone on improving or enlarging the existing one – perhaps even building a second city – or on something else altogether.

There are people who benefit from war. The US benefited from both WWI and WWII – by staying out for as long as possible and selling goods to the European participants. The US was the metaphorical Mr Gain, the glazier. Not only did being Mr Gain of WWII drag the US out of the Great Depression, WWII accelerated the transfer of wealth, economic dominance and power from Western

Europe to the US so that it became the most dominant power on earth. But the majority don't benefit. They pay for it with their savings, lost opportunities and, often, their lives. Glasgow, and other industrial cities like it, were very much Mr Loss and Miss Doubt in the whole process.

This same theory does not just apply to war. It plays out every time government offers subsidy, stimulus and any other types of help. Subsidy – and indeed taxation – is the taking of money from one group and giving it to another. Those receiving the subsidy benefit. We might be shown numbers to prove how these incentives have brought benefit. But what about those who paid for it? These numbers never show us the unseen costs, Bastiat's 'what you don't see'. They never show us Mr Loss or Miss Doubt – the people who missed out. Unfortunately, there is no way to audit this 'what might have been'. You can only speculate.

When cost is unseen and unproven, an illusion of 'costlessness' is created. But there are always costs. There's always a Mr Loss and a Miss Doubt. The American economist Walter E. Williams says:

> How many times have we heard 'free tuition,' 'free health care,' and free you-name-it? If a particular good or service is truly free, we can have as much of it as we want without the sacrifice of other goods or services. Take a 'free' library; is it really free? The answer is no. Had the library not been built, that $50 million could have purchased something else. That something else sacrificed is the cost of the library. While users of the library might pay a zero price, zero price and free are not one and the same. So when politicians talk about providing something free, ask them to identify the beneficent Santa Claus or tooth fairy.[33]

One of the aims of this book is identify the 'tooth fairy' – Miss Doubt – and defend her. Man's productivity has dramatically increased over the last 100 years, and over the last 40 in particular. The two main facilitators of this increased productivity have been oil and the microchip. They have, effectively, brought down the cost of food, energy, industrial goods – just about everything. It has been estimated that we now spend 40–50% of our earnings in the West on food, clothing and shelter, as opposed to 80–90% in 1900.[34] Not only do we spend less but, generally speaking, quality is higher. Productivity has improved, costs have fallen, earnings have risen, yet, in the West, we are mostly poorer and more indebted than our parents. We shouldn't be. It should be the opposite.

This is all caused by hidden costs of tremendous proportions – a colossal, multi-generational 'Miss Doubt' factor at play. Despite the cost of most things falling, there is one cost that has risen: the cost of the state.

In the opening paragraphs of his book *The End of Politics*, Conservative MP Douglas Carswell states:

> The biggest purchase Western man will ever make is not your home or your children's education, it is government. $36 of every $100 an American earns now goes on government, £46 of every British workers' £100 and €59 of every French or German worker's €100 ... In 1900, a British household typically spent 8.5% of what they earned on government – a figure little changed since the days of the medieval tithe. In the United States and Europe, households spent between 5 and 15% of earnings on government.[35]

It is not simply that we spend more of our earnings. Earnings have increased and so, as Carswell says, 'the total resources allocated to government have increased by a magnitude of 30 to 40 times what they were'. But every time the state takes money from you, it creates a Mr Loss and a Miss Doubt.

Of course, government is giving us more than it used to. We all enjoy a little of Mr Gain's privileges: health care, education, social security and infrastructure, for example. But government is not giving us anything like 30 to 40 times more services – '30 times more officialdom maybe', Carswell notes. Some of the services it gives us are simply not very good. They have not seen anything like the improvements and the falls in cost that have been seen in areas in which government does not get so involved. Other 'services' it gives us are actually harmful, as I'll demonstrate later in the book. And there is also the issue of waste.

I want to come back now to the story of Glasgow, to speculate for a moment and consider the unseen costs – the unaudited 'what might have been'.

Let's imagine the state had never got involved and Glasgow, as it was in the 18th and 19th centuries, was left to itself. With no government involvement, the increasing numbers of disputes between Glasgow's workers and employers in the early 20th century would have had to be settled between themselves. Would employers have continued to put their employees in such awful conditions? If they did, would employees have gone elsewhere? Would pay and conditions have improved as mankind advanced, economies grew and people became more prosperous? We will never know.

More significantly, Glasgow would never have got so involved in the two World Wars. Its people did not vote for them. Without these wars, governments would never have been under the same pressure to provide welfare. Without the subsidy from welfare, dependency would not have been able to expand in the way that it has; money and other resources would never have been taken from taxpayers, from future generations and all the other places government sources it – all of whom would now be in a stronger position, instead of increasingly dependent themselves. A vicious cycle was created – with Mr Loss and Miss Doubt taking greater and greater losses – and it has never stopped spiralling.

Even if shipbuilding was destined to move East, and that is arguable, Glaswegians had repeatedly shown that they are a highly entrepreneurial, formidable people able to successfully deal with change and evolve. They adapted when the tobacco industry was killed by the American War of Independence. They lost their trade winds advantage when the development of steam ships put an end to the Age of Sail, but adapted again. As the 20th century progressed, Glasgow would have had to continue to adapt and modernize. History suggests it would have done so successfully – had government not got in the way with its wars and subsidies.

Perhaps the city wouldn't have been able to continue growing, but instead would have had to contract. That would have been painful, yes. It would have forced economic migration and the death of some businesses. But these have happened anyway. What would have emerged might have been smaller, but it would also be leaner, more efficient, self-sufficient – and not a drain on everywhere else.

Instead, welfare has meant that things can limp on. It has led to an acceptance of reduced circumstance that has trapped people, and not only created an underclass but empowered it to grow – the very opposite of what welfare's founders intended. Now the situation is such that any re-adjustment process will be extremely painful, many times more painful than it should have been.

Billions of pounds have been spent in Glasgow on infrastructure, housing, benefits, health, education, subsidy and other attempts at regeneration – all with the very best intentions. But more and more people have fallen into welfare rather than escaping from it. As Ronald Reagan once said, 'We should measure welfare's success by how many people leave welfare, not by how many are added.'[36] The UK has already spent more money than it has on its various schemes and, in the process, enslaved ourselves and the next generation to taxes and debt. Why not try something else?

It was Albert Camus who said, 'The evil in the world almost always comes of ignorance, and good intentions may do as much harm as malevolence if they lack understanding.'[37] With all that money that has been thrown not just at Glasgow but at all of former industrial Britain, no influential policy-maker appears to have considered, 'Who pays?', 'Who loses out by this?', or 'What will the side-effects be?'. What about Mr Loss and Miss Doubt?

This is why I argue that the best thing that government can do is nothing. It should stop intervening through wars, the welfare state, subsidy, regulation, taxation, planning and all the other ways it finds to interfere. These actions have unintended consequences.

Glasgow could have sorted its own problems out. It still can. There's enough character, enterprise and invention there to do it. If Glasgow is to revive and grow, great. If it is to shrink, so be it. Death is a part of life. Don't create zombies. The best way for government to help people is not to.

3   The Freedom That Dare Not Speak Its Name

How to Make Progress and Prosperity Inevitable

Prosperity comes from everybody working for everybody else.
Matt Ridley, scientist and author[38]

In his compelling book *The Rational Optimist*, Matt Ridley demonstrates how by doing something no other animal does – by exchanging things – *Homo sapiens* overtook the stronger Neanderthals and, indeed, the rest of the animal kingdom, to become the dominant species on earth. He states that: 'There was a point in human pre-history when . . . people for the first time began to exchange things with each other, and that once they started doing so, culture suddenly became cumulative, and the great headlong experiment of human economic "progress" began. Exchange is to cultural evolution as sex is to biological evolution.'[39]

This applies not just to the exchange of objects, but the exchange of ideas, knowledge and information, of skills and services – just about anything. 'If I catch the food, you cook it' means that I could specialize in catching – and become better at it – while you could specialize in cooking and become better at that. With my superior catching and your superior cooking we both now enjoy considerably better lifestyles, and mankind also progresses through the subsequent improvement of catching and cooking techniques. It is through exchange that man has progressed to the extent that we now take for granted such luxuries as electricity and running water that were unheard of to people not so long ago.

We are only able to do what we do today because of what was done in the past. It is only because of the cumulative work of millions of people – from Steve Jobs to Alan Turing to Shakespeare to millions of people who I'll never know or even hear of – that I am able to write this book on this computer. I don't know how to build a computer; I don't know how to extract the oil necessary to manufacture its component parts; I can't make paper or ink or printing presses, yet, because of the cumulative effects of the exchanges of millions of people, I'm now able to exchange my work – itself the product of studying the work of many others – with you.

Writing to the scientist Robert Hooke in 1676, Isaac Newton famously described the same phenomenon. 'What Descartes did was a good step. You have added much several ways . . . If I have seen further it is by standing on the shoulders of giants.'[40] That expression is famously now also associated with Einstein, Oasis – it's even quoted on the £2 coin.

The collective intelligence of mankind is far, far greater than what can be held in the mind of even the brightest individual that ever lived. This collective intelligence keeps on growing. There is no limit to it. 'The extraordinary thing about exchange,' says Ridley, 'is that it breeds: the more of it you do, the more of it you can do. And it calls forth innovation.'[41] The more we exchange, the more we progress. This accumulation of intelligence over generations has led to a situation where, even a hundred years ago, to quote the French philosopher Ernest Renan, 'The simplest schoolboy is now familiar with truths for which Archimedes would have sacrificed his life'.[42]

But the reverse applies as well. When we stop exchanging, there is regression. As Ridley argues, 10,000 years ago rising seas isolated Tasmania from mainland Australia. Cut off, the possibilities for exchange diminished. Technologically, the Tasmanian people actually regressed.

Exchange is limited under oppressive, totalitarian or bureaucratic regimes, which is why they are overtaken by freer neighbours. To an extent, this is what happened in Glasgow: government intervention in all its many forms created barriers to exchange that didn't exist elsewhere and Glasgow was left behind.

It follows, therefore, that for individuals, families, communities, nations – indeed mankind – to prosper, progress and fulfil their potential, there need to be conditions that are optimal for exchange. It really is that simple – and creating these conditions should be the primary agenda of every policy-maker and leader in the world.

This means a marketplace where, from tax to tariff to bureaucracy, there are as few barriers to exchange as possible. It means a marketplace where there is trust and confidence. It means a marketplace in which ownership of property is clear and secure. It means a marketplace where participants can operate without coercion or crime; where good practice is rewarded and bad practice meets with failure. It also means a marketplace whose medium of exchange – money – is dependable.

I'm talking, of course, about a free market.

Is this Capitalism?

There is no pure free market economy.
Jeane Kirkpatrick, former US Ambassador to the United Nations [43]

Many associate the term 'free market' with exploitation and the rampant greed of the 1980s Thatcher–Reagan era – of yuppies, Harry Enfield's 'Loadsamoney' and Michael Douglas as Gordon Gekko in *Wall Street* declaring, 'Greed is good.' Though they came to be called that, these were not free markets in the purest sense; they were not 'capitalist'. What was born under Thatcher and Reagan in the 1980s was something different; a form of 'crony capitalism'. The term 'free market' and, indeed, the term 'capitalism' were both corrupted; they are now wrongly associated with exploitation.

A simple example of a free market transaction might take place in my local shop. The keeper sells loaves of bread for one money unit. I want a loaf, I am happy to pay that price and I buy one. The transaction takes place voluntarily; it involves us and us alone, and we both find benefit – that is key: I now have some bread; the shopkeeper has some money. Another simple example: I see a company is advertising for a writer for which it is prepared to pay X amount of money. I am looking for work and am happy to sell my labour for that fee;

the company likes my writing – my labour – I am employed by said company and we both benefit – they from my writing, me from their payment.

As soon as there is any kind of intervention or coercion, that market is no longer 'free', in the pure sense of the word. Tax is one way governments intervene in the market place. I always loved Walter E. Williams's demonstration of this:

> Suppose I hire you to repair my computer. The job is worth $200 to me and doing the job is worth $200 to you. The transaction will occur because we have a meeting of the mind. Now suppose there's the imposition of a 30% income tax on you. That means you won't receive $200 but instead $140. You might say the heck with working for me – spending the day with your family is worth more than $140. You might then offer that you'll do the job if I pay you $285. That way your after-tax earnings will be $200 – what the job was worth to you. There's a problem. The repair job was worth $200 to me, not $285. So it's my turn to say the heck with it. This simple example demonstrates that one effect of taxes is that of eliminating transactions, and hence jobs.[44]

That tax has become a barrier to exchange: it has the very opposite effect of encouraging it.

Almost every transaction that takes place today involves a state intervention of some kind: we must use government money – the pound, the dollar and the euro are all government monies and not freely chosen by market participants – and most transactions involve tax. Whatever your views on the rights and wrongs of a particular tax, taking money forcefully from one group and giving it to another is a form of coercion or extortion, with another body arbitrarily deciding what money that you have earned should be spent on. It is not free. This is perhaps why Jeane Kirkpatrick, Ronald Reagan's US ambassador to the United Nations, was moved to say, 'There is no pure free market economy.'

Most dealings with the government are not of the free market. You pay for government services whether you want them or not:

if you don't pay tax on your earnings, you face fines and even jail. Subsidy, regulation, taxation, legislation, monetary policy, welfare: these are all ways through which, rightly or wrongly, government intervenes in the economy – the market place – over which we are given no power except for a vote in an election every four or five years. Whether you agree with its policy or not, your dealing with government is not voluntary, but coercive. Government is the very antithesis of 'free market'.

The Thatcherite and Reaganite booms of the 1980s and '90s are perceived as 'free market' because a lot of de-regulation took place. They even branded themselves as 'free market'. But they weren't. First, because government – which, as I say, is not of the 'free market' – was actually expanding in the West, as were its agencies. State spending was growing, welfare was growing, stealth taxes were increasing, more and more people were employed by government, and more and more people were becoming dependent on it.

Second, because of money. In a 'free market' those operating in it decide what they use as money. It might be paper, gold, shells, feathers, a digital code. But then, just as now, we had to use government money (actually, the currency laws are a bit more complicated that that, but the point remains).

*

State protection, welfare and subsidy are, more often than not, a well-meaning attempt to help a group of people, but one of the unintended side-effects is that they lay the foundations for special interest groups to rise up – groups who benefit from the subsidy and then tend to lobby for more of it. Such lobbying, known by economists as 'rent-seeking', sees people try to gain a share of wealth that has already been created. Rather than actually build new wealth, instead they try to manipulate and exploit an existing social, economic or political environment. If they are successful, rent-seekers (a term you are going to hear a lot in this book) are then given some special privilege – a subsidy, a grant, favourable legislation, exemption from some kind of tax that others have to pay – and wealth is redistributed to that special interest group. This is not free market capitalism, but crony capitalism in another guise.

In the UK, for example, we have some theatre that is subsidized and some that isn't. Some would argue that the subsidized group deserves this help. That may or may not be so. But as soon as you declare one group is deserving and another isn't, as well as distorting the market, you descend into the realm of moral hazard. Who is government to declare which groups are worthy and which aren't? Why is one play worthy and another not?

Using my example of theatre, the group that is subsidized is now able to pay more and so acquire better talent, premises, advertising and so on than the unsubsidized group. Audiences are usually attracted to the theatre that has the better talent, the more persuasive advertising and so on, so that is where they spend their money. Meanwhile, as well as losing their audience, the costs of the unsubsidized group are also pushed up – they have to spend more to compete with the subsidized group for the various services they need. They might then have to put up their ticket prices. Higher ticket prices are, generally, harder to sell and limit the range of potential customers to a wealthier demographic. All in all, subsidy makes it now more difficult for the unsubsidized group – which is squeezed on both sides – to operate than it otherwise would have been. Subsidy actually creates barriers to exchange – the very opposite of what is intended. Many unsubsidized groups now go out of business and the subsidized group finds itself with a greater market share, often a monopoly. People then say, thank goodness for the subsidized group, otherwise we would have no artistic theatre of merit.

Theatre is already a hard enough business to be successful in without subsidy making it worse. Yet the huge majority who work in the arts, even if they don't receive subsidy, see arts subsidy as 'a good thing'. Yes, subsidy might benefit the Royal National Theatre and whoever else receives it, but it is detrimental to everyone else. As David Boaz, vice-president of US think-tank the Cato Institute says, 'Taxing your competitors to subsidize your industry is a rent-seeker's dream.'

Just as the man from the council always spends his budget to make sure he gets it next year, so are subsidized groups motivated to actually get costs up in order to secure further subsidy next year. The cycle is perpetuated.

This practice of seeking some kind of privilege and then exploiting it once it has been granted is entrenched in Western economies. All sorts of dogma (opinion presented as fact) and memes get spread about how this or that particular group must receive special favour. Bankers, for example, leaned on policy-makers to bail them out in 2008. Otherwise, they said, 'the whole financial system comes crashing down.' Celebrities get together every few years and persuasively lobby parliament that the arts must have more subsidy or we risk 'losing London's status as the theatre capital of the world'. The BBC maintains that the licence fee is essential to preserve the status of 'the best broadcaster in the world'. Doctors must be paid a certain wage and given other benefits 'or their services will be lost'. We must spend more to 'preserve the NHS, otherwise we lose the greatest health service in the world'. If we build many more homes, 'our beautiful countryside will be destroyed'. Governments must 'do more to tackle global warming' and 'fund recycling and alternative energy initiatives' otherwise the world is going to end. You may or may not agree with the arguments – I make no judgement – but they are all areas in which dogma is rife, government intervention widespread and rent-seeking endemic. Bankers, home-builders exploiting planning restrictions, lawyers cashing in on legal aid, government quangos and bureaucrats, doctors benefiting from NHS pay systems, councils dishing out overpriced parking tickets, state TV broadcasters, theatricals enjoying subsidy, or, simply, the unemployed – they all benefit from government intervention and protection in various ways. The amazing thing is that often the dogma is believed and spread by people who actually lose out by the intervention. Almost every theatrical I've ever met, for example, speaks in favour of the National Theatre and its subsidy, even if they've never had a job from it, are penniless and struggling to get work due to the fact that other opportunities in theatre are now so limited.

Rent-seeking is extremely lucrative for some, but it is not productive – in fact, it is destructive: it sucks capital from productive endeavour elsewhere and distorts markets. It is a barrier to exchange. Worse yet, as Anthony Ogus argues in his paper 'Corruption and Regulatory Structures',[45] 'Rent-seeking may, indeed, impose costs to the economy as high, if not higher, than those arising from corruption.'

Next time you are going about your daily business, keep an eye out for those who are either enjoying some sort of government-granted privilege, or pushing for more of it; look at how many things that exist in the world are a product of some kind of rent-seeking. It will terrify you how proliferative and ubiquitous it is. Whenever you hear phrases such as 'I know my rights', 'where's there's blame, there's a claim', 'unfair dismissal', 'health and safety', 'equal opportunities', I'll bet the issuance of some kind of government-bestowed privilege or protection is never far away. From parking and speeding fines to media licensing and pharmaceutical patenting to defence and infrastructure contracts, rent-seeking is everywhere. What's more, we are all at it to a greater or lesser degree; we all like to sip at the trough of government largesse.

But where we are given no special privilege, we have to operate by different, freer market rules and, *in addition*, subsidize rent-seekers that don't. I use the example of theatre, but far worse is the dual standard that is applied to banks. Profits are privatized (banks and their employees keep any profits made) – but risks are socialized (if the bank fails, the bank is bailed out). Without the real risk of failure – a natural regulation that a normal market would impose – recklessness is actually incentivized. Bail-outs, for example, had the opposite effect to that which was intended. Instead of reforming the system, they have made it worse. Changes in regulatory systems are now regarded as the answer. But Mother Nature has given us a very effective regulator already: it is called bankruptcy.

The situation with government institutions is more perilous. They are sacrosanct. Many of them are so incompetent and inefficient – the Inland Revenue, for example, Transport for London, or the NHS –

that they would have long since gone bust had they operated in a normal marketplace. Instead the government throws more and more money at them and they shuffle on with costs ever rising, impervious to the forces that would otherwise make them cheaper and more efficient. They cannot die. Many of these are the 'entrenched systems' – as I mentioned in the prologue – that need to be changed.

When government seeks to redistribute wealth, despite good intentions, they end up creating systems that are easy to manipulate; they create an environment that rent-seekers can exploit. The system under which we operate is not capitalist. There has been a systemic failure – absolutely, yes; however, that failure is not the fault of capitalism. It is 'crony capitalism' that has failed.

How Greed is Gaia

All the impediments to exchange spring from the state, for which
man in his ignorance of Natural Laws is to blame.
E. C. Riegel, author[46]

Charles Darwin's theory of natural selection drew in part on his study of economics, in particular the work of Thomas Malthus. Since the 1990s, and probably earlier, we have seen this reversed with economies now interpreted in biological terms. They are seen as living, breathing, evolving ecosystems. One of the pioneers of this was Michael Rothschild, who published *Bionomics: Economy as Ecosystem* in 1995. In his preface he writes, 'A capitalist economy can best be comprehended as a living ecosystem. Key phenomena observed in nature – competition, specialization, cooperation, exploitation, learning, growth, and several others – are also central to business life. Moreover, the evolution of the global ecosystem and the emergence of modern industrial society are studded with striking parallels.'[47]

I would like to consider Western economies in this light.

First of all, there is the issue of central planning. You cannot plan an ecosystem in the way that you might a farm. If there's one thing ecosystems do constantly, it's change: they evolve, they adapt, they shrink, they grow. Yet despite the obvious hazards of rigid planning in a world of constant change, in the West we increasingly adopt a fixed, top-down, one-size-fits-all approach – from the Chancellor and the central bank basing all its policies around an arbitrary target of a certain level of economic growth – usually 2–3% is deemed the right amount, for some reason – to the Department of Education setting its syllabus to determine what we learn, to the local council and its urban planning. No planner can possibly know all the facts, knowledge is dispersed and incomplete, the facts might be constantly changing, and said planner cannot possibly know what inventions and innovations are about to happen, nor account for other unpredictable things people are going to do. So how can they be sure they are making the right plans?

Take invention and discovery. The internet, as we know, has changed the world in myriad unforeseen ways, but even the internet was not planned, let alone the way it has unfolded – it was only invented as a means for the US military to share information. Penicillin was stumbled upon because Alexander Fleming didn't clean up his workstation one day; Coca Cola was invented by a pharmacist trying to make a cure for headaches; plastic by a man at home who thought he could make a bit of money if he came up with a cheaper way of insulating electronics than the 1907-standard, shellac, made from Asian beetles. The inherent unpredictability of invention means you need an economic system that is inherently flexible. Plans and mandates and targets and policies can all get in the way of that.

I'm not saying you shouldn't attempt to plan things; of course not. But there must be flexibility, a flexibility that does not exist in state systems as they now stand.

Centrally planned economies are always outperformed by disorganized, apparently chaotic market systems. South Korea, for example, is some 15 times more prosperous per head than its neighbour to the north. In the Soviet Union, time and time again, bumper wheat harvests never made it to the shops. There was no incentive in the form of trade and profit to calculate prices for freight trains, flour mills and so on – the various stages of the process to get to the eventual consumer. While the wheat sat unconsumed, the Russian starved. I am reminded of Thomas Jefferson's line, 'Were we directed from Washington when to sow, and when to reap, we should soon want bread.'[47] Evil though the word may be to some, profit – not planning – is what makes the economic ecosystem function.

Capital is like food. Usually, but not always, it will come in the form of profit. Without it businesses perish. The possibility of failure – of losing money – is as important a driver of efficiency and good practice as the possibility of gain. It guides investment, labour and production. If there is no longer a need or a customer for something – if that something no longer produces food – investment, labour and production will quickly move on. This makes the capitalist jungle inherently flexible. Loss-making firms die – and that might create grave problems for those involved, yes – but that is a necessary part of life. It is a waste to produce what is not needed.

However, an entity which is not dependent on profit, but on legislation or on some other decision within government for its food, has no such pressure on it. It must convince some policy-maker, rather than the market, that what it does is necessary. But the policy-maker – or planner – does not know as much as the market. He might think there is a need (perhaps he has been taken in by persuasive lobbying) when really there isn't. As long as the entity secures its funding, it can carry on doing what it does forever. The state can go on spending money on something irrelevant, unwanted and unneeded for generations. But this means capital is sucked away from other potentially productive endeavour, it creates a Mr Loss and a Miss Doubt and the ecosystem suffers.

In the same vein, Ridley writes, 'Because it is a monopoly, government brings inefficiency and stagnation to most things it runs; government agencies pursue the inflation of their budgets rather than the service of their customers; pressure groups form an unholy alliance with agencies to extract more money from taxpayers for their members. Yet despite all this, most clever people still call for government to run more things and assume that, if it did so, it would somehow be more perfect, more selfless, next time.'[49]

In *Obliquity*, the economist John Kay calls for 'order without design'. He writes:

> Evolution has a much better sense of what is good for us than we do ourselves. It is hard to overstate the damage done in the past by people who thought they knew more about the world than they really did. The managers and financiers who destroyed great businesses in pursuit of shareholder value. The architects and planners who believed buildings could be drawn on blank sheets of paper, and that expressways should be driven through the hearts of communities. The politicians who believed they could improve public services by the imposition of multiple targets. Acknowledging the complexity of the systems for which they were responsible and the multiple needs of the individuals who operated these systems would have avoided these errors. Such acknowledgements might also have avoided the gravest cases of public bad decision making of the last decade: the Iraq war and the credit expansion of 2003–7. Both these developments were predicated on a knowledge of the world that the decision makers did not in reality possess.[50]

The clash between the laissez-faire, non-interventionist style of government that I am advocating, as opposed to statists who, in general, feel governments should 'do more', reflects the clash between what philosophers call Natural Law and Positive Law – between Naturalists and Positivists. Positive Law, a term first used by the political philosopher Thomas Hobbes in his *Leviathan* in 1651, derives from the verb 'to posit', meaning to put in place. It means a law established by government and refers not just to laws but to legislation, regulations, decrees, orders and so on, which often grant or take away privileges from certain groups or individuals. Natural Laws, of which Hobbes's rival John Locke was a proponent, on the other hand, exist whether or not government enforces them; they are inherent – they're not conferred by an act of legislation.

It is Natural Law that we are born, that we grow, eat, sleep and reproduce, that we are social animals that live, for the most part, and support each other in groups; that we look after our children; that we have access to air, water and the natural world; that we do not murder people; that we do not enslave them; that we keep the profits of our endeavour; that we are free to live and pursue happiness, as long as it does not impinge on the liberty, life and happiness of others – and so on. Even the need for justice may be innate, as is suggested by the way children instinctively demand fairness.

It is Positive Law, however, that we must pay taxes, show official proof of who we are if we want to go to another country, use government money, pay penalties if we breach edicts. There is no government in the natural world that regulates the distribution of goods and benefits, or bestows certain groups with favourable legislation. According to Locke, who is now seen as the father of Classical Liberalism (now called Libertarianism) the role of government should be to enforce Natural Laws and no more. In my view we need to get ourselves back under the rule of this Natural Law – not just the role of the state, but in the whole way we live our lives.

The fairest, freest system – and the simplest to govern – must surely be one in which the rules are the same for all, and where we have equality. The best way to achieve that is with a market as free of intervention as possible, and with fewer, simpler regulations because as soon as one group is granted some privilege, an imbalance is created.

*

If you leave an economy alone and 'let nature take its course', won't the weak just get trodden on? This was Hobbes's fear and why he advocated his Positive Law. It was a means to keep people, who act mostly out of self-interest, well behaved. Without Positive Laws, the fear is those ruthless laws of the jungle – 'dog eat dog', 'kill or be killed' and 'every man for himself' – will take hold. The English philosopher Herbert Spencer, in his *Principles of Biology* (1864), reflected the view that Nature is cruel and heartless when he coined the phrase 'survival of the fittest'. But I suggest this is not a fair view. The natural world is also co-operative and symbiotic, with all sorts of species supporting each other in millions of weird, wonderful and, often, yet-to-be-discovered ways, while at the same time acting in their own interests. The jungle is in fact one of the richest, most fertile and most diverse places on earth. There is often order behind the apparent chaos – we just can't see it.

The BBC series *How Nature Works*, the international version of which I narrated, considers this very subject: the interconnectivity and interdependence of nature. One episode looked at grizzly bears in Alaska. In autumn they catch tonne after tonne of salmon, eat just the brains and eggs, the most fatty parts of the fish, and dump the rest on to the forest floor in what seems to be the most wasteful way. Thousands upon thousands of barely eaten salmon carcasses lie there rotting, as various slugs move in. But the rotting salmon, we discover, provides essential nutrients for trees and other plant life without which they would not survive the harsh Alaskan winter. When the snow melts, these same nutrients, now processed by the slugs and plants, are washed back down the river and into the ocean, where they provide essential food for the next generation of young salmon.

These same processes can be seen within individual beings, which are, in fact, communities of millions of cells, all interconnecting and supporting each other in ways we don't even yet know about.

Even predation reflects this co-operation and symbiosis. Lion eat antelope, and, in doing so, regulates the antelope population. This in turn protects plants and trees from being over-eaten. In other words, predation maintains the balance of nature – yet that balance is constantly evolving. It is part of nature's self-regulation. 'Since 'tis Nature's law to change,' wrote 17th-century poet John Wilmot, 'Constancy alone is strange.'[51]

If economies and societies are living, breathing ecosystems, then, left to their own devices, without intervention and interference, they can and do work in the same co-operative and symbiotic way as nature.

Death is a part of life. It is essential to the jungle's system of self-regulation and evolution. Bad businesses and obsolete practices must be allowed to wither and sometimes die. That is Natural Law. They cannot be propped up and bailed out, for that way zombies lie. Zombies hinder the birth of newer, better businesses, in the process Joseph

Schumpeter famously described as 'creative destruction', because they devour capital. The entrepreneur Luke Johnson writes, 'One of the wonderful things about markets is that they self-correct ruthlessly: companies that fail to serve the customer will be overwhelmed by rivals – and go bust – and see their assets reallocated.'[52] It is when there is perceived to be no potential loss that you get misallocation of capital, malinvestment and bubbles.

Extrapolate this natural, free-market efficiency through the billions of lattices of global trade and you have – to quote James Lovelock's 'Gaia principle' – the potential for an enormous, efficient 'self-regulating complex system'. It is a wonderful thought.

'We have always known that heedless self-interest was bad morals,' said Franklin D. Roosevelt. 'We now know that it is bad economics.'[53] This is a view held by many. In the jungle every plant and creature is acting out of self-interest, just as people do in a free market, or in any market, but consider a certain dynamic: in a crony capitalist, social democrat society, in which everyone is trying to secure themselves a piece of the government pie, this self-interest comes at somebody else's expense – I must have a subsidized theatre, therefore you must pay more tax; but in a free society that same self-interest brings benefit to others. As the moral philosopher Adam Smith so famously said back in 1776, 'It is not from the benevolence of the butcher, the brewer, or the baker that we expect our dinner, but from their regard to their own interest.'[54] The better a service they offer, the more custom they will receive.

When I buy something from you, I am not acting in your interest, but in mine – and you are not acting in my interest, but in yours. That is the dynamic. When this exchange occurs, we both benefit – yet there is this flawed but pervasive idea that when an exchange happens, somebody loses. As Johnson writes, 'Plenty of opinion-formers in places like Brussels and Whitehall too often think the world is a zero-sum place: they believe that each commercial success is bought at the cost of someone else's failure.'[55] Exchange is not zero sum: there is no loser, but the opposite. I get your product; you get my money. We both benefit. Not only does each participant benefit from an exchange, mankind also does through progress. This process of mutual benefit works right the way through the expanse of global trade. From the extraction of natural resources through machines and industry to the consumer at home, every exchange of goods, ideas or services brings some kind of benefit to the participants, as well as progress to mankind. It is monopolies and rent-seekers' profits that come at somebody else's cost.

Economist Walter E. Williams describes the dynamic beautifully:

It's popular to condemn greed, but it's greed that gets wonderful things done. When I say greed, I don't mean stealing, fraud, misrepresentation or other forms of dishonesty. I mean people trying to get as much as they can for themselves. We don't give second thought to the many wonderful things others do for us. Detroit assembly-line workers get up at the crack of dawn to produce the car that you enjoy. Farm workers toil in the blazing sun gathering grapes for our wine. Snowplow drivers brave blizzards just so we can have access to our roads. Do you think these people make these personal sacrifices because they care about us? My bet is that they don't give a hoot. Instead, they along with their bosses, do these wonderful things for us because they want more for themselves.

People in the education and political establishments pretend they're not motivated by such 'callous' motives as greed and profits. These people 'care' about us, but from which areas of our lives do we derive the greatest pleasures and have the fewest complaints, and from which areas do we have the greatest headaches and complaints? We tend to have a high satisfaction level with goods and services like computers, cell phones, movies, clothing and supermarkets. These are areas where the motivations are greed and profits. Our greatest dissatisfaction is in areas of caring and no profit motive such as public education, postal services and politics. Give me greed and profits, and you can keep the caring.[56]

If I invent a magnificent machine that, say, takes used tyres and converts them into an incredibly powerful energy source, then, yes,

I might make a great deal of money from it, but it also brings great benefit to those that buy it. As a consequence of this wonderful machine I have invented, somebody else can now go and invent a better one, which will further benefit mankind – as well as render mine obsolete.

In his little-known book, *The New Approach to Freedom*, economist E. C. Riegel says:

> Natural Law, inspiring personal enterprise, induces man to help himself by helping others. To advance himself, he must contemplate and gratify the wants of others, who in turn gratify his wants through the process of specialization of labour and exchange. Thus we see that personal enterprise is co-operative and social. The individual cannot determine his vocation or activity in contempt of the wishes of his fellows, for it is they who decide the value to them of such activity and reward him accordingly. Every man is the servant of every other man. This is the law of life. Therefore the most intelligently selfish individual is the most socially minded, productive, creative . . . Competition compels co-operation, for he who will not deal fairly is defeated by his competitor. Therefore, that exchange that operates under the freest competition is the fairest.[57]

The societies in which people have best escaped the evils of poverty have been those in which free exchange has been most possible. The societies which have been worst off have always been those that do the opposite – the ones that restrict exchange and restrict freedom. The evidence of history is overwhelming.

Great achievements have never been made by government committees or bureaucrats – they have been made by individuals pursuing their own interests, even if the interest is altruism. Albert Einstein, Isaac Newton, Steve Jobs, Michael Faraday, Mohammed Ali – show me a great man and I will show you an individual pursuing his own interests. The greatness comes when those interests bring some kind of mass benefit.

Profit need not necessarily entail exploitation. It is – in the right environment – a reward for good practice. This dynamic was described by Adam Smith in *The Wealth of Nations* as 'the invisible hand': 'Every individual . . . intends only his own gain, and he is in this, as in many other cases, led by an invisible hand to promote an end which was no part of his intention.'

It is human nature to act out of self-interest. You can't regulate against human nature. Far better to have a system by which that self-interest brings benefit to everyone, a system by which, as Gordon Gekko said, greed *is* good. That, in my view, is a system based on Natural Law.

It is naïve to pretend that people don't attempt to take advantage of others. Of course they do. People will try to pay as little as possible and charge as much as possible. The market is the balance. Some employers will try to pay their workers as little as possible, but if those workers feel they are being exploited, and they are unable to negotiate their pay higher, they need to take action: perhaps leave and find other employment elsewhere; re-train so they have more desirable skills; or even form unions to protect their own interests – but if those unions then push the price of their members' labour too high, fewer among them will be employed, in which case they're not protecting the interests of their members (forming unions for mutual benefit and protection is fine, as far as I'm concerned; it's when unions start dictating to governments that you pass through the gates of rent-seeking hell). The onus is on both unions and employers to get the balance right. This is one of the reasons I like employee-owned businesses – the co-operative or John Lewis model – where ownership of the company is shared among those who work for it. Under this model, it seems, the right balance between conditions, pay and profit is found naturally. It was common and successful in the 19th century with the co-operative societies. But, somehow, in the first half of the 20th century, the notion of employee-owned business morphed into the nationalization of business, which, ultimately, kills it.

'People must help one another,' said poet Jean De La Fontaine. 'It is nature's law.' It is important to understand that profit is not the only motive by which people act, even if they are acting in self-interest. The unregulated (because governments haven't been able to keep up with it) land of the internet is probably the best example of a free market that exists in the world today. As we all know, it is the most fantastic medium in which to exchange anything from ideas and knowledge to services and products. All sorts of amazing communities have risen, far-flung connections have been made and businesses grown. It has taken care of all sorts of minority needs and niche markets in a way that a government never could. Far from being suppressed, minorities have actually thrived thanks to the internet. It has brought colossal progress.

Despite the fear that this unregulated place would become a haven for crime and ruthless exploitation, in many ways the opposite has happened. It has brought out the best in people. YouTube, Twitter, Flickr, LinkedIn and Freecycle, are just some of the plethora of sites with large followings through which users voluntarily share things – information, ideas, news, videos and pictures, contacts, goods – with no expectation of financial profit. In many cases people do it simply for enjoyment, sometimes it's for status. Humans have a need to give, share and exchange of their own volition, even when there is no profit. The mind boggles at the amount of information that has been shared through the net. Wikipedia has become the most wonderful reference tool perhaps ever invented; it evolves every day; almost all the information there has been compiled gratis. The open source software movement and Linux, through which programmers quite selflessly share ideas and improvements, have made marvellous computer applications, all available for free. Often these applications are superior to those marketed commercially. The simple use of feedback and reviews on sites like eBay and Amazon has led to high standards of behaviour between buyer and seller, standards that are constantly improving. User reviews on sites such as TripAdvisor have forced better practice on to all sorts of different businesses selling to the public, especially hotels and restaurants. It all goes to show how an unregulated environment quickly self-regulates – and that self-regulation evolves organically, as the environment evolves. Co-operation and virtue are as much a part of human nature as anything else.

I am overstating how good the internet is. It is far from perfect, of course. It is also a forum for foul, violent, abusive and often malicious language; for false rumour and fraud; an opportunity for the grooming of the young and innocent for sex. The internet has facilitated hundreds of despicable practices. Am I in favour of any of these things? Never (except the occasional foul language). But I suggest the positives of the internet far outweigh the negatives.

If a market is free, an exchange must take place voluntarily. With theft, tax, slavery, or fraud (the thing you're buying doesn't do what you were led to believe it would), the exchange is not 'free', nor is it mutually beneficial. It is exploitation or worse – and it leads to loss, not gain. In the real world, exploitation can descend into slavery (as, for example, seems to be the case with the building of Dubai, where captive immigrant labourers have had their passports confiscated). It is not only criminal in ordinary terminology, but a gross violation of the principles of the free market. It is coercion of the worst kind. Tragically, it seems that the world and, as importantly, the Dubai authorities are desensitized to what is going on. For a free market to flourish, property rights need to be respected, defended and safe. That extends to one's own body. Slavery is, in effect, a violation of somebody's property rights over their own body. In this regard government has a role to play. Not by implementing price controls or regulations that hinder new entrants to a market, but by protecting property rights and enforcing contracts. The protection of property rights is key. This is one of the few areas, as I see it, where the state has a role, although the more extreme argue that the free market can deal with this issue too.

Consider this passage from Fyodor Dostoevsky's *Crime and Punishment*:

> If I were told, 'love thy neighbour', what came of it? . . . It came to tearing my coat in half to share with my neighbour and we were both left half naked. As a Russian proverb has it, 'Catch several hares and you won't catch one.' Science now tells us, love yourself before all men, for everything in the world rests on self-

interest. You love yourself and manage your own affairs properly and your coat remains whole. Economic truth adds that the more better private affairs are organized in society – the more whole coats, so to say – the firmer are and the better is the common welfare organized too. Therefore in acquiring wealth solely and exclusively for myself, I am acquiring, so to speak, for all, and helping to bring to pass my neighbour's getting a little more than a torn coat, and that not from private personal liberality, but as a consequence of the general advance. The idea is simple, but unhappily it has been a long time reaching us, being hindered by idealism and sentimentality. And yet it would seem to want very little wit to perceive it.[58]

Prosperity, I'm about to suggest, leads to higher standards. I'm not suggesting for a moment that prosperous people are any better than those who aren't. But the same person, when prosperous, will have higher standards than when he isn't – because he can afford higher standards.

Prosperous people tend to be happier. They live longer. There are lower death rates as a result of disease among the prosperous. Polio, typhoid, cholera, yellow fever, typhus, malaria are all but gone from the first world. Measles, mumps, rubella, influenza are nothing like the problems they once were. The great disease threats in the west of recent years, AIDS, SARS or swine flu, for example, never had the decimating effects that were feared after their outbreaks. Prosperity has even led to lower murder rates. Pieter Spierenburg shows, in his *A History of Murder*, that the crime was, per person, ten times as common before the Industrial Revolution in Europe as it is today.[59] This ignores those killed in wars, but even wars tend to take place in less prosperous locales, even if the perpetrators, governments usually, are rich.

Indur M. Goklany's recent paper 'Death and Death Rates Due to Extreme Weather Events' reveals how deaths resulting from extreme weather events have declined by 95% since the 1920s.[60] There are no fewer events, but now, as a result of better technology, forecasting is better, warnings are disseminated earlier, leading to more preparation time, there are better emergency services and so on. This is a consequence of prosperity.

The 2011 Tohoku earthquake in Japan killed fewer than 20,000 people. It had a magnitude of 9.0, the most powerful known earthquake ever to hit Japan, the fifth most powerful ever known. In Haiti – the poorest country in the Western hemisphere – an earthquake a year earlier had a lower magnitude of 7.0, yet it killed over 300,000. Of course it is much more complicated than this simplistic comparison – the epicentre is key – but the point about the prosperous being better equipped remains.

The effects of prosperity are moral as well as practical. Not only do people live longer, but prosperous societies are less tolerant of an array of things no longer considered acceptable – pollution, child labour, child molestation, sexism, and racism, for example. There's even an argument that it was prosperity that put an end to slavery in the UK in 1833 (long before the days of invasive government). Thanks to the Industrial Revolution – which saw innovation and improvement in machinery, tools, chemical manufacturing and iron production processes, water and steam power, and the transition to coal – man became dramatically more productive. He could now afford *not* to have slaves in a way he couldn't before – and so he campaigned to have the practice made illegal. Yet forms of slavery still exist in Africa today, where there is not the same prosperity.

Luke Johnson writes:

> Anti-capitalists suggest that the solution to inequality is re-distribution – which actually means levelling down . . . Business is a fantastic technique for someone from a modest background, with minimal education, to improve their life and get ahead. Entrepreneurs often have few qualifications and would have been unable to enter more 'noble' professions such as politics, law or academia. Perhaps that is why so many of the intellectual elite have always looked down on those in trade and industry. They resent the fact that in the capitalist system, uneducated but

energetic individuals can reach positions of power and wealth through sheer effort.[61]

But capitalism in its most ideal form does not necessarily exalt material gain above spiritual success. It exalts peaceful co-operation between producers and suppliers without coercion, theft, and rent-seeking. Affluence then allows more time to pursue spiritual and other such affairs, if so desired.

If you extrapolate this notion of both sides benefiting through exchange to every lattice of the global economy then you see how quickly mankind can progress when there are no barriers to this exchange. The policy of every government should be to encourage exchange in every way it can and remove every possible barrier. The way to do this is to *remove* itself from the market – fewer taxes, simpler taxes, less protectionism, less subsidy, less planning, and fewer targets. It is through exchange that people prosper and progress. The chain is simple. Self-interest and a free market lead to exchange, which leads to progress and, in turn, to prosperity. Crony capitalism is one of the fundamental causes of the mess in which we now find ourselves. Genuine 'free market capitalism' – the economic environment that most reflects the efficiency, co-ordination and symbiosis of Natural Law – is the cure.

7 Deadly Wins For a Free Market:

1   It is the fairest system to all.
2   It is the only system flexible enough to adapt to changing conditions – because it is inherently flexible.
3   It is the most efficient and least wasteful system. Thus it is the most harmonious with nature.
4   It is the easiest and cheapest system to administrate because it requires little administration.
5   It is the system by which people become the most prosperous – and the least dependent on government. As a result of their prosperity they are able to exchange more and become more prosperous. A virtuous circle is created.

6 It is the system that brings the best out of people. It raises standards of behaviour. There is more trust, more giving, more kindness. People become entrepreneurs, not rent-seekers.

7 It is the system that brings the most progress, and therefore that which best benefits mankind.

4 Why Your Family is Getting Smaller: The Unspoken Truth

Joint income mortgage and debt servitude to a bank instead of having a family is the new norm.
'Democorruptcy' (internet forum poster)[62]

What is the average number of children in a middle-class family? 2.4 is the number you think of, the number embedded in our minds. But this actually harks back to pre-WWII days. Of families with children, the average US family unit now has 1.8 children, the UK 1.7.[63] If you include families without children, there is less than one child per family unit.

Across the West, the overwhelming reason why parents are having fewer children is money. In the UK, 60% of parents with one child and 64% of those with two cited money as the reason they have not had, and were not going to have, more.[64] A 2013 report from the Centre for Economics and Business Research shows it now costs over £222,000 to raise a child to the age of 21. The insurer Aviva, however, calculated in 2011 that the number is even higher – £270,000. Neither figure includes school fees. In the US the cost is a similar $235,000 to raise a child to the age of 18 – $270,000 if you live in New York or Boston.[65]

The numbers that follow focus on the UK – but rest assured, the issue at the heart of this chapter applies across the West. Before we start, I need to define 'poor'. The widely accepted definition, and the one we'll go with here, is living on less than 60% of the average (median) household income.

According to the Department of Work and Pensions, 'Families with four or more children account for less than 5% of all families, but more than 20% of poor children.'[66] A 2006 study of child poverty in the UK by the Joseph Rowntree Foundation showed that 50% of children from families with four or more children are poor. I think that's amazing: 50%. It says, 'A child in a 4+-child family was between 280–800% more likely to be poor than a child in a one-child family – other things being equal.' Forty-two per cent of all poor children come from large (three children or more) families, while parents were more likely not to be working and have a 'lower level of educational achievement'.

In the UK, over 42,000 families with five or more children receive out-of-work benefits (3% of claimants). More than 1,000 families have at least eight children. There are some 680 people on incapacity benefit – i.e. deemed unable to work – who nevertheless have seven or more children under 16.[67] An inflammatory article in the *Daily Mail* in 2010 showed one family, the Smiths, taking home £95,000 per year in benefits – equivalent to pre-tax earnings north of £150,000 – to look after their ten children.[68] (I should say at this point, as far as I'm concerned, people can have as many or as few children as they want. I am looking at a different issue.)

Despite the income that families such as the Smiths can receive, the Rowntree study blames the benefits system for favouring small families. It calls for increased benefits. In my view this thinking is backwards. Children in large families are more likely to be poor not because of lack of benefit, but because *only* families on benefits – as well as the very rich – have the means to support large families.

The short of it is this: on a proportional basis, those on benefits are more likely to have more children than those not on benefits. Those not on benefits are having fewer children and having them later in life. The reason is money, and the biggest bill in their life is, of course, the state.

The government is administering a system that takes money from one group of people – the middle-class taxpayer, for the most part – the economic realities of whose situation mean they are having smaller and smaller families, and handing it to another, who, in many cases, are not exercising the same restraint. And why should they? The economic reality of their situation is that they can have as many children as they want and then be supplied with money, accommodation, health care and education. What's more, should it emerge that their children do not work either, they too will be subsidized. It's no wonder that this group of people expands, while the other – the middle-class family – contracts. Effectively we have a system whereby one group of people has the amount of children it can have limited in order to pay for another group to have more. It is also a highly unnatural situation. It is entirely a consequence of the Positive Law that is government policy.

Iain Duncan Smith, the UK government's Work and Pensions Minister, is trying to address this issue by capping benefits. He's making himself unpopular in certain quarters by doing so. At the other extreme, people are calling for sterilization. It is not for the government, a bureaucrat or anyone to dictate how many children a family should or shouldn't have. It is absolutely, fundamentally none of its business, yet it is imposing its views on this matter onto others through regulation, taxation and benefits. I say, why not let the economic laws of nature be your regulator and don't intervene at all? Why not let everybody live by the same rules?

At present a vicious cycle is being perpetuated. If you are born into an environment where welfare dependency is the norm, you are then several times more likely not to work and to become welfare-state dependent yourself. The country as a whole becomes more burdened as this group increases and the self-sufficient quarter contracts.

The group of people who have limited the amount of children they have according to their heavily taxed, financial circumstances are the Mr Loss and Miss Doubt in all of this (those receiving benefits are Mr Gain). What if we don't tax them? Suddenly Mr Loss and Miss Doubt have more capital – twice as much in some cases. If they feel they want bigger families, then, as God said to Noah, 'be fruitful and multiply'. This self-sufficient, self-reliant and in many ways this more deserving social sector (because they give more than they take) is now in a position to expand, should it see fit. Not only is such a system more natural, I suggest it is for the greater good and the health of society.

Without welfare it wouldn't be possible for the dependent group to expand. The group would not be able to support itself. It would have to learn to do so, to tighten its belt where necessary, to work, to behave more prudently and to become either self-reliant or reliant on family or community. And thus the size of this group shrinks. This might seem a rather terrifying and ruthless argument. What about those who really can't help themselves? Do we let them perish, according to the idea that only the fittest survive? Of course, we do not. Am I advocating no welfare? No, I am not. I am simply saying that *government* is not the best provider of welfare. Yet, at present, it has a monopoly. Later in this book I'll explain how a freely chosen and highly efficient system of welfare will develop quite organically – if only the state would just stay out of it.

Part II

Money and Tax:
Why You'll Never Be One of the 1%

5   The Essential History They Never Teach You

All the perplexities, confusions, and distresses in America arise,
not from defects in their constitution or confederation, not from a want of
honour or virtue, so much as from downright ignorance of the nature
of coin, credit, and circulation.

John Adams, second president of the US[69]

The gulf between rich and poor is the largest it has ever been, yet it continues to increase all the time. The richest 400 people in the world have assets equivalent to the poorest 140 million.[70] The wealthiest 1% of Americans pocket a quarter of the country's income. Through such means as property, bank accounts, investments and art, they control as much as half of the nation's total wealth. That share of wealth has doubled in the past four decades. In the UK the divide is even greater.

The Greek historian Plutarch declared that 'an imbalance between rich and poor is the oldest and most fatal ailment of all republics'. He is purported to have claimed that the difference in earnings between those at the bottom of an organization and those at the top should be six times. The great American financier J. P. Morgan (once the richest man in the world) reportedly said it should be 20 times.

In 2011 Jamie Dimon of the firm J. P. Morgan was paid $22.9 million; John Stumpf, chief executive of Wells Fargo, $17.9 million; Curtis Arledge of BNY Mellon, $17.9 million; Lloyd Blankfein of Goldman Sachs, $16.2 million. Adriana Vasquez, a contract cleaner in the J. P. Morgan Chase Tower in Houston, earned $8.35 an hour.[71] Generously assuming that Jamie Dimon put in a 70-hour week, 50 weeks a year, his earnings equate to over $6,500 an hour – almost 800 times what Vasquez was paid. When the gap in earnings is so vast, Dimon and Vasquez have almost become different species. In the UK in 2011, HSBC chief executive Stuart Gulliver was paid around £8 million – over 500 times what an HSBC call-centre worker in

Swansea earns. I do not see that gulf in earnings as healthy.

Government has taken it upon itself to redistribute wealth from top to bottom through taxation, legislation, benefits, the welfare state and so on. Yet the more it has done this, the greater the gap has become. As government has grown, so has the gap between rich and poor.

'There's no way!' exclaimed rapper Tupac Shakur in a 1992 interview with MTV, 'There's no way that these people should own planes and there're people don't have houses. Apartments. Shacks. Drawers. Pants! I know you're rich. I know you got 40 billion dollars, but can you just keep it to one house? You only need one house. And if you only got two kids, can you just keep it to two rooms? I mean why have 52 rooms and you know there's somebody with no room? It just don't make sense to me. It don't.'[72]

I'm going to show you how this gap – this skewed distribution of wealth – is a simple but inevitable consequence of our system of money.

My kids are forever asking me, 'What is money?', 'How do you "make" money?', 'Who decides what *is* money?' I can remember asking the same questions. Unanswered, they seem to fade away as you get older. (I was once told that the thin silver strip that runs through a note was silver and that was what gave money its value. As a matter of fact, that thin silver strip just makes money more difficult to counterfeit.)

The answer is that government and banks 'make' money, and I suggest that many of our problems lie in the economic distortion this privilege has created. The key to rebalancing the unequal distribution of wealth does not lie in higher taxes, in bigger benefits or in government clamping down on a particular group. It lies in a simple reform to our system of money; a simple reform that spreads power, removes privilege and liberates exchange.

Even in the world of economists, so few think to question money, yet every transaction that takes place involves it. Money is to an economy what blood is to a body. It is essential that it is healthy. The money we use today is diseased and riddled with infection.

But before I outline the big fix, I need to explain how what we have came about.

From Stone Age Man to Isaac Newton

In a basic agricultural society, it's easy enough to swap five chickens for a new dress or to pay a schoolteacher with a goat and three sacks of rice. Barter works less well in a more advanced economy. The logistical challenges of using chickens to buy books on Amazon.com would be formidable.

Charles Wheelan, public policy lecturer[73]

Besides barter, the first forms of money were 'commodity money' – shells, cocoa beans, feathers, bits of metal, tobacco, even whales' teeth.[74] They all represented some form of value. At one stage Roman soldiers were paid in salt – from which we derive the word 'salary'. Later forms of commodity money have taken the form of cigarettes or cognac. But it seems that early traders also used accounting systems to record credits and debts, as David Graeber explains in his book *Debt*.[75]

Metals were the most popular and successful forms of commodity money – for five good reasons. Metal has intrinsic and universal value; it's standardized and constant – copper or gold don't change, they're copper or gold wherever you are; metal is durable, divisible and its value is almost all-encompassing. Different things have different costs. Not only can metals be divided – one ounce buys you four times as much as a quarter-ounce and so on – but different metals have different value. Gold is worth more than silver, which is worth more than nickel, which is worth more than copper. Copper and nickel were used for low-value transactions – and still are today – while silver and gold were used for more expensive.

It is thought the first coins were cast around 700–650 BC in the eastern Mediterranean. Certifying weight and metal content – with the coin issuer's stamp further endorsing the metal's purity – coins would bring confidence (what monetary historians call 'surety') to a transaction. In fact, the names of most currencies today denote either the metal, the issuer, or the weight of metal. For example, the words 'silver' and 'money' are interchangeable in some 90 or more different languages – 'argent' in French, 'plata' in Spanish, 'shekel' in Hebrew. The Dutch 'guilder' means simply 'golden'. The UK government calls its bonds 'gilts', which also means golden. The Scandinavian 'krona' refers to the crown, the issuer's stamp. The German 'mark' and the French 'franc' are also words that denote the authenticity of the issuer and thus the metal content of the coin.

The phrase 'one pound sterling' once meant a pound of sterling silver. The Italian and Turkish 'lira', the French 'livre', the Spanish 'peseta', South American 'peso', and Arabic 'dirhem' all refer to weight. Even the dollar derives, it is believed by some, from the world 'thaler', an ounce weight of silver, originally coined by one Count Schlick in the 16th century. From the other side of the world, the Thai 'baht' was also a unit of weight. The Chinese 'yuan' and Japanese 'yen' both mean 'round shape' – referring, of course, to the shapes of coins.

There are also early examples of 'fiat' currencies, meaning currencies whose worth is declared by some ruling diktat or law, rather than on the underlying value of the metal. Examples include a system in Sparta, somewhere between 750 and 415 BC, using iron disks; one in Athens based on copper; and one early Roman system somewhere between 700 and 150 BC, based on bronze tablets, and then coins.[76] In these cases the value of the metal in the coins was actually less than the 'face value' that was stamped on to them.

For day-to-day transactions gold was the least effective of the metals. Even a small, one-eighth-ounce, gold coin – about the size of a penny – is worth a great deal (about £150 or $200 at today's prices). Before the 20th century there would have been only about one quarter-ounce per person on the planet, and so the more common metals – copper, nickel and silver – were more useful. But, for precisely the same reason – that even a small amount of gold is worth so much – gold was the most effective of the metals as a store of wealth. The practice of wearing jewellery, a means to store wealth as well as to display it, is born of this. A half-ounce piece of jewellery around your neck might be worth the equivalent of, say, a five-pound (two-and-a-half kilo) block of copper – which is considerably less portable.

But you cannot store all your wealth about your or your partner's neck – particularly if you have a lot of it, or if you like to patrol the shadier parts of town at night. You need some safe location to store it. Hence the emergence of banking.

The word 'bank' is said to have its roots in the benches – 'banche' – of the money-changers of 14th-century Florence, on top of which they would make their transactions.

But the practice of banking may even pre-date the casting of coins. In ancient Mesopotamia and Egypt, receipts were issued for grain stored. When the receipt changed hands, ownership of the stored commodity changed hands too. They were probably the first example of paper money. In Egypt, by about 300 BC the various grain banks or granaries had been transformed in a network, with the centre – where all the accounts were recorded – in Alexandria. That was probably the first example of a central bank.

The huge variety of unstandardized coins that were circulating from the time of ancient Greece onwards gave rise to another role for bankers – the infamous money-changers. Despite the bad press they have had over the years, not least in the Bible, they were performing an essential service. Different coins contained different amounts of different metal. This meant there would be constant doubt and suspicion in the marketplace as to the value (i.e. the metal content) of a particular coin. With no standardization, someone had to be responsible for exchanging them. I suspect that much of the moneylenders' unpopularity lay in the fact that, in telling you the value of your money, they were often bringers of unwanted news.

Paper currency, it seems, found use in the East long before it did in Europe. First recorded in 7th-century China under the Tang dynasty, by the 11th-century Song dynasty its use had become widespread. Kublai Khan – the first emperor of China's Mongol dynasty – issued paper money known as the 'chao'. The 13th-century Italian explorer, Marco Polo, marvelled:

All these pieces of paper are, issued with as much solemnity and authority as if they were of pure gold or silver . . . with these pieces of paper, made as I have described, Kublai Khan causes all payments on his own account to be made; and he makes them to pass current universally over all his kingdoms and provinces and territories, and whithersoever his power and sovereignty extends . . . and indeed everybody takes them readily, for wheresoever a person may go throughout the Great Khan's dominions he shall find these pieces of paper current, and shall be able to transact all sales and purchases of goods by means of them just as well as if they were coins of pure gold.[77]

From there the practice of using paper money spread to the Mediterranean – Italy in particular – and eventually to Britain. As early as the 16th century in England – and probably before – goldsmiths would issue receipts in exchange for gold stored with them, known as 'running cash notes'. Over time, though initially only for larger transactions, it became more convenient to trade these goldsmiths' receipts in the market place – just as in Egypt – instead of the actual gold (or grain). With paper replacing metal, money was evolving from commodity to representative.

Goldsmiths were now, in effect, bankers. Some began to make money by lending out certificates – paper – against depositors' gold. This would become one of the building blocks on which banking was built. The goldsmith – we'll call him a banker now – paid the depositors one rate of interest to store their gold with him and then lent at a higher rate. The difference was his profit. In 17th-century Britain there was so much coin clipping and counterfeiting that paper from a reputable bank was in many ways preferable to actual coinage.

In 1694, the Bank of England was formed by a Scot, William Paterson, to raise money for King William III's war against France. It issued paper notes in return for deposits of gold. Like the goldsmiths' receipts, the transaction was based on a promise to pay the bearer on demand the sum of the note. Thus the note could be redeemed at the bank for gold or coinage by anyone presenting it for payment and the notes were used as money. But the Bank was issuing more notes of credit than it had gold to back them. Initially the scheme was a great success: the navy was funded. But all this newly created paper money circulating in an economy, without a corresponding growth in the number of goods and services available, quickly led to rising prices – what we today call inflation. Prices doubled in under three years. Something like £1.2 million of gold was deposited in ten days, but the Bank's obligations rose from £1.2 million to £16 million in the same time.

When prices are rising rapidly, a common psychological consequence is that people feel a need to catch up. Get-rich-quick schemes often emerge to meet this need. The late 1600s saw a spate of them. One was a venture that proposed to drain the Red Sea and recover the gold that Moses had left after he parted the waters all those years before. I can just imagine the promoter pushing that idea.

Isaac Newton took much of this in hand when he went to work for the Bank of England in 1696, becoming Warden, and then in 1699, Master, of the Royal Mint. At the time of his appointment there was monetary disorder. The currency had been weakened by clipping and counterfeiting during the Nine Years' War against France; the Bank had created more notes than it had gold to back them. Inflation raged. Newton began to fix this by recalling and replacing all the coins in circulation and then redefining the shilling, pound, and penny, so that 21 shillings and sixpence would stay equivalent to one gold guinea (about a quarter-ounce of gold). This 'great re-coinage' would give England, then Scotland – and, eventually, the world – a standardized system of money built on gold. He had to revalue gold upwards to do it (and it caused a temporary flight of silver from the UK) but Newton's gold standard would become the bedrock of the British money system – and, eventually, world trade – for the next 200 years.

The system was not perfect. Government spending on the Napoleonic Wars led to inflation at the turn of the 19th century and another 'great re-coinage' in 1816. But it was considerably more successful than France's, which saw a total economic collapse in 1720 with the bursting of the Mississippi Bubble, hyperinflation, revolution, monetary collapse in the 1790s and the consequent rise of a dictator in Napoleon. (Incidentally, monetary collapse almost always seems to be accompanied by a dictatorship of some kind, as well as war, though the order in which the members of this unholy trinity arrive varies.)

In the 19th century the pound, thanks to the constancy of its gold backing, would become the global reserve currency (as the dollar is today). This stability allowed the British banking system and commerce to flourish and dominate on an international scale. The world trusted the integrity of British money – and by extension the integrity of Britain, its people and its products. In many ways the success of the British Empire can be traced back and attributed to the consequences of Newton's standardization of money.

From Honest Gold to Filthy Lucre

With the exception only of the period of the gold standard, practically all governments of history have used their exclusive power to issue money to defraud and plunder the people.
Friedrich Hayek[78]

This practice of banks issuing and lending out paper representing more gold than they had on deposit was gradually legalized and regulated. Limits were agreed on the amount of paper money that could be printed and lent. Usually the ratio was nine loaned paper units to one actual unit in gold. That means there would only be enough money to repay about 10% of the bank's customers at any one time. This is known as 'fractional reserve banking' – where you only need to hold on deposit a fraction of the paper money or debt you put out. This is in contrast to full reserve banking, where all of a depositor's money is kept on hand in cash, and where a bank would need to ask the permission of savers before it could make loans to borrowers. Even today, if you deposit money in the bank, it is no longer your property, but that of the bank – over 70% of UK citizens are not aware of this, according to a recent survey, even though the rule goes back 200 years.

The fractional reserve system may seem rather fraudulent – and in a way it is. Why should banks have this privilege to create money from nothing and then charge interest on it? William Paterson himself is reported to have said, 'The bank hath benefit of interest on all moneys, which it creates out of nothing.' Nevertheless the system worked reasonably well under the gold standard. New money supply did not get out of control (as it has done with the arrival of electronic banking).

The entrepreneur and gold-dealer Paul Tustain writes:

It is pure nonsense to say that a gold standard means all money should be backed by vaulted gold. Suppose it was. It would prevent a man with a paid up £100 million property portfolio from borrowing £10,000 from his bank to pay someone £10,000 to build a garden shed. A monetary obstruction to this deal just isn't going to be tolerated, and it's a stupid idea to suggest the deal should be blocked simply because the consumer (rich property owner) or his bank currently has no gold at hand. It was precisely this sort of economic blockage that caused people to create money in the first place, and if you try to stop willing and credible exchangers from using one type of money they'll simply abandon your money, and either use someone else's or create their own. The gold standard did not require every single banknote, and every single accounted Pound in every single bank account, to be backed with specific gold. If that had been the policy, there would have been no money for our rich, property owning shed-buyer, and the gold standard would have been abandoned in a few days to be replaced by something which allowed wealthy people to buy things. The point of the gold standard (and it was a good point) was to create a yardstick. It tied money to something real and more-or-less stable, but it did not insist on every unit of account, and every banknote, being a unique representation of a specific physical gold stock held by the Central Bank. So we can allow banks to support free trade by creating money (even under a gold standard). Banks just need to know that if collateral needs to be liquidated they'd better be very confident it will raise sufficient money on whatever yardstick is being used. Otherwise it's curtains for all their shareholders' equity.[79]

Runs on banks – when everyone tries to withdraw their money at the same time – could become a serious problem with this fractional reserve system, so it became common practice for central banks to support local banks with loans of gold in an emergency. But a central bank protecting other banks is the state protecting one special interest group. In doing so it makes itself vulnerable to lobbying, rent-seeking and other forms of 'crony capitalism'. That is, unfortunately, how the system of banking has evolved to the point where central banks across the West bailed out bank after bank in the crisis of 2008–9.

The rather elastic use of paper money tied to gold certainly made trade and exchange more possible, and it accelerated man's astonishing progress through the 17th, 18th and 19th centuries – the commercial expansion, the Industrial Revolution, the scientific advances, everything. The problem has been the abuse of the system. Issuing more paper credit than you have money to back it is a cause of this persistent cycle that has blighted mankind with inflation, booms, bubbles and busts (Newton himself is said to have been caught up in one of the most famous of all, the South Sea Bubble in 1720).

Compared to the 20th century, prices were stable under Newton's standard, but there were still problems. Government warmongering was expensive. In the 20 years from 1694 to the war of Spanish Succession in 1714, national debt grew from next to nothing to 60% of gross domestic product (GDP). In other words government debt was equivalent to 60% of all the goods and services the UK produced in a year. With the Carnatic Wars in India, the Seven Years War against France and the American War of Independence, national debt had grown to 156% of GDP by 1784. Military spending continued to grow as the French Revolution unfolded, and it exploded with the Napoleonic Wars. By 1816 national debt stood at 237% of GDP. It all led to the second 'great re-coinage' in 1816, with silver coinage and the gold sovereign re-introduced. The United Kingdom then entered a 'golden age' of prosperity and relative peace, which saw national debt paid down to a manageable 25% of GDP by 1914.

The government monopoly on creating money was further strengthened in 1844 when the Bank Charter Act declared that no bank other than the Bank of England could issue paper notes, depriving private commercial banks of their power to do so. As well as giving the Bank of England an effective monopoly on the printing of new notes, the act restricted the number of notes in circulation.

At any given moment during the 19th century, the Bank of England only had gold to back about 25% of the paper money it put out. Towards the end of booms and periods of commercial expansion this went as low as 15%. During contractions the figure went as high as 50%.[80]

By the 20th century, the fractional reserve system had become the dominant monetary system of the world. But simultaneously, another more dangerous problem was developing. The amount of gold-backing was shrinking. The British came off the gold standard in 1914 with the advent of WWI. The Bank of England website states that the reason for this is that 'the Government needed to preserve its stock of bullion and the Bank ceased to pay out gold for its notes'. The Bank was printing money to pay for the war and didn't want a run on its gold, thus breaking the promise you see on every note it prints to 'pay the bearer on demand'. The German government did the same and also departed from its gold standard. From 1914 the UK and most European currencies were no longer backed by anything tangible. They had become 'fiduciary' – or faith – currencies, otherwise known as 'fiat' currencies. Ironic, that a broken promise should be replaced by something that requires faith.

In 1925 Winston Churchill put the UK back on to the gold standard in an attempt to restore Britain's place as a centre of finance. But he put the UK on at the pre-WWI rate – £4.25 per ounce – which did not reflect the new money that had been created since 1914. To put the country on at a different rate would have been an admission that the currency had been devalued, which, for various reasons – pride among them – the British authorities did not want to do. The effect was for the pound to become severely overvalued against other currencies. UK exports became expensive – and uncompetitive – while America's, whose industrial infrastructure was in better shape after WWI anyway, grew cheaper. The result was a deflationary slump in the UK and a boom in the US – one which got out of hand and eventually led to the crash of 1929 and the subsequent depression of the 1930s.

In 1933 the UK came off the gold standard once again. It has never returned to it. Meanwhile, in the US, which was deep in post 1929 crisis and depression, President Franklin D. Roosevelt made it a criminal offence for Americans to own gold, even though the dollar was on a gold standard. Executive Order 6102, which Roosevelt signed in April 1933, forbade 'the Hoarding of Gold Coin, Gold Bullion and Gold Certificates within the continental United States'. Within less than a month any American individual, partnership, association or corporation was required to hand over their gold and be given a little over $20 an ounce in exchange. Eight months later, in January 1934, the Gold Reserve Act revalued gold from $20.67 to $35 an ounce. Roosevelt, effectively, stole twice from his citizens. First, taking their gold, then devaluing the money he had given them in exchange. He did it because devaluing money was his method of dealing with the 1930s depression. Does this sound familiar?

In 1944, towards the end of the WWII, there was another development: delegates from 44 nations met in Bretton Woods in New Hampshire to negotiate and establish a monetary order between the major industrial countries. The result is known as the Bretton Woods Agreement. The US dollar became the global reserve currency, pegged to gold at $35 an ounce. Other currencies were valued against the dollar. The USA and Switzerland were now the only major nations left with a currency tied to gold.

Throughout the 1960s, the US developed and expanded its system of welfare. It also went to war in Vietnam. The government didn't have sufficient gold to pay for either. Indeed, under President Johnson and then Nixon, many more dollars were issued or printed than the US had gold to back them. The French, under Charles

De Gaulle, began demanding gold in exchange for their US dollar holdings at the agreed fixed rate $35 per ounce. On the black market gold actually commanded a higher price. Initially, the US delivered, but eventually, in 1971, as a run on the dollar gathered speed and faced with the rising cost of the Vietnam War, President Nixon removed the dollar from the gold standard altogether. This move was a direct breach of the US Constitution which clearly states that nothing but gold and silver should be money. Article I, Section 10, Clause 1 reads: 'No State shall . . . coin Money; emit Bills of Credit; make any Thing but gold and silver Coin a Tender in Payment of Debt.' America's Founding Fathers, having seen currencies collapse, wrote this clause with good reason, it seems.

After 1971, for the first time in history (with the exception of the Swiss franc) no currency on the planet, nor any small fraction of any currency, was backed by gold or any tangible commodity. The basic nature of money had changed again. A new era was beginning.

6   A Promise of Nothing

So you think that money is the root of all evil.
Have you ever asked what is the root of all money?
Ayn Rand, *Atlas Shrugged*[81]

When a country 'comes off the gold standard', money then becomes what the Bank of England calls 'fiduciary': based on good faith. The Bank of England also declares, rather vaguely, that money is backed by 'securities' (securities, in this case, usually means government bonds – i.e. debt – of various types). This type of money is also known as currency by government edict or decree – 'fiat' money ('fiat' is a Latin word meaning 'it shall be so' or 'let it be so'). In other words it is money by law. It is the law that backs this money and gives it its worth.

Fiduciary or fiat currencies have worked many times in history (including now, to an extent). Money can be anything, in theory – even nothing. The key is that enough people have to believe in this money for it to function. The problem with faith-based currencies is that, when people lose faith, there's not a lot else left.

On a £20 note it says, 'I promise to pay the bearer the sum of twenty pounds'. But 20 pounds of what? The answer is 20 pounds of nothing. In effect, that note is not even nothing, but a promise of nothing. How sublime that faith money should be inscribed with an empty promise. Yet this global system has functioned for over 40 years. It has created many problems, which I'll explain, but it has survived and grown to become the norm. The world – apart from a few on the fringe – believes in this money and uses it.

One of the reasons it has survived so long is government enforcement. In the past, people had the choice to refuse privately created bank credit notes, but now US legal tender laws declare that citizens must accept this government-edict money – this fiat or fiduciary currency – as payment. UK tender laws are a little more vague. By law, the pound must be accepted in payment of debts. But any monies may be used for other transactions, as long as the appropriate taxes for the value of the transaction are duly paid (this applies to barter too). The pound ends up being used out of sheer convenience. The status of government money is also protected by the fact that taxes must be paid in that money.

The value of the currency is determined by how it trades against other fiat currencies on international currency markets, and thus by the status of the issuing country. The Singapore dollar is strong at present, for example, due to the strong economic performance of that country. The US dollar, the global reserve currency, is protected by US economic might, but also to an extent by the US military. (Did you know that shortly before the US invaded Iraq, Saddam Hussein pledged to sell oil in Euros?[82] Some say the US invasion had more to do with protecting the hegemony of the dollar than anything else.)

Only the government and its central banks have the power to actually issue and print fiat money (notes and coins). But banks create it when they make loans. Many find this hard to believe, but they do. In simple terms, say I want to buy a house. I go to the bank with this proposal; they create the money by entering new numbers into my bank account. I sign a contract promising to repay this money, plus interest, over the next 25 years, and the bank receives the deeds to the house as collateral in case I can't pay. I then pay the bank interest on this money that didn't previously exist. Meanwhile, the money that has been created for me to buy a house then goes to the vendor, who takes it into the economy and then spends it on whatever he sees fit (often another house, which will help to push house prices up further).

There is an idea that successful business ventures create money. This is not necessarily so. Successful businesses generate revenue yes, they make profit, but they don't actually create new money – they just get existing money from their customers. However, if the business borrows from a bank, if they issue bonds or their customers borrow to make payments, new money is created. It is lending that actually creates new money.

Just over 2% of UK and US money is actual cash printed by government. About 97.5% is now electronic, in the form of bank deposits on bank balance sheets, created, mostly, by banks through lending. Hence this system of money under which we operate is a 'debt-based fiat currency'.

There is a finite amount of gold in the world. So, under a gold standard, money supply is limited (assuming the standard is not abused). As there is nothing tangible to fiat currency, there is no limit to the amount that can be created. This makes inflation inevitable. To combat this, we have seen the growth in importance of central banking's role since 1971 to manage inflation and, more importantly, 'inflation expectation'. But the measures they use do not track money creation, only the prices of certain goods.

In the 40 years since 1971, money creation has seen the amount of money circulating in the UK grow at 11.5% per year. Yet official measures say inflation from 1989 to 2012 has averaged just 2.8%.[83] This is because the official measure, known as consumer price inflation (CPI), only looks at a basket of consumer goods and services, which – thanks to competition and increased productivity – have, in many cases, not risen in price. Some items – clothes, furniture, electrical goods, food and so on – have actually fallen in price. In the UK (though figures are similar for the US) only about 10% of all money created between 1997 and 2007 went into consumer goods, according to research by think tank PositiveMoney, so CPI only measures the effect of 10% of money creation. Inflation measures do not take into account areas where government runs up deficits – in education and health, for example (in the NHS prices have risen by an average of 14% over the last 18 years). CPI does not take into account house price rises – yet between 1997 and 2007, 40% of newly created money went into residential and commercial property. 37% of newly created money goes into financial markets – no wonder the financial sector has grown – yet CPI does not include financial assets. It's all part of the great obfuscation that is, deliberately or otherwise, taking place. Just 13% of newly created money between 1997 and 2007 went into real businesses that actually create jobs and boost economic growth. (The numbers are similar for the US.) Our system of money is not greasing the wheels of exchange, as it should and once did. Instead it is causing asset price inflation, and making Western economies dependent on this inflation.

The irony with fiduciary money is that the more there is, the more faith in the money falls away. When faith in it goes, its value disappears at alarming and dramatic speed, and you fall into the hyperinflations that blighted Weimar Germany in the 1920s, and Zimbabwe and Argentina more recently. Hyperinflation is psychological as much as it is mathematical. The numbers are such that it could happen now in the West. It is mass psychology that is preventing it. Perhaps that's why so much effort goes into 'managing inflation expectation'.

When you combine this debt-based fiat system with the practice of fractional reserve banking, the potential to create money suddenly multiplies many times over. A bank once made a loan by printing numbers on a piece of paper against gold in its vault; as long as the borrower was able to spend the piece of paper and didn't ask for the actual gold, the bank would not be too restricted in how much it could lend, but there was restraint. Now that gold backing has gone and those pieces of paper money have been replaced by electronic numbers in bank accounts, the money-creation process has become even easier. As long as no one demands the actual notes from the banks, the bank doesn't need to have the money before it makes the loan. In the UK, by 2007, the government had only created a total of about £50 billion in cash and £20 billion in central bank reserves – enough money to finance 10% of one year's expenditure. The credit money created by banks at that point had reached over £1,600 billion (Thanks to money creation through quantitative easing (more on this later) that figure is now above £2,000 billion.[84]) In most nations, mad dictator countries excepted, banks have been the biggest money creators.

Now that most money is electronic, the 1844 Bank Charter Act that said only the Bank of England could issue notes has become irrelevant. I remind you of that alarming statistic: 97% of money in the UK and in the US is created digitally by banks, and most of this money is created when people go into debt to them.

As well as the evolution of electronic money, the 1980s and 1990s also saw deregulation in the banking sector. In the UK in 1986 we had the 'Big Bang'. In the US, 1999 saw something similar – the repeal of the Glass-Steagall Act. These new laws meant that ordinary high street (or commercial) banks – where most people deposit their savings or have their current (checking) accounts – were no longer separated from investment banks (what goes on in the City, in Wall Street and elsewhere). So now somebody in the investment bank could make a bet on the stock market, say, or invest it in some venture, using money that your proverbial Aunt Mabel had deposited there. (I am not wildly against this deregulation, as long as, one, it is transparent, which it isn't – people don't realize what goes on with their deposited money – and, two, banks are allowed to go bust if they overdo it, which they aren't – they get bailed out. If they were allowed to go bust, they would operate in a different, more responsible way.)

Due to clever means of leverage and complex derivatives, ways have been found to lever the fractional system even more, so that by 2008 some institutions were levered by many more times than the original 10:1 fractional reserve ratio. When there is that much leverage in the system and money is not going into real businesses but instead into financial speculation, you just need a bet to go against you by a small amount and suddenly entire banks – indeed the whole system – comes under threat. That, in a nutshell, is what happened in 2008. Bankers then bullied politicians into bailing them out, otherwise, 'the whole system comes crashing down'. It was a classic example of a privileged, rent-seeking, special-interest group manipulating governments.

We have an over-leveraged and highly vulnerable financial system, which has got itself into a bog of too much debt. The whole thing operates using this intangible system of money that is based on law and faith and nothing else. Banks and governments have the privilege, which nobody else enjoys, to create and issue money. Banks also have the legal privilege to lend other people's money – without even having to ask their permission (remember, depositors no longer own the money, banks do). All that newly created money has gone into houses and financial speculation, rather than genuine wealth-generating businesses. As new money gets created, existing money is devalued. The system is destructive.

The rest of us must not only use this constantly devalued money to save and spend, but we must do it while central banks set interest rates. In other words, they set the price of borrowing money. If some central planner were to set the price of shoes or cars or any other item, most would think it not only absurd, but also highly impractical. The market sets the price. If the goods are in short supply, their price rises; if they are plentiful, their price falls. If a central planner sets the price of anything – unless he sets the exact right price every time, which is highly improbable – a distorted situation is created. If the planner sets the price too low, businesses will struggle to sell goods – because they can't profit at that price. They may even stop supplying them altogether. If the planner sets the price too high, the reverse happens, there is excess supply – and you get your European butter mountains. The market is a better pricing mechanism.

Why should the price of money be any different? In many ways the price of money is the most important price of all, so it's even more important that the price is set by the market, rather than the artificial situation of a central planner's office. The fact that central planners are unelected makes it even more worrying that they hold responsibility for setting the price of money.

If the Bank of England or the Federal Reserve Bank – perhaps leaned on by a government that wants to create a boom in time for its next election, or is under some sort of pressure from the media to 'do something' – sets the price too low, people may borrow more than they otherwise would. Borrowing entails the creation of new money, and new money leads to higher prices. Higher prices often attract speculation, even if the assets are unnecessary and unwanted – which leads to further borrowing and money supply growth. Such malinvestment is a terrible waste of resources and usually leads to loss of capital. It causes artificial booms and subsequent busts.

If the Bank sets the price of money too high, you get the reverse – nobody borrows, exchange dries up and you get some kind of deflationary collapse. This is, broadly speaking, what happened when Churchill put the UK back on the gold standard back in 1925 at too high a rate.

Money has become a political tool: policy-makers use it and manipulate it for their own political agenda. This system of money and finance is not an unregulated free market, but protected crony capitalism. It is immoral, deeply unfair and highly perilous. It is exploited by rent-seekers. But because it is monopolist or, more accurately, duopolist, when the system comes crashing down, the wrong people – the innocent – pay.

That, broadly speaking, how is our system of money has come to be and how it works. It is an inefficient system; it causes waste, malinvestment and all sorts of economic injustices. The asset booms it has created have alienated an entire generation and consigned them to debt servitude. It was born out of political expediency. Money should be money and nothing else.

7   How Money Is Theft

Lenin was certainly right. There is no subtler, no surer means of overturning the existing basis of society than to debauch the currency. The process engages all the hidden forces of economic law on the side of destruction, and does it in a manner which not one man in a million is able to diagnose.

John Maynard Keynes, economist[85]

Since that fateful day, 15 August 1971, when President Nixon closed the gold window and made the dollar no longer convertible into gold, debt has grown exponentially. In 1971 there were fewer than $70 billion in circulation in the US. Today the number is around $2.7 trillion (2,700 billion) – a near 40-fold increase. The reality may be that there is many times more money in circulation than that. It is virtually impossible to put a number on it. UK money supply has also grown many times faster than the economy from £31 billion in 1971 to just under £2,100 billion (£2.1 trillion) today – a 67-fold increase. In July 1971, US government debt was $412 billion. Now it is $16 trillion – i.e. $16,000 billion – another 40-fold increase. In 1971 the UK government's debt was £33 billion. In 2012 it will have reached about £1.1 trillion, about a 35-fold increase.[86] And these figures do not include unfunded liabilities; even the UK government's own Office of National Statistics has estimated that the real debt may be four times higher than the official figures suggest.

I would like to show you what happens when new money gets created, how insidious the process is, how, in this crony capitalist system, it harms and impoverishes the innocent. If there is one section of this book it's vital to understand, it is this. This process is, as I see it, behind the economic distortion we have in our world today.

There is considerably more money in the world than ever before, as I have outlined, but are we any richer? Looking at a typical Western European or North American family, we are richer in the sense that we have more things than we did a hundred years ago, but that is due to man's increased productivity and the technological advances he has made – most of which derive in some way from fossil fuels and the invention of the microchip.

Though there is more money in the world, we are, in most cases, in more debt than we've ever been. We have gone from a situation where one parent worked to where both parents need to, just to maintain a middle-class lifestyle. In relative terms, the under-thirties, thanks to their debt, are the poorest they've ever been. In London, most people in this age group believe they will never be able to own a house. Most delay starting a family to much later in life as a result. Given man's dramatically increased productivity, I find it incredible that most of us in the West are poorer than our parents.

The simplest consequence of all the newly created money that has poured into the economy since 1971 has been to push up prices. Sometimes it has been house prices that have risen, sometimes it has been commodities, sometimes the stock market; always it's been the cost of government, and it never stops growing. Wages have risen less often. The prices of most things are many times higher now than they were ten, 20 or 40 years ago in nominal terms, even if their relative cost of production has fallen. In other words, your pound note or your dollar bill buys you much, much less. This relentless fall in the purchasing power of money, otherwise known as inflation, is as certain as death and taxes. In fact it is a tax.

Imagine a tiny economy. There are 20 people in it. Of these, ten each have $1 in cash, so there is $10 in the entire economy. The other ten people each have an asset – these are the only assets in the economy and are each priced at $1. People quite happily buy and sell these assets for $1 each. If more assets appear in this economy, but the amount of money stays finite, the cost of assets will fall. But let us assume for now no new assets enter the economy.

One person – Mr King – is suddenly able to magically create another $10 from nowhere. He decides to go out and spend some of this new money. He buys an asset for $1, which the vendor is happy to sell because, based on the knowledge the vendor has, that is the fair market price. Except that it isn't because there is no longer $10 in the economy, but $20. At $1 the vendor has sold his asset too cheap – and he has received devalued money in exchange.

Mr King then decides to outbid the others and offers $1.50 for another asset. This vendor is delighted, sells, probably feeling rather clever, and makes off with $1.50, but even he has sold his asset too cheap. Mr King, meanwhile, is becoming asset rich. The other vendors hear assets are now trading for $1.50 and now expect that price, which Mr King is happy to pay. In other words, asset prices are gradually rising to reflect the new money in circulation.

There are some big losers in this process – the people who each had $1. The purchasing power of their money is now no longer enough to buy an asset they were previously able to buy. Ultimately, their purchasing power will halve because there is twice as much money in circulation. They haven't acted imprudently in any way – they haven't even acted – yet they are made poorer by this process of other people creating new money.

What about the people holding the assets? How have they done? Eventually, asset prices in this economy will rise to $2 – there are ten assets and $20 in circulation. The price of their assets should rise to reflect this extra money in circulation, so – as long as they didn't sell – they come out even. They might think they are richer because their asset now costs $20, but this is a delusion: it is the same asset. They have just survived the inflation, nothing more. If, however, they were one of the early vendors who sold for $1 or $1.50, now they cannot afford to buy back the asset they previously sold. They are 'priced out' and poorer.

Meanwhile, Mr King has done extremely well. He benefits, of course, as the recipient of a load of newly created money. But he was also able to buy assets for $1 and $1.50, before they rose in price to reflect the new money in circulation, so, with his assets now valued at $2, he profits from the asset-price inflation too. Wealth, which was originally spread evenly through our tiny economy, has insidiously transferred *from* cash-holders and those who sold their assets early *to* Mr King.

As a consequence of this process not only has wealth transferred, but those operating in our tiny economy no longer focus on making things. Instead they look for signs of future money creation and speculate on those signs, because there is more money to be made that way.

There we have the dynamic of Western economies over the last 40 years. It is impoverishing – particularly to those people who have savings or are on fixed incomes. Prices spiral further and further out of reach. Wages have not risen concomitantly. People have taken debt to afford the things they were previously able to buy, more people in the home have had to work, the younger generation have been priced out altogether. Many assets progress beyond people's reach altogether – in the case of London, most locals would not now be able to buy the house in which they live. Those who sold are now priced out.

The process is continuous and relentless. It effectively redistributes wealth from one group to another. And the longer it goes on, the more enslaved people become to debt. Writing in 1921, Keynes explains: 'Governments can confiscate, secretly and unobserved, an important part of the wealth of their citizens. By this method they not only confiscate, but they confiscate arbitrarily; and, while the process impoverishes many, it actually enriches some . . . Those to whom the system brings windfalls . . . become "profiteers" who are the object of the hatred of the bourgeoisie, whom the inflationism has impoverished . . . the process of wealth-getting degenerates into a gamble and a lottery . . .'[87]

Let's consider the three groups from our scenario in the context of the broader economy, starting with asset holders.

Goods of which there is a finite supply – houses in exclusive areas, for example, antiques or works of art (a great investment for the super-rich) – have risen dramatically in price over the past 40 years. Every year some new record is broken at an art auction somewhere. But it is still the same painting, piece or house. It hasn't changed. There have been no modifications. So the owner hasn't actually become any wealthier (unless his business is actually trading houses, antiques or art). He may feel like he's richer, particularly if his asset has grown in price by more than money-supply increases, but really he has simply survived this process of money devaluation. This is why, broadly speaking, assets such as houses and works of art have been a much better place to store your wealth than cash, even if that cash pays interest.

One of the psychological consequences of seeing the purchasing power of your money fall is the desire not to get left behind, so people kept buying assets rather than hold savings, sometimes taking on debt to do so, all of which, of course, causes asset prices to rise further. This can snowball into a boom, eventually a bubble – and then a bust.

It happens time and time again, particularly with houses. I am 42 and I can clearly remember two housing boom-and-busts. In many ways a house is a liability and should be a depreciating asset. A house costs money to run and maintain. As it gets older you have modernizing, refurbishing and maintenance costs. Yet prices constantly rise – the creation of credit keeps pushing them up – until you get a credit contraction. So our system of money and banking actually causes this boom-bust cycle in real estate. (Planning laws restrain the amount of new houses that can be built, yes, this is another factor, but between 1997 and 2007 for every four new people added to the UK population, three new homes were built. Money creation is what has made them so unaffordable.)

The groups who benefit the most are those who are able to create new money (Mr King) – or those who get it early. They can buy assets before they rise in price to reflect the new money in circulation.

Who are these groups? Who is Mr King?

One group is, of course, the government. It hasn't done anything productive to earn money. It hasn't had to work hard or invent something or start and run a business. By virtue of being the government and having a monopoly on money, it can tax it, print it – or find other more opaque ways to create it, such as quantitative easing. 'When you start printing money,' said the Bank of England's Paul Fisher, 'you create value for yourself. If you can issue a thousand pounds of IOUs to everybody, you've got a thousand pounds for nothing.'[88]

In the past many governments have spent money before it's even been created, particularly during wars – by so-called deficit spending.

If you, or I, or any other business spend more than we earn, we go bust. But not the state.

Banks are the other prime beneficiary.[89] Not only can they create money, but they can then charge interest on this new money that didn't previously exist.

The next beneficiaries are those receiving this money early. They can go out and spend it in the marketplace before the cost of goods and services have risen to reflect the new money in circulation. The older generation is one example. They were able to buy assets – houses, in particular – a long time ago before all this new money had been created. They now enjoy the price rises. So our system of money is a direct cause of the wealth divide between generations.

This process is known as the 'Cantillon Effect', after Richard Cantillon. Having purchased shares in John Law's notorious Mississippi company in 1719, he noticed that the paper money that government was creating, backed by shares in the company, didn't reach everyone at the same rate. The well-connected got the paper first, but the time it reached those at the bottom of the chain – the labouring classes – it had lost value. Eventually, it became worthless. Writing in *MoneyWeek* magazine, Bill Bonner says:

> A version of the Cantillon Effect was observed in Soviet Gulags and German concentration camps. Victims reported that those who were close to the kitchen were more likely to survive. The food often ran out before it reached those who worked in the fields and forests.
>
> Now, we have the central banks running their printing presses – effectively giving money to their friends in the banking industry. From there, it seeps into the whole financial community, boosting prices for financial assets, which are owned by . . . you guessed it . . . the 10%.

Housing tends to be a beneficiary of this new money-creation process. If people could buy houses only with cash, or using money that others had actually saved (i.e. if credit was in line with earnings), prices would be much lower. They would remain in line with savings and there would be a natural limit on how much money is available for mortgages. But that isn't what happens. More and more money is created, bearing little relation to actual savings, and it is pushed into the housing market, which then drives up prices. This process goes on and on so that everyone associated with the housing market and its new higher prices benefits – be they estate agents, builders, mortgage brokers – until the expansion of debt stops. The housing market is one of the easiest ways an ordinary person can get close to the 'soup kitchen' and expose themselves to the benefits of money-creation.

Think of all the other areas where new credit is created – corporate finance, venture capital, bond markets, for example. These are all areas where huge sums are made by participants. It's because the people involved are close to the new money (credit) creation point.

The military is another beneficiary, arms dealers in particular. The government borrows, money is created and then spent on arms or tanks or ships – and the arms dealer makes good. The same goes for all those on lucrative government contracts – doctors, lawyers and those involved at the top end of the huge spend that is infrastructure. But however money is created – be it through lending, money-printing, deficit-spending, quantitative easing or any other form of bail-out – banks are always at or near the top of this money-lending pyramid. Meanwhile, those who are furthest from this issuance of new money are the big losers. These are the holders of \$1 in cash in our earlier scenario. These might be people on fixed salaries, those who live in remote areas, far from the banking centres – farmers or fishermen, for example. (You only need look at the north–south divide in the UK to see this at work). By the time this newly created money has filtered through the economy to reach them, the prices of the things they want to buy have risen, their money buys them less and their wages are broadly unchanged. In some cases, they have to take on debt just to be able to afford the things they were previously able to buy – which means they have to go back to the banks.

Now consider the group of people who are furthest of all from the creation of new money – those not yet or only recently born – the young, in other words. They have no assets and no cash – just debt.

In reality, all that this process of money-creation does is continuously redistribute wealth from the bottom to the top of the money-issuing pyramid. Those at the top get richer, those at the bottom get poorer – and the gap between rich and poor gets bigger. This is not the free market at work, but a gross, unintended economic distortion caused by the colossal government intervention that is the duopoly that banks and the state have on money.

The gap between rich and poor was the single most-cited complaint of the 'Occupy' movement that gathered such momentum in 2011. Politicians are forever going on about the gap. All sorts of remedies, usually involving increased taxation and regulation, have been suggested and, in some cases, implemented. But you cannot tax and regulate your way to prosperity. This is recognized only by a few diehard economists in the nether regions of the internet – many of them operating under a school of economic thought known as the 'Austrian School'. The gap is a simple and direct consequence of this process of new money creation. It distorts economies. It causes boom and bust. And it is inherently unjust – benefiting that favoured small group that can create money, or are close to its issuance, at the expense of everyone else.

Despite this, money-creation is the response to the current crisis that many seem to want. The world's most powerful banker Ben Bernanke, chairman of the US Federal Reserve Bank, actually believes in it. In 2002 he said, 'The US government has a technology, called a printing press (or, today, its electronic equivalent), that allows it to produce as many US dollars as it wishes at essentially no cost.'[90] The printing press is what he and his UK counterparts keep resorting to.

Governments' response to this crisis has been to bail out the banking system, the car industry, almost anything they can. They have already spent, even in inflation-adjusted terms, many times more than was spent on the Second World War in its entirety. The money has effectively, as US Congressman Ron Paul is so fond of saying, been 'created out of thin air'. We do not yet know what the consequences of this money creation will be. Part of the reason this has not resulted in major inflation is that the currency is still trusted (inflation also being a psychological event), but also that governments have not been able to create money as fast as credit has contracted. Many in the private sector have paid down debt, cut costs and conserved capital. Banks have tightened lending. Once banks become significant net creators of capital again, and people expand their borrowing, inflation, and even hyperinflation become more likely.

I remind you of that alarming statistic – the richest 400 people in the world have assets equivalent to the poorest 140 million. One thing that this system will continue to do, as sure as night follows day, is further exacerbate the gap between rich and poor – and it is happening on a global scale. Those furthest from the issuance of new money – in the outer reaches of Africa, say – get poorer as those closest to its issuance (Wall Street and the City) get richer.

As a child in the 1970s and 80s I can remember hearing people complaining about it on TV, yet the gulf between rich and poor keeps on getting wider. It will continue to do so until we reform our system of money, banking and credit. All attempts by government to deal with this through taxation or legislation have failed – and will always fail, because they erect barriers to exchange. The answer is not more taxation, legislation and regulation. It is less.

Is it any wonder that the government (now as much as 25% of the country's workforce) and finance have both grown so disproportionately large? Government, and for the large part finance, are both 'rent-seeking' industries. They re-allocate existing wealth, rather than create new wealth (remember, just 13% of new money creation goes into real business). Too much talent and too many resources have gone into unproductive sectors at the expense of the genuinely productive. Consider our 'Miss Doubt' from the second chapter. Where might our manufacturing or other industries now be, if all that talent, capital and effort had gone to her instead of to rent-seeking?

The only way to create real new wealth is to grow stuff, make stuff or mine stuff. Everything else is simply the transference of wealth from one group to another. Thanks to our system of money and banking, we have transferred all our wealth to a small percentage of society – and impoverished a generation in the process.

8   The Biggest Murderer in History

Who controls the food supply controls the people;
who controls the energy can control whole continents;
who controls money can control the world.
Henry Kissinger, 56th US Secretary of State (attributed)

When one body has the ability to create money, it gives them a disproportionate amount of power. I would like to look now at some of the consequences of that power. I want you to imagine for a moment that money is independent. Banks can't create it, nor can governments. I also want you to imagine that all taxation is transparent. The costs are seen and felt. There are no stealth taxes, there is no deduction of income tax at source, there is no taxation via inflation, or running-up of never-ending deficits (the British government has run deficits in 38 of the last 40 years; the US in 36 of the last 40). Thus you have a situation where government (and banks) can't create money to devalue their existing debts and they can't raise taxes. Suddenly, they can only spend money they have. If, once a government spends that money, it is gone, they would suddenly have to operate under the same rules as the rest of us. If we consistently spend more than we earn, we go under.

In such a scenario, WWI – perhaps the most terrifying and unnecessary war in British history – could never have happened. Neither the British nor the German governments had the money, or gold, to pay for it. Both came off the gold standard and printed the money they needed. Had either government not had the power to print money or create debt – i.e. if they did not have control of money – the war would have had to stop. Imagine that – the war really *would* have been over by Christmas. All those millions of young men would never have died; all that unnecessary grief, destruction and ruin. Think about the implications. What did WWI lead to? German reparations, which led to Weimar hyperinflation, which led to the rise of Hitler and so on. Glasgow could not have got into its current state.

The same goes for almost all wars – WWII, Vietnam, Iraq, you name it. No war has ever been fought on a cash basis. Costs are concealed by deficit spending. If taxes had to rise concomitantly in the same year that wars were being fought, people would not pay. Instead, the cost is added to the national debt. People don't have to pay £10 billion this year; instead they pay an extra £500 million every single year for eternity in interest on the national debt. Take away this power to create money and run deficits, and you suddenly limit the scope of the war to the amount of money the government has. In other words you limit government power – and you limit the damage that they can do. That alone is reason enough to separate money and state.

It is commonly said that 'religion is the cause of all wars'. As a percentage of global population involved, the five biggest wars in history were the An Lushan rebellion, the Mongol conquests, the Qing conquest of the Ming dynasty, WWII, WWI and the conquests of Timur. Not one of these was primarily religious. Of the worst 20 wars in history by death toll, only three could be classed as religious – the Taiping Rebellion (1850–64), the Thirty Years War (1618–48) and the French Wars of Religion (1562–98).[91] Governments and leaders are the cause of most wars, with clashing ideologies and races, as well as conquest, usually the fundamental reasons. In fact, there would be far fewer wars if people stuck to the guidelines of their religions (war is a direct breach of the Sixth Commandment, for example).

It is government control of money that makes these wars possible. 'Without the money-counterfeiting tool of government,' wrote American economist E. C. Riegel in 1949, 'there could be no war except by popular mandate, because the price would have to be consciously and immediately paid. The would-be war-maker first of all conquers and subdues his own people by the narcotic of counterfeit money. If the people would hold the veto power of war, they must deny to their government the power to counterfeit money.'[92]

If there really is a need for an army, perhaps to defend against threat of invasion by another state, the market will meet that need. But, at present, which nation state is going to invade Britain or the US?

'The paper money of the Soviet Republic,' wrote Bolshevik economist Evgeny A. Preobrazhensky in 1919, 'supported the Soviet Government in its most difficult moments, when there was no possibility of paying for the civil war out of direct tax receipts. Glory to the printing press! To be sure, its days are numbered now but it has accomplished three-quarters of the task. In the archives of the great proletarian revolution, alongside the modern guns, rifles, and machine guns which mowed down the enemies of the proletariat, an honorary place will be occupied by that machine gun of the People's Commissariat of Finance which attacked the bourgeois regime in its rear – its monetary system – by converting the bourgeois economic law of money circulation into a means of destruction of that same regime and into a source of financing the revolution.'[93]

Look how that turned out. The consensus is that Stalin and his policies went on to kill 20 million people. In his book *Lethal Politics*, historian R. J. Rummel of the University of Hawaii, argues that this 20 million figure is wrong, calculating the real figure to be 43 million.

Who would have thought that systems of money and banking affect war and peace? But they do. Abuse of money is a force for war. Independent money is a force for peace. The cost of war is usually met by people who, for the most part, never wanted war in the first place – paid for by loss of life and through destruction of communities, families and wealth. The cost of the war is met by our Mr Loss and Miss Doubt from chapter 2, while Mr Gain makes good.

Since 1971, when the last official link between gold (an independent money) and money was broken and the world made the final move to this debt-based fiat system of money, a number of apparently unrelated trends have accelerated. I want you to consider some of them. I see 15 August 1971 as one of those days the points on the railway – the railroad switch – were changed and the hurtling train that is mankind accelerated further down the wrong tracks.

First, there is the endless sea of debt. Debt has become so normal that the difference between debt and money has become blurred. The only way to service the existing debt of the system is for that system to take out more debt, hence this obsession there is with what they call economic growth – really debt expansion. But at what cost?

With this expansion of money and debt – and of government – we have seen unprecedented acceleration in: financial inequality, malinvestment, working hours, wage slavery, divorce rates and the dissolution of the family, wars, frauds and bubbles, and the destruction of the environment. They are linked.

As debt expands, so the cost of servicing debt increases and you have a never-ending bubble of expansion requiring endless growth, for people to work harder and harder and business to expand and expand – whether expansion is appropriate to circumstance or not. It all comes at the expense of other areas of our lives.

Governments worldwide are trying to keep the system going. They're encouraging lending, slashing interest rates, buying their own debt, creating money through quantitative easing, the long-term refinancing operation (LTRO) and 'Operation Twist', and central banks are printing money to buy government debt. All of these operations – just different forms of new money or debt creation – will prove wasteful and damaging. They will already be having unintended consequences that we do not even know about. They all interfere with the natural purging process of a free market. Companies that have acted irresponsibly should be allowed to go bust. It may be painful, but that is the natural way of things. The hole they leave will be filled by another company that has behaved responsibly and prudently, and the world will be a better place for it. Death is part of life. Zombies are not. Failure is key to progress.

When one body has power over money, that power will inevitably get abused, either by incompetence, as is usually the case, or by something worse. Examine the methods of any and every dictator and you will see that control of money has been his most essential tool. The best way to stop the abuse of power is to spread it as widely and as thinly as possible. This is, in fact, the Marxist ideal – giving 'power to the people'. Let us have socialism, but without the state. As the motivational speaker Michael Cloud once said, 'the problem isn't the abuse of power. It is the power to abuse'. Government is not the means to achieve the socialist ideal of equality. Let us have money that is independent – a money that no single body has the power to print or create. Then no group will have special privilege. The rules will be the same for everyone.

Man has tried to give 'power to the people' through the Soviet and left-wing means of expansive government, regulation, taxation, central planning and the welfare state. But this has had, counter-intuitively, the opposite effect. Broadly speaking, Soviet Russia first made everyone poor – then it created the oligarchy, which is about as far from the original Marxist ideal as you can get. We need to do the opposite – to reduce the power of governments and banks. Independent, freely chosen money is the route to liberty and prosperity.

Many will see some of the ideals of this book as just that: ideals, unrealistic and impractical given the current situation. They may be right. But the simple step of moving to independent money is not so impossible to realize.

9   Why Metal Is Armour Against the State

In the absence of the gold standard, there is no way to protect
savings from confiscation through inflation . . . This is the shabby secret of
the welfare statists' tirades against gold. Deficit spending
is simply a scheme for the confiscation of wealth. Gold stands in
the way of this insidious process. It stands as a protector of property rights.
If one grasps this, one has no difficulty in understanding
the statists' antagonism toward the gold standard.

Alan Greenspan, former Chairman of the US Federal Reserve[94]

I like gold. But I am not one of those who believe that gold and only gold should be money. In fact, I think virtually anything can be money. If two people want to use air miles to effect a transaction, or whales' teeth or online barter points, then that is up to them.

In the UK, if we effect a transaction in some other currency, we are bound by law to translate the value of that transaction into government money and then pay the appropriate taxes. It is onerous. Most don't bother. In the US you are not even allowed to do that. You must use dollars.

I'm going to outline some of the arguments as to why the world should go back to using metal as money – not just gold, but metal. Ultimately, though, this is a decision the market should make. You're going to read some – forgive the pun – shining praise of gold, so let me reiterate here: gold is not the be-all-and-end-all. It does have a lot going for it, in my view, but it is not the only solution.

The chief reason I like metals is that they're independent. No one body has control over their supply. You can't print metal, so it limits what government can do and the system isn't complicated by excess concentrations of power. The author Chris Powell wrote the following on his blog in April 2012:

Perhaps first is that gold as money is the primary mechanism of enforcing limited government, and limited government is the first characteristic of civilized government. The distance between gold as money and unlimited fiat money is the distance between limited government and unlimited government, between democracy and totalitarianism.

The trend toward unlimited government lately has become overwhelming, from the stupid imperial wars being waged by the United States every few years to the comprehensive surveillance undertaken under the 'Patriot Act' to the 'financial repression' that even a recent member of the Federal Reserve's Board of Governors complained about a few months ago.

Gold remains a protector of individual liberty as well as a power that competes with government's power.[95]

Professor Walter E. Spahr, Chairman of the Department of Economics at NYU from 1927 to 1956, said about the gold standard:

It represents integrity. It insures the people's control over the government's use of the public purse. It is the best guarantee against the socialization of a nation. It enables a people to keep the government and banks in check. It prevents currency expansion from getting ever farther out of bounds until it becomes worthless. It tends to force standards of honesty on government and bank officials. It is the symbol of a free society and an honorable government. It is a necessary prerequisite to economic health. It is the first economic bulwark of free men.[96]

How, many ask me, can metal function today as money? It's archaic. I remind them of three primary functions of money.

1   To be a medium of exchange.
2   To be a store of wealth. I might not want to spend money I have just earned till tomorrow, next year or my retirement. I need the purchasing power of my money to last over time.
3   To be a unit of account. This is so I can value the goods or services you offer – and the ones I do; so I can measure profits, losses, liability, assets, relative value and so on.

To explore point one: of course, we no longer carry gold and silver coins on our person. We carry less paper than we used to and all but the smallest transactions now take place digitally. The speed at which a digital payment can be made (for which we have entrepreneurs and inventors, not governments and banks, to thank) – and the instant divisibility of modern money, from trillions down to pennies and cents – has been a marvellous facilitator of trade.

It's quite simple to set up a global electronic payment system using metal as money. In fact such systems already exist for gold and silver. The reason they are not yet more commonly used is because of legislative rather than practical issues. They work as follows.

Metal is safely stored – and properly audited with serial numbers and so on – in vaults around the globe. Ownership of the metal is then transferred instantly by digital transaction. Let me give you an example. There is a silver bar, weighing ten ounces, stored in the ABC vault. It is registered in my name. I buy something from you worth five ounces. With my card, or phone app, I instantly transfer the ownership of half that bar to you.

I suspect the storage costs would make this process uneconomic for copper and nickel transactions – though I am happy for some entrepreneur to prove me wrong on this – but for silver and gold transactions it is simple. Ownership of a metal bar – that doesn't move but stays in the same vault – is actually easier to record and execute than the transfer of money from one bank to another. Money could be paid and received as instantly as it is today. It's easy under such a system to involve no bank at all – and thus not to have to pay a share of all those expensive salaries, buildings and processes.

Such a system would improve international payments. Currently the process of transferring money internationally is drawn-out and expensive. It can involve at least two banks, sometimes more, waiting for money to clear, foreign exchange (forex) transfers, commission and goodness knows what else. It's archaic and typical of the megalith that is the state and banking. But metal is the same worldwide – you wouldn't need national currencies at all. You merely transfer ownership of metal. So metal can actually work better than fiat currency as a medium of exchange – if allowed to do so.

Next we consider the second point: to be a store of wealth. How does gold do this?

Spandau Ballet sang, 'Gold, you're indestructible' and indeed it is. It's immutable. It doesn't tarnish. As the recent discoverers of Iceni gold buried in Norfolk found to their delight, you can dig up a gold coin buried in the ground a thousand years ago and it would be more or less intact, unoxidized and unblemished. Indeed, there are some who argue – though how you prove this, I have no idea – that, as gold has virtually no industrial use, it doesn't get consumed, so almost all the gold that has ever been mined still exists somewhere in the world today. What about your paper £5, or your computer digit representing £5 stored on some hard drive somewhere? Where will they be in ten, 50 or 100 years' time?

Just as gold lasts over time, so does its purchasing power. An ounce of gold would have bought a Roman Senator a toga and sandals; it would have bought the 18th- or 19th-century gent a very nice suit and shoes from his tailor on Savile Row; and, today, the sterling equivalent (£1,000/$1,600) still buys your important man-about-town a respectable suit and shoes. In fact, it might easily buy you three sets or more, given the improvements in the efficiencies of clothes manufacturing.

A story from the Old Testament mentions that King Nebuchadnezzar of Babylon was able to buy 350 loaves of bread with an ounce of gold. If a large loaf now costs about £1.50, 350 loaves would cost about £525. An ounce of gold costs about £1,000. So gold buys you more bread now than it did in the Old Testament – as it should: with modern farming and production methods, bread is cheaper.

According to the Koran, a gold dinar would buy you a lamb (back in the 6th century AD). The modern equivalent still does today.

So gold buys you as much bread, meat and clothing as it ever has. Its purchasing power has hardly changed over millennia. As stores of wealth go, that's hard to beat.

Let's now look at the price of energy. The oil price always goes up, right? In 1972 a barrel of oil cost 0.06 ounces of gold. In 2012 a barrel of oil costs – you guessed it – 0.06 ounces of gold. That's not far off what it cost in 1942 or 1902 either. I reiterate: if you measure oil in metal, the price is – give or take a few per cent – the same as it was ten, 50 or 100 years ago. The price of oil does fluctuate if you measure it in gold, but it stays within a range – from about 0.16 ounces to 0.04 ounces.

But the price of oil in US dollars has gone from $3.50 a barrel in 1972 to around $100 now. That's something like a 3,000% rise – or a 96% loss in purchasing power. The same goes for all modern government currencies, which buy you less and less each year: less house, less chocolate bar, less anything. In 1971, I could have taken my son to the FA Cup Final for £2 (now over £100). The Mars bar I bought him at half-time would have been 2p (now 60p). The beer I bought myself would have been 11p (now £5 a pint at Wembley). The gallon of petrol I needed to get me there and back would have been 33p (now £7). And the house we went home to would have been something like 40 times cheaper.[97]

Average earnings have increased too, but by far less. They have risen from around £2,000 in 1970 to about £25,000 today. The differential has been covered up by more debt, longer working hours, more women in the workplace and so on (no, I am not against women working).

Purchasing power declines as more money is created. The only times at which government money's purchasing power has been constant was when it was tied to a gold or metallic standard. How much better for world trade would it be if prices remained as constant as they are in gold? Then relative value really would be simple to determine.

Which brings us to money function number three: to be a unit of account. Again, in my view, metals trump government currency. A piece of copper, nickel, silver or gold is the same wherever you are in the world – be it in Africa, Asia or America. It is still a piece of copper, silver or gold. It's constant. Its value remains the same. It might buy you more in one place and less in another, but that's the whole point of having a constant unit of account. It's to measure relative value. How much more beneficial would it be for global trade to have one metallic standard by which we all operate, rather than business being susceptible to the vagaries of the foreign exchange markets?

I've lost count of the times where an investment I've made abroad has done well – it's risen, say, 20% – only for the currency to fall by 20%. I've given back all my profit in forex losses. I've encountered so many businesses that have gone under simply because of currency fluctuation. In fact, currency fluctuation is one of the biggest problems for any investment abroad. Forex complicates business unnecessarily and it's entirely a product of the inconstancy of government money. People make fortunes trading forex; it's one of the biggest markets in the world – but it is not a productive business. It does not create new wealth. It does not bring something new to the world. It merely redistributes existing wealth. It's now an essential service, yes, but in many ways it's another form of rent-seeking. Metal eliminates all of that – and makes proper productive business endeavour so much more possible. (As a side note, metal also simplifies the study of history. Using something tangible and constant, you have a much better measure of real historical price. Instead we have to measure things in 'inflation-adjusted' terms or 'relative to GDP' which is so much more complicated than it need be.)

This relative constancy of gold and other metals is due to the fact that there are limits to how much metal you can mine. In other words, the supply of metal money is constrained. The same cannot be said of government money. Of course, if significant new gold deposits were suddenly found, inflation could become a problem. The discovery by the Spanish of all the gold and silver in the Americas meant that Spain suddenly found itself flooded with money, leading to inflation in the 16th and 17th centuries: ultimately proving to be one of the main factors in the decline of the Spanish Empire. However, despite huge amounts being spent on exploring for metals, repeated studies and declarations by senior gold mining executives all indicate major deposits are proving harder and harder to find, while grades (the amount of metal in rock) are falling. The sudden discovery of immense gold and silver deposits is unlikely to happen, unless, of course, there is some technological breakthrough – some wheeze to mine asteroids or under the sea (work is already happening here) perhaps. But don't hold your breath.

The fact the metal is expensive to mine is both a bane and a boon as far as its use as money is concerned. A bane in that money has a cost to bring it to existence; a boon in that its very cost gives it value.

One premise of this book is one of moving from Positive to Natural Law. Government fiat currency is the very essence of man-made Positive Law. Metal – gold in particular – is very much the money of nature's choice. In gold, nature has given us something that is almost eternal. It is so rare that it has great value – so much so that it is prohibitively expensive to use in industry, hence the reason so little of it gets consumed. Its only real use is to be a store of wealth. Nature has also given us something the supply of which grows at the same rate as the population – in fact it has grown ever so slightly quicker; until 1900 there were about 0.40 ounces per person, and now there are about 0.75. Cumulative world gold supply and world population grow at roughly the same rate.[98]

The common criticism of gold as currency is that there is not enough of it to go around. There is, in fact, more than there has ever been, but it is its very scarcity that gives it its value. There is plenty to go round if it is left to revalue upwards to levels at which people are happy to spend it rather than hoard it.

But how can gold be nature's money of choice, given the damage gold mining can do? This is a valid and important question. The environmental damage from irresponsible mining can be devastating and long-lasting. Forests can be ravaged. Toxic chemicals are sometimes dumped into waterways, destroying fish stock and poisoning the water. Workers are sometimes forced to labour under the most inhumane conditions. What goes on in mining camps can spread into and often destroy the social fabric of local communities through the introduction of alcohol, drugs and prostitution.

How does one ensure that mining is carried out responsibly? Mining, for some reason, attracts the irresponsible. I say this as someone who has experience in the industry. I don't know why but mining, throughout history, has attracted – as well as brilliant entrepreneurs – all sorts of scoundrels. It is part of the game. Hence Mark Twain's 'A mine is a hole in the ground owned by a liar.'[99]

There are many examples of communities that have benefited hugely through the responsible exploitation of their natural resources. But too often, sadly, the reverse is true. Informal, artisanal, unlicensed – and sometimes even properly licensed – mining can have dreadful consequences. Mining practices have improved greatly in recent years – in part this is due, I expect, to regulation; more likely it is down to increased awareness and better education as to the consequences of irresponsible mining, as well as better practice through greater prosperity. But there are still too many examples of bad practice. Though standards are improving, the bottom line is this: the damage done by gold miners is nothing compared to the rape of the earth and the destruction of communities – and indeed humanity – caused by the endless expansion of debt and the malinvestment it creates.

An essay I wrote for *The Idler*, 'Why Gold Is the Currency of the Free', ended as follows:

> Gold is true. It is incorruptible. You can't print it. It is a rare, useless, inanimate object, but it is constant, immutable and nobody else's liability. It imposes a discipline on people and governments, so they can't spend recklessly. Spending, no matter how well-intentioned, creates problems. Gold is a restrictive monetary system, but it is a fair, free and honest system. It all starts with money: values, morals, behaviour, ambitions, manners, everything. Money must be sound and true. At the moment it is neither. Society is corrupt as a consequence. As Dorothy is repeatedly advised in *The Wizard of Oz* (an allegory about the monetary system and the fraud that is the dollar, 'The Emerald City') the time has come once again to 'follow the yellow brick road'.[100]

Gold on its own is not enough. It's too restrictive and too inflexible. It could create as many barriers to exchange as it frees up. But gold will always have a large and important role to play in the monetary system.

Metals, however, could work.

Why We'll Never Find El Dorado

You have to choose [as a voter] between trusting to the natural stability of gold and the natural stability of the honesty and intelligence of the members of the Government. And, with due respect for these gentlemen, I advise you, as long as the Capitalist system lasts, to vote for gold.

George Bernard Shaw, playwright and co-founder,
London School of Economics[101]

Governments were held in check – to a degree – when the world was on a gold standard in the 18th and 19th centuries. The problem was, they kept finding ways around it – printing more money than they had gold, coming off the gold standard when it suited them, deficit-spending and so on.

Some are calling for us to go back to a gold standard now. But at what rate? If governments set the rate too low, the deflationary slump could be immense. If they set the rate too high, they could cause a global run on currencies. So what is the 'right rate?' How on earth does anyone decide? One possibility is simply to value gold at the current market rate. The problem with this is that the amount of gold in the world bears no relation to the amount of fiat currency that has been issued. Another formula would be to divide the amount of money on issue by the amount of gold in the vaults of its central bank.

The US monetary base – the amount of US dollars on issue – is $2.6 trillion. There are 261 million ounces of gold in Fort Knox. (Though this gold has not been properly audited in 50 years, we will assume it is there). If this monetary base were to be 100% backed by gold, then the gold price would be $2.6 trillion divided by 261 million ounces, which is $10,000 an ounce. (The current gold price is about $1,600 an ounce). So $10,000 an ounce is one possible rate at which to return – a rate that would make current holders of gold very happy, I'm sure.

Another possible rate would be to divide total US government debt ($16 trillion) by its gold – in other words revalue gold up to a level at which the US could pay its debt off with its gold. $16 trillion divided by 261 ounces is $61,303 per ounce. However, the US could pay off its debt with other things apart from its gold, so let's stick with the idea of the monetary base for now.

I should stress that the current monetary system is complicated – it is very hard to actually define what is money, what is debt and what is derivative. Tom Fischer, professor of mathematics at the University of Würzburg, prefers to use what is known as 'money with zero maturity' (MZM) as a measure of the US monetary base, saying:

> MZM, i.e. financial assets redeemable at par on demand, is what the Federal Reserve system has to underwrite in the case of a banking crisis, to avoid panics. If the central bank fails to underwrite sufficiently large parts (potentially all) of MZM, a panic might ensue where money could be withdrawn in such large amounts that it could become systemically dangerous. The Fed therefore has no choice: it has to underwrite MZM.[102]

Current MZM stands at just under $11 trillion. Divide that by the 261 million ounces of US gold and you arrive at a figure of $42,000 per ounce.

Another idea, proposed to me by leading gold data expert Nick Laird (who runs the data website sharelynx.com) runs as follows. The reaction of governments to this crisis has been, among other things, to try and create inflation. Interest rates have been slashed to get people borrowing and banks lending; savers have been forced to speculate by the negative return they are getting on their money; we have quantitative easing and all sorts of other forms of money creation. This is all because, as a result of excess debt, the world is severely undercapitalized. Many people who own gold are waiting for higher prices before they sell. They may not want to sell at the current price of $1,650, but they might be happy to at $10,000 or $42,000. They would then go out and spend and invest that money. The effect of an official, upwards revaluation would, simply, be to recapitalize the world and lay the foundations for another period of economic expansion. It's a transparent way of creating the inflation that governments and central banks are trying to create surreptitiously.

These suggestions have little more than a cat's chance in hell of getting through. To officially revalue gold from $1,650 to $10,000 – let alone $42,000 – would be such a shameful admission of the devaluation of money that has gone on that no policy-maker would undertake it. Indeed, it may totally undermine public confidence in money, one of the essential triggers of hyperinflation.

There would also be media outrage at the injustice, which would cause all sorts of problems for a politician. How, the outcry would be, can the government so transparently benefit one particular group – those who own gold? Far more likely would be some kind of confiscation – such as that which happened in the US in 1933 – or simply going back onto a gold standard at too low a rate.

What's more, though it would benefit me personally (as I own some gold) it is not the solution I favour. This would mean government 'fixing' something – which contradicts the free-market principles of this book. A government gold standard is, in my view, preferable to what we have now – it worked well in the 19th century – but it still involves too much government. It is not freely chosen by the market.

10   The Points on the Railway That Can Save Us All

There are no tyrants among men; there are only tyrannies, and the mother of tyrannies is money monopoly . . . Not money, but a false money system is the root of all evil . . . If money is to fulfil its function as the liberator of exchange, it must be protected from pollution by false issuers, and it must also be free to draw its supply from all worthy sources. The broader its base, the higher can be its apex and the greater its service to mankind.

E. C. Riegel[103]

Ending the monopoly that governments and banks have on money is changing the points on the track – my 'railroad switch' – that I alluded to at the beginning of this book. Governments and banks will then be forced onto the same playing field as the rest of us, operating by the same rules – the quite natural rules – of a free market. Once the field is level, the rest will follow and society can re-balance itself. But how to end this monopoly?

Earlier on, I outlined the idea of adopting a global metallic standard. It seems the fairest way to an independent, standardized global system of money. As E. C. Riegel writes in *Flight From Inflation*, 'Since money is but the mathematics of value, there is no more justification for the nations of the world to have separate monetary systems than separate systems of mathematics'.[104] But the broader market may not like my idea. If money is metal then there is a cost of production to it. Perhaps that's inefficient.

Perhaps the broader market will prefer some kind of digital money system, such as Bitcoin. Bitcoin has had a lot of publicity in recent months. It is a currency that is not created and controlled by central banks or by mining, but by cryptography – by a code. I can send you a payment as an email attachment, I can pay you via a smartphone or a computer app, without the need for bank or any other financial institution to get involved. In other words, it is money without governments or banks. Wonderful!

My first thought when I came across Bitcoin is that it is a scam. I'm less sure now. More and more businesses are starting to accept it as payment. It is a beautifully simple and quick way of conducting international transactions. However, it is the first currency of its kind and, as such, very much an experiment. It has survived and grown; and is now very much in the public consciousness. Time will tell if it works. But one thing is for sure, the bigger it grows, the more governments will try to stop it.

The world of mobile phone apps is also muscling in on money and payment in an unstoppably rapid way, particularly in Africa. Perhaps some form of digital mobile phone currency will arise that people prefer.

These are all possible solutions. None of them should be forced on us. We should be able to choose our money freely, just as we choose what books to read, what food to eat and what films to see – just as we were always free to choose what money we use before states took control of the system. Here is a simple, organic solution, one that will be palatable to an uncomprehending media and populace; one that will be easy to implement and one that is fair.

Firstly, governments need to relax and repeal their legal tender laws to allow other forms of money to compete in the market place. People can buy things, save (i.e. store wealth), be paid and pay taxes in a range of different currencies, whether they are national currencies such as the dollar or pound, or alternatives, such as gold, silver or Bitcoin. This way, choice is reintroduced. Any gains made in these alternative currencies, if they rise in value against local government currency, should not be liable for tax. This is so as not to penalize people for using alternative money.

The English MP, Douglas Carswell, has already made proposals about this in British parliament, while the former congressman and presidential candidate Ron Paul has made similar suggestions in the US, saying:

The obvious solution is to legalize monetary freedom and allow the circulation of parallel and competing currencies. There is no reason why Americans should not be able to transact, save, and invest, using the currency of their choosing. They should be free to use gold, silver, or other currencies with no legal restrictions or punitive taxation standing in the way. Restoring the monetary system envisioned by the Constitution is the only way to ensure the economic security of the American people.

After all, if our monetary system is fundamentally sound – and the Federal Reserve indeed stabilizes the dollar as its apologists claim – then why fear competition? Why do we accept that centralized, monopoly control over our money is compatible with a supposedly free-market economy? In a free market, the government's fiat dollar should compete with alternate currencies for the benefit of American consumers, savers, and investors.[105]

If my shopkeeper only wants to accept pounds and I am happy to pay him in pounds, then we have a trade. If he wants to accept silver or Bitcoin or some locally issued bill of credit, and I am happy to pay in those currencies, so be it.

It sounds chaotic, but the market would quickly make it efficient – more so than the current system. On a recent trip to Istanbul I noticed how traders in the Grand Bazaar will accept dollars, euros, Turkish lira, pounds, Russian rubles – anything, as long as it means trade for them. It is as simple for digital payments. These can be as easy as using an Oyster card, a debit card or a mobile phone app.

Problems arise around the barrier to exchange that is taxation. The constant need to translate sales tax, income tax, duty and so on back into local government currency is onerous, but this can be dealt with electronically with the development of the right app. What's more, as I am about to argue, governments must dramatically simplify and lighten their tax load.

This is not a campaign to destroy the pound or the dollar – governments can go on issuing these, if they see fit. It is simply to give everyone else the option of which currency we want to pay, be paid and save in. A bit of competition from other currencies – whether they are other national currencies, privately issued bills of credit, computer or metallic currencies – will force better practice on to all issuers of money and drive down costs. The inferior currencies will simply be forced out of the market place by the fact that no one will use them – unless they improve. In a world with choice, the market will probably turn to and use the soundest forms of money: gold and silver – but I don't know that for sure. Meanwhile unsound government currencies will no longer be propped up by the private sector, which currently has no choice but to use them.

E. C. Riegel made suggestions in this regard in the 1940s, and the idea was taken up in 1977 by Friedrich Hayek in his paper, 'Denationalisation of Money'. The paper's premise is that private businesses should be allowed to issue money, deciding how to do so themselves, instead of a national government imposing its money on everyone in the economy by force.

In his 2011 speech in the House of Commons, Carswell stated:

> If the Bank of England keeps printing off more money – more quantitative easing, more loose monetary policy – there may be a fall in the value of its currency, but not necessarily in the value of the currency that the rest of us choose to use. At the click of a mouse, people and businesses would have an alternative. Incidentally, our ability to opt out as individuals and businesses from the MPC's [Bank of England Monetary Policy Committee's] monetary monopoly might encourage it to stop taking liberties with our currency.[106]

Such is the rate at which the internet is spreading freedom and at which technology is advancing, and the rate at which currencies are being debased, competing currencies may be inevitable anyway, whether governments want them or not. Far better, I would have thought, to embrace the inevitable rather than fight it and cause a whole load of expensive, unwanted consequences.

The second step we need to take is an end to compulsory fractional reserve banking. I said earlier that most people don't realize this, but when you deposit money in a bank, that money becomes the property of the bank. What's more, the bank does not need to ask your permission to lend that money out. We need to return ownership of people's money to them. I'm not suggesting that we end fractional reserve banking – just that we restore choice. There should be accounts in which the customer owns the money and, probably, has to pay for banking services in fees; and others in which the bank is free to lend your money – and neither you nor the bank gets bailed out in the event that the bank over-extends itself. Thus good practice is forced on all, banks will have to clearly state what type of account it is and transparency ensues. The end result will mean that debt is suddenly backed by savings – by real money – rather than backed just by more debt in this endless pyramid we currently have. In other words, debt will become sustainable.

Carswell has suggested a bill here. His proposal is that you have to give the bank express permission – by ticking a box when you open an account – to go on and lend your money out. If they don't have your permission, they can't lend your money out. Speaking in the House of Commons in 2010 he said:

> My Bill would give account holders legal ownership of their deposits, unless they indicated otherwise when opening the account. In other words, there would henceforth be two categories of bank account: deposit-taking accounts for investment purposes, and deposit-taking accounts for storage purposes. Banks would remain at liberty to lend on money deposited in the investment accounts, but not on money deposited in the storage accounts ... Far from anti-free market, my proposal enshrines the individual property rights. Rather than undermining Western capitalism, my proposal attempts to address the problem of crony corporatism, which gives the free market such a bad name.[107]

His bill did not get through. On the positive side, however: the seed of the idea is planted.

These two steps – allowing people choice in what money they use and in how they bank – are simple to implement. They will be less problematic than, say, more contentious issues, such as anti-fox-hunting laws or gay marriage. In implementing them, we wrest control of money from government and banks. In wresting control of money, we wrest control of power – and return it to the people.

Governments and banks will lose the privileges they have abused and they will be forced to operate by the same rules as the rest of us. The playing field is level again. The train is re-routed. We are back on the path to a society that is more fair, transparent and prosperous.

7 Reasons To Like Independent Money:

1 It limits what governments can do. Wars immediately become less possible, as does waste.
2 Power is spread, not concentrated.
3 Money is just money. It is no longer a political tool that is manipulated to suit a political agenda.
4 The insidious, destructive forces of inflation and the social inequality it creates are no longer felt.
5 If you debase money, you debase society. With honest money, a virtuous circle is created.
6 The market is the best arbiter of what is good money. Let the market decide.
7 With sound money, people are more likely to save. With savings grows strength.

11   Our Immoral System of Tax

The income tax has made more liars out of the American people than golf has. Even when you make a tax form out on the level, you don't know when it's through if you are a crook or a martyr.

Will Rogers, comedian

How has the state grown so big? Nobody voted for it to happen – not consciously, anyway. But every time calls for more schools, more health care, more police – whatever the issue of the day is – are met, the state grows. None of this could happen without the state's monopoly on money. The practice of deficit spending, its ability to create money and inflate, fractional reserve banking and systems of government debt have all given the state inordinate power.

Between March 2009 and September 2012, £375 billion was created through the practice of quantitative easing to help the UK – or, rather, certain privileged bodies – through the financial crisis. With around 25.5 million households in the UK, that is £14,705 each. Can you imagine the response if each household had been transparently presented with a bill for £14,705 (about $24,000)? Voters would not have allowed it. Government has been able to grow so big because it conceals its costs.

Monetary manipulation is everywhere. Stealth taxes abound. Inflation is not measured properly; even its meaning has been distorted. Our proverbial Miss Doubt goes unaudited. Public borrowing means costs are not felt now, but later – often passed on to the next generation. Governments have hidden debts in 'off-balance sheet' liabilities, a practice that would not be acceptable if they were to operate by the generally accepted accounting principles they themselves set for corporations. Unequal taxation is everywhere. Income tax is deducted at source, so workers never actually see their money taken from them. Taxes are raised in small increments, so people don't notice and you suffer 'boiling frog syndrome' (if a frog is placed in hot water it jumps out, but in cold water that is slowly heated, it does not notice and is boiled to death). As Jean-Baptiste Colbert, Controller General of Finances for Louis XIV, so famously declared, 'The art of taxation consists in so plucking the goose as to get the most feathers with the least hissing.'[108]

Our systems of taxation are perhaps even more insidious than our systems of money. Across the Western world, taxes need to be lower, simpler and more transparent. Taxation reform is almost as easy as reforming our system of money. It's not a vote-loser, necessarily. It is another potentially huge 'game-changer'. It's obvious that it needs doing. Yet politicians do not do it. I wish I knew why.

In the UK we have income tax, National Insurance, value added tax (VAT), council tax, corporation tax, business rates, fuel duty, capital gains tax, stamp duty, and inheritance tax. We are taxed on the interest on our savings, even though we have already been taxed on our earnings. We are taxed on our dividends, even though the corporations that pay those dividends have already paid tax on their profits. We are taxed on our death, even though we have paid tax all through our life. The story is the same in the US and across the West. I am with Milton Friedman when he said, 'I am in favour of cutting taxes under any circumstances and for any excuse, for any reason, whenever it's possible.'[109] There are too many taxes. There are too many inconsistencies. There are too many mistakes. There is too much complexity and red tape. Avoidance and evasion are everywhere. All sorts of market distortions and crazy schemes have been invented in the quest to pay less tax. Unproductive – rather than productive – enterprise is incentivized. Government taxes where it can, rather than where it should. The answer lies in a wholesale simplification of the system.

Income tax was first introduced to the UK during the Napoleonic wars; it was abolished in 1816, reappeared briefly in the 1840s, but was here to stay from 1907–09 onwards thanks to the efforts of David Lloyd George, Winston Churchill and their 'People's Budget'.

Income tax was introduced in Australia in 1907, in the US in 1913 and in Canada in 1917. The Founding Fathers of the US never intended for Americans to be taxed on their labour; but in 1913 the 16th Amendment to the Constitution declared: 'The Congress shall have power to lay and collect taxes on incomes, from whatever source derived, without apportionment among the several States, and without regard to any census or enumeration.' Now, 47% of US Federal Tax receipts come from individual tax, with another 33% from payroll taxes. In the UK, income tax is about 30% of total tax revenue; National Insurance is 19%.

It was with the introduction of income tax that the tide changed and the move towards ever-bigger government began. It is no coincidence.

In the UK, income tax is the largest source of government revenue. Along with National Insurance, it is levied at source through Pay As You Earn (PAYE). Of the £153 billion it levied in income tax in 2010–11, £130 billion was levied at source. In other words, the worker never even received the money for which he worked.

The super-rich find ways of avoiding tax through off-shore vehicles and so on. Ordinary workers paying income tax are easier targets. Those paying the top rate are never the most numerous in a society, so targeting them for higher rates of tax can even make you popular. Just 10% in the UK pay over half of all income tax – others enjoy the profits of their labour, while, as they are merely 10% of the electorate, high earners carry low democratic influence. In the US, as Mitt Romney declared to his great loss in the run-up to the US elections, 47% of Americans pay no income tax at all. The top 1% contribute 20% of all tax revenue, while the top 20%, who earn 55% of revenue, contribute 70% of tax. As George Bernard Shaw once said, 'A government with the policy to rob Peter to pay Paul can be assured of the support of Paul.'[110]

It will always be a fact of life that some earn more than others. They might work harder, they might have gone to a better school or university, they might have had a lucky break, nature might have bestowed them with some great talent, they might just have been born at the right time. In many ways the current system of taxation is an attempt to redress that imbalance, by taxing the successful more than the unsuccessful. There is plenty to be said for that sentiment. I suspect, however, the reality is rather less benevolent – governments will elicit tax where it is most easy to do so. Income tax is easy to collect. But as money gets devalued while tax bands remain unchanged (or change at a slower rate), more and more people will find themselves in that top band, forced to pay more and more taxes as, life around them gets more and more expensive. The middle class will be further squeezed and stretched.

I have three strong moral issues with income tax. First of all, tax is not of the 'free market'. It is not freely given, but is coerced and extorted. There are similarities to protection money: you pay the Mafia or you will be beaten up; you pay taxes to the government or you will be arrested. Secondly, it is not just that the services I receive from government in exchange for my taxes are not good value for money, it's that my labour is often funding things I am morally and ideologically opposed to – wars, for example, or inefficiency and bloated bureaucracies. Too small a portion of my paid tax actually gets through to something that I might actually support. I'm minded of Thomas Jefferson's, 'To compel a man to furnish contributions of money for the propagation of opinions which he disbelieves and abhors, is sinful and tyrannical'.[111] The third problem is that we are taxed on our labour – on what we produce. The harder we work the more productive we are likely to be, yet the more we get taxed. In other words, we are penalized for being productive and successful. I think that's unhealthy. I'm convinced it's better for the soul to produce rather than consume, that happiness lies in production not consumption; it's certainly better for the economy to produce rather than consume. So foster productivity and don't tax people on it, is my view. 'To tax the larger incomes at a higher percentage than the smaller is to lay a tax on industry and economy; to impose a penalty on people for having worked harder and saved more than their neighbours,' says John Stuart Mill in *Principles of Political Economy*.[112] We'll come to taxing unearned wealth later in the chapter. If, on the other hand, you tax consumption instead of production, people will have a choice as to whether they pay tax or not; they don't *have* to consume if they don't want to. Untaxed on their productivity and offered the opportunity to make their own choice, people will be empowered. In a world of excess consumption and, according to some, fast-diminishing resources, I'm sure this would be a better route.

I also question the efficacy of taxation. It's good for government and its agencies, yes. But is it good for people? If you keep taking from one part of society and giving it to another, the set you take from will get smaller and weaker. The set you give to will grow. The revenue generated has gone towards schools and hospitals, yes, but more has gone on officialdom. All, in my view, are too expensive. The taxed are now less likely to be able to afford education or health care themselves, so they use the government option and become dependent on it. Meanwhile, with fewer and fewer customers, the non-government option finds it harder to survive. So taxation becomes counter-productive. The more one is taxed, the less capital one has for spending or investment, which hampers potential economic activity, and the less one is incentivized to go out and act in a capital-producing way. The government and its agencies have become Mr Gain; the rest Mr Loss and Miss Doubt.

Why Tax Avoidance Is Your Patriotic Duty

This is a question too difficult for a mathematician.
It should be asked of a philosopher.
Albert Einstein (when asked about completing his income tax form)[113]

Ease and simplicity have disappeared from our modern system of tax. In the UK, our tax code is 11,000 pages long. That's too complicated – by about 10,990 pages, I'd say. The US tax code, at 67,204 pages, is six times longer – 'about as long as 112 copies of James Joyce's *Ulysses*,' observes blogger Scott Simon, 'with 1,638 different tax forms'.[114] When you have a complicated system, it will inevitably be exploited. Error becomes not only commonplace, but unavoidable. We now even have a UK Office dedicated to Tax Simplification.

Let's look first at blunders. In 2010 it emerged that some 15 million people were on the wrong tax code. That's 25% of the population! In 2011 around six million people found themselves in line for tax rebates after HM Revenue and Customs (HMRC) made a computer error. But the amounts do not justify the cost of repairing all the errors – in response to the mistake, an HMRC spokesperson stated that 'each person should receive on average a couple of hundred'. A further one million are thought to have underpaid. HMRC now has to go back and repair errors for 2007–8 and earlier. Meanwhile 146,000 pensioners were to receive letters after mistakes in the taxing of their pensions meant they had underpaid. How much does all this cost to administrate? In 2012 in the UK some one million letters to the taxman were left unanswered.[115] Three of them were from me.

Fraud and evasion is everywhere. A recent *Telegraph* headline ran, 'Tax evasion costs Treasury 15 times more than benefit fraud.' According to 2010 data from the National Fraud Authority, tax evasion costs the Treasury £15.2 billion in lost revenue, while benefit fraud costs £1.1 billion every year. Now more regulation is being introduced and billions are being spent to tackle evaders. They have it backwards again. The problem is not evaders. The problem is the system. Tax evasion is the consequence – one of the many – of a system that is too onerous and too complicated. Some evade tax just because they cannot be bothered with the administration of it.

In his book subtitled *The Story of Taxation* Charles Adams notes that mankind, when over-burdened with taxation, resorts to one of the three Fs: Fight, Flight or Fraud.[116] From the Occupy movement to tax evasion, the black market, non-domiciles (or non-doms), off-shore companies and accounts, to large corporations operating in one country but being 'based' in another, we have a proliferation of all three in the West.

Our system of taxation is also inconsistent. Large corporations, which have set up entire departments to deal with the taxman and fight him, often find themselves better treated than small businesses and individuals, who are hounded over insignificant amounts. In December 2011 a committee of MPs criticized 'unduly cosy' deals between HMRC and large firms (Goldman Sachs and Vodafone in this example) over £25 billion worth of unpaid tax.

The aim behind quantitative easing and artificially low interest rates is to get the economy ticking over again, to get banks lending and put money in people and small businesses' hands. Why not just tax people less? That's surely a quicker way to recapitalize the economy. Rather than taking money from people, redistributing it and printing more of it, why not let people spend their own money themselves? They've worked for it, after all.

Flat Tax: Simple and Obvious. Why Don't They Do It?

Whoever hopes a faultless tax to see,
Hopes what ne'er was, is not, and ne'er shall be.
Alexander Pope (quoted by Charles Adams)[117]

It's difficult to see an end to income tax. It's too easy to collect. But shifting to a flat-rate tax is a possibility. It is simpler to administrate, it's simpler to understand and it's the same for everyone. But there is a crucial proviso: it should be lower than the current rate.

For example, let's presume that in this scenario the first £15,000 ($24,000) you earn is untaxed. You then pay a flat 15% rate on earnings above that level. Corporations pay the same rate as individuals. Why they are currently taxed less, I've never understood – is it simply because individuals are relatively easy to tax, and corporations can bully governments with the threat of basing themselves elsewhere?

In the short term, it might create a shortfall in government revenue, but governments run deficits anyway. With more cash in their pockets, people will have less need of government services, so government spending can easily and quickly be cut. In the medium term it will attract such a flood of business here, and bring so many evaders and avoiders back into the system, that revenue may actually increase with the boom it would create. Government revenue does not necessarily fall if you cut tax, even to such low levels, counter-intuitive though it may seem. The reverse is often the case, as happened in the US under Ronald Reagan, for example. There is less avoidance and evasion –

people, it has been proven, are happy to pay tax if they think it's fair; companies and individuals suddenly have more capital to spend and invest, so the economy becomes more buoyant; and industry quickly relocates from abroad to a low-tax environment. With our existing infrastructure and expertise, this would be rapidly become the case.

In Russia, revenues from Personal Income Tax rose by 25.2% in 2001, the first year after the Federation introduced a flat tax, followed by a 24.6% increase in the second year, and a 15.2% increase in the third year. Consider the relative wealth of somewhere like Hong Kong, which caps its income tax at 16%.

All those accountants, lawyers and tax experts – often intelligent people who spend their entire working lives looking at legitimate ways to manipulate the system through off-shore accounts, off-shore companies, non-dom status and so on – would suddenly have the opportunity to put their creativity and entrepreneurial skills into something that is actually productive.

Writing in *MoneyWeek* magazine in 2006, Tim La of the Adam Smith Institute says a flat-rate income tax 'is simple, transparent to the taxpayer and easy to manage, with low administrative costs'. He continues:

> it enhances the incentive to work; if it is extended to investment income it encourages the saving and investment necessary to stimulate economic growth in a competitive global market; it attracts entrepreneurs from abroad to a business friendly environment; it provides the conditions for increased employment; counter-intuitively, and given a sufficiently generous non-taxable personal allowance, it favours the lower paid over the affluent; and it quickly leads to higher tax receipts that enable government spending elsewhere.[118]

The problem with a flat-rate tax is finding a chancellor of the Exchequer brave enough to push it through. George Osborne looked extensively at the idea while in opposition, but, after making some positive noises, changed tack. I wish I knew the reason why, but I'd bet it was political, not economic.

Given the chancellor's job, not something I particularly want – with the remit that I can't abolish all government (as, in my more extreme moods, I would like) I would have a flat, 15% tax across the board. Not just income and corporation tax, but for VAT, capital gains, and duty. Then tax is simple, fair and consistent.

Kicking a Family When It's Down

The happiest mourner at a rich man's funeral is usually Uncle Sam.
Richard 'Olin' Miller, academic[119]

Less than 1% of people own 70% of all land in the UK. Around 6,000 or so landowners – aristocrats, large institutions and the Crown – own about two-thirds of the UK (40 million acres). Just 20 landowning families have inherited an area bigger than the entire counties of Kent, Essex and Bedfordshire.[120]

There are 60 million acres of land in the UK, and the population is 65 million – yet the average Briton lives on 340 square yards. 60 million people live in 24 million homes, which occupy just 7.7% of the land – 4.4 million acres. The average density of people on one residential acre of British land is 12 to 13.[121]

Ownership of the countryside is exclusive. Just three in every 10,000 enjoy that privilege. Each UK home pays an average of £550 per year on average in council tax, while each landowning home receives £12,169 per year in subsidies and, in addition, a similar amount from the EU. In England alone, as much as 50% of the land is still not registered.[122]

I'm all for the family unit, I'm all for wealth being passed from parent to child, rather than to government, but I'm *not* for 70% of the acreage of Britain being owned by 0.6% of the population. I'm *not* for 158,000 families owning 41 million acres of land while 24 million families live on four million acres.[123] In Spain the numbers are even more alarming: 70% of the land is owned by 0.2%. The unequal distribution of wealth is one of the fundamental economic problems of our times. It is one of the key themes of this book. Inheritance tax is seen as way to fix this, as a way to stop the super-rich families taking hold of huge swathes of land and keeping it for generations. But the above figures show that it clearly hasn't worked. It has not cured the problem of 'unearned wealth'. Instead it has just further eroded the prosperity of the middle class. It's another case of 'right goal, wrong route'. I'm going to suggest a solution to this in the next chapter, but first I want to consider the damage caused by inheritance tax.

Inheritance tax makes up 1% of UK government revenue. All wealth over a £325,000 threshold is taxed at 40%. In the US, there is currently a $5 million exemption, after which tax is applied at 35% – rather more generous. This could soon revert back to the pre-Bush-tax-cuts rate, which would be a $1 million exemption and a 55% tax.

The family is, in my view, the most natural and, indeed, most efficient unit for people in which to live, thrive and look after each other. But the trend of the past century, as the state has grown, has been that families have gradually become smaller and more disparate. They are started later in life. Many of the responsibilities that once lay with the family are now taken on by the state. One of the things I see happening in life after the state is that the family unit grows strong again. But inheritance tax, I suggest, is actually an attack on it. A family is already weakened by the death of a member; for part of his or her wealth then to be taken from the family and given to the state is a second and unnecessary blow.

The boom in UK house prices has been such that an ordinary four-bed house in a London suburb now costs in excess of £1 million ($1.6 million) – not some mansion, just an average, suburban, four-bed family home in London. Prices have risen to these absurd levels because of easy credit, loose monetary policies, the ongoing devaluation of money and planning laws restricting the building of new homes. When the owners of that four-bed home pass away, their children will now face a bill in excess of £270,000 ($440,000). Unless the children can afford to pay this, they will be forced to sell the family home. And wealth passes from the family to the state.

It makes it hard for a family to take root in an area over generations, which in my view is a natural and healthy thing to happen. The heirs, in many cases, will then find themselves priced out of the area in which they grew up. This isn't owing to market forces, but state forces – taxation, devaluation of money and so on. Moreover, as government devalues money, but tax bands stay unchanged, more and more wealth passes to the state. But, yet again, this transfer is not transparent, but furtive.

It's a common, even clichéd, complaint, but I agree with it: you have paid tax on your earnings all your life, why should you then have to pay tax on it again when you die? It is your absolute right to pass on your wealth – which is not 'unearned', but very much 'earned' – to whom you feel fit, without any interference. Why should someone else, who you never knew nor had any dealings with – somebody whose values or behaviour you may not agree with – be entitled to a share of the proceeds of your life's endeavour? To those that receive it, this is 'unearned wealth'. The descendants who receive the inheritance haven't necessarily earned it either. But your descendants are a part of you, they are very much the focus of your own efforts and goals. To want to look after them is natural and normal.

Government would be far better off dealing with the causes of asset price inflation and the intergenerational divide it has created, rather than focusing on inheritance tax.

Someone from a wealthy family may have an advantage over somebody from a poor background, yes, but not always. The latter may be more ambitious and hungry for success; the former may be more complacent. But the free world is the most likely world in which you can remedy any disadvantage of birth. The free world is the world in which you can exchange your way to prosperity. You are less likely to remedy that disadvantage in a world of debt, taxation, financial repression and intrusive government.

The Freest and Fairest of Them All

*The tax upon land values is, therefore, the most just and equal of all taxes.
It is the taking by the community, for the use of the community,
of that value which is the creation of the community.*

Henry George, economist[124]

I'm sure that the reason so many are in favour of inheritance tax is an instinctive objection to people enjoying 'unearned wealth'. This objection is not new. In 1848 the philosopher John Stuart Mill felt that 'It is not the fortunes which are earned, but those which are unearned, that it is for the public good to place under limitation.'[125] Sharing 'unearned wealth' is precisely the scope of land value tax (LVT). I would like to show you how, by taxing land instead of labour – resource instead of productivity – wealth may be redistributed fairly and organically.

LVT existed in the UK in the 17th, 18th and 19th centuries. However, the idea is now alien to many; it is a fundamentally different way to think about taxation. It's not an easy concept to grasp, which makes it a difficult 'sell' for a politician looking for simple sound bites and electability. If I were trying to get elected, I wouldn't use LVT as my main selling point. Should the idea ever get real traction, it will meet with considerable opposition from those with vested interests. Nevertheless, it is a potential re-router of the runaway train.

The 19th-century American economist Henry George, one of LVT's most influential proponents, also called it the 'single tax' because it replaces all other taxes. UK Business Secretary Vince Cable has spoken in favour of the Mansion Tax, which derives from LVT. But Cable wants it *in addition to* other taxes. LVT should replace other taxes. There would be no income tax, no VAT, no National Insurance, no inheritance tax, no fuel duty, no corporation tax, no business rates, no stamp duty, no alcohol tax, no capital gains tax and so on.

The philosophy behind 'Georgism' is that wealth you earn or create is yours. You do with it as you see fit. But the wealth that *nature* has given us, in particular land, is unearned. No individual or company made the land; there is no cost of production to it: nature gave it to us, so it should belong to everyone. By building or farming or mining on it, many have improved it, but the land itself was always there. LVT ignores the house, the farm or the factory, whatever is on the land. Tax is paid simply on the rental value of the land itself. If the annual rental value of the land is £100, the tax payable would be a percentage of £100.

Some land is more valuable than other land, it has a higher rental value. But as it is the needs of the community that push the value up, the land value should go to the community and not the individual.

The 17th-century proponents of LVT were known as the physiocrats – physiocracy meaning 'government of nature'. The 'unearned wealth' given to us by nature belongs to the community, or so runs the thinking: the mineral wealth, the airspace, the broadcast spectrums, the space orbits. Why should the oil under the sands of Saudi Arabia belong to a few princes? It is unearned wealth that should have been spread among all its people. Of course, there are huge costs and expertise that go into finding and extracting minerals, just as building and flying a plane or transmitting through a broadcast network involves great expense and technological innovation. Such endeavours, if taken on successfully, are compensated commensurately by the reward of profit in the market. But if you want the right to exclude others from a plot of land – i.e. for it to be 'yours' – and you want government to protect your title to that land, then a rent needs to be paid to the community that reflects the value of that land. Once you've paid that rent, the profits of your endeavours are yours.

Here's a simple explanation of how LVT would work. Every parcel of land in the country is assessed for its rental value – not the buildings, crops, drainage or anything else – just the land. If the land is undesirable scrubland in a remote location with no planning permission, it will have low rental value. If the land is in a prime area, is very fertile or is rich in minerals, demand for access to these features will be high, so the land's rental value will be high too. Valuations are based on current market evidence. If there are two parcels of land in the same street, both the same size and with the same planning potential, yet one is developed and the other not, they are still both given the same rental value. Tax is then levied as a proportion of the annual rental value of that land.

A four-bed family home of around 2,000 square feet (185 square metres), in a pleasant part of London, might have a rental value of around £35,000 per year; similar property in an undesirable part of the country rents for £10,000. The difference between the two, around £25,000 per annum, gives you a rough guide to the premium that the London land commands, i.e. the land value of the London property. You would then pay a percentage of that land value of £25,000 in tax each year. That is the only tax you would pay.

What percentage? That depends on how much government needs for its spending. In 2011–12 the total UK government revenue from tax was about £550 billion. It is not going to spend anything like that in my brave new world, because it is going to do a lot less, but we'll use that figure for now. If it were to levy £550 billion in LVT, you would add up the annual rental value of all the 60 million acres of land in the UK. The rate is that total annual rental value divided by the amount government needs. If the total annual rental value of all the land in the UK is £5.5 trillion and the government needs £550 billion, then the rate of tax payable will be 10% of annual rental value. If the total rental value of all UK land is £1.1 trillion, then rate of tax payable would be 50%.

If a government is going to try to levy a 50% LVT, then good luck to it in trying to persuade its people. That is one of the many beauties of LVT. It is direct and transparent. There is no concealment. The cost is felt directly by those that pay it. A government spending too much will find itself quickly pressed by its electorate to stop doing so.

In the UK at present, a building plot – the land – 'now constitutes between half to two-thirds of the cost of a new house', says Kevin Cahill. He continues: 'An acre of rural land worth £5,000 becomes an acre of development land worth between £500,000 and £1 million once planning permission is obtained.'[126] In December 2011 there were 662,105 vacant homes in the UK, according to the Halifax Empty Homes Survey. The necessity to pay tax on land will deter people from sitting on undeveloped property waiting for its value to appreciate. Instead it will pressure existing landowners either to put the property to good use, or to make way for someone who will. It might cause dilapidated inner-city sites, for example, to be redeveloped, which in turn reduces strain on green-field and other environmentally sensitive areas. LVT makes for more efficient use of land and existing resources. I see it as a morally preferable use of the coercive force of taxation to income tax.

Inheritance tax has failed to redistribute the 'unearned wealth' of the 50% of UK land that is unregistered and that 70% of the land that is owned by 0.6% of the population. If those lucky people, companies or trusts who own this land want exclusive rights to it, pay tax on it to the community. If they don't want to pay tax on it, sell the land to someone who is happy to. This is a quick, efficient route to redistribute this 'unearned wealth' through the community via natural market forces, rather than by the incompetence and moral minefield that is state reallocation. 'This is a natural source of public revenue,' writes Henry Law of the LVT campaign, which is promoting the adoption of land value taxation in the UK and trying to improve understanding of its economic benefits. 'All land makes its full contribution to the Exchequer, allowing reductions in existing taxation on labour and enterprise'.[127]

LVT, which Milton Friedman described as 'the least bad tax',[128] is a simple tax to administrate. Once the system is in place, revaluation of land, which would probably have to take place annually, is the only issue. Not only is there less bureaucracy, there is very little evasion. Land cannot be hidden or moved offshore. It could also stimulate economic activity away from costly centres towards depressed, remote areas, where land has little or no value, thus bringing all sorts of badly needed revitalization. Again, the effect would be to spread wealth and power.

Speculation in real estate, often a consequence of loose monetary policies, is probably the single biggest driver of the boom-bust cycle. It is extremely damaging to an economy. Look no further than the recent sub-prime mortgage crisis and its consequences in the US, or to Ireland and Spain, for examples of this. In London we have an entire generation that is alienated because houses are unaffordable to them. In the UK, the average age of the first-time buyer is now over 40. LVT, because it forces efficient use of land as well as taxing it, knocks the speculation out of house prices.

'Tax land, not labour', runs one of the LVT campaign slogans. It is a tax on consumption, not production. See it as a fee, based on the current market value, for the right to occupy exclusively a piece of the land that belongs to everyone.

The idea of the proceeds of LVT going into a central government pot may seem contradictory to some of the other minimal-state views I am propounding. What does government then do with its revenues from LVT? This raises the question, 'What is the state for?' – something I discuss in the final chapter. Government should spend that money on whatever is deemed right at the time: it might be spent on roads or infrastructure; it might be spent on the protection of people's private property rights; or it might simply be returned to shareholders – the people – in the form of dividend. Now that really would be socialism!

Singapore currently operates something close to my ideal system of taxation. It operates a land value tax, based on projected rental values of the properties. Its income tax rises incrementally according to earnings to a limit of 20% for residents on earnings over S$320,000 (c. US$250,000). Its corporate tax is capped at 17%. It has very high motor taxes to curb car ownership and congestion. Its VAT is 7%. It has no capital gains tax, no inheritance tax and no tax on dividends.

What are the consequences of a tax regime like this? Recent data from the World Economic Forum (the Global Competitiveness Report) ranked it as the second most competitive country in the world after Switzerland. Singapore 'has the highest rank in terms of the trust in politicians and is also number one in terms of the quality of its legal and administrative frameworks. Singapore also ranks near the top in market efficiency, infrastructure, higher education and financial markets development.'[129] It has the third highest GDP per capita at purchasing power parity (PPP) after Qatar and Luxembourg, according to the International Monetary Fund (IMF), and third highest PPP gross national income per capita, according to statistics from the World Bank (again after Qatar and Luxembourg).[130] Qatar has huge oil reserves; Luxembourg is a haven for large corporations wishing to avoid or minimize tax. Singapore beats the likes of Kuwait, Norway, UAE, Brunei, Hong Kong and Switzerland.

Low tax, flat tax, simple tax and land value tax all work. Why don't we do it?

Nine Reasons To Like LVT:

1 It doesn't tax productivity. You keep what you earn.
2 Unearned wealth is shared by the community.
3 You are taxed on the land you use: on what you consume.
4 It is transparent. Costs are felt, not hidden, so government spending is checked.
5 Once the system is in place, it is simple to administrate.
6 There is little tax evasion or avoidance.
7 It makes for more efficient use of land than we have now.
8 It disincentivizes speculation in houses.
9 Taxes are lower; people are empowered.

Part III

Pillars of the State?

12   National Health Sickness

The British welfare system has created more invalids
than the First World War.
Theodore Dalrymple, author and psychiatrist[131]

If governments and their activities are suddenly limited, what then happens to those essential services they deliver? What happens to health, education and welfare? We start with health.

The National Health Service (NHS) was born in 1948, just after WWII, and unveiled by Aneurin 'Nye' Bevan with the words, 'We now have the moral leadership of the world'. It is regarded by some as the finest achievement of the Labour Party. In many ways it dates back further – to 1911 and David Lloyd George's National Insurance Act. Regarded as the largest 'single-payer' health care system in the world (where funding comes from one source), with 1.7 million employees, it is currently the world's fifth largest employer, behind the US Department of Defence, the People's Liberation Army of China, Walmart and McDonald's.[132] It employs more people than: China National Petroleum Corp, the State Grid Corporation of China, the Indian railways and Indian Armed Forces, and has one employee for every 12.6 full-time UK workers in the country (or one for every 17 workers, if part-timers are included).[133]

The NHS has saved many lives. It is possible to have any ailment treated competently – something that, of course, often happens. My argument is, simply, that a much better service could be provided at a much lower cost.

Let us consider some of its shortcomings. There is the waste – the notorious IT project being the most famous example. It was intended to allow for electronic records, digital scanning and integrated IT systems across hospitals and community care. Originally budgeted at £2.3 billion in 2002, it soared to more than £12 billion – although some estimates put costs far higher – before being scrapped in September 2011 without ever being properly used.[134] More than £12 billion (about US$20 billion) and nothing to show for it! That was enough, commented one newspaper, to pay 60,000 nurses for ten years. Imagine if that money had never been taken from taxpayers – what might they have done with it? Many might even have been able to pay for their own health care. The alarming truth is that it's now considered normal for a government project to run over budget.

Then there's the neglect. The most infamous recent example is the terrible story of Kane Gorny, who died of thirst in St George's Hospital in south London after nurses repeatedly denied him water. He resorted to calling 999, from his own bed, to ask for water, but the police were denied entry to the hospital. Later, as his devastated mother sat with her son's dead body, a nurse asked: 'Have you finished? Can I bag him up now?'

As a result of the incident, just one nurse was demoted. The others are all still working in health care. Malpractice and neglect may lead to expensive legal suits and compensation, but it rarely ends with the dismissal of the perpetrators, who are just moved sideways. Even the serial killer Dr Harold Shipman – who is said to have been responsible for the deaths of over 250 people, and had 459 people die while in his care between 1971 and 1998 – had not been struck off the General Medical Council's register by the time he was given 15 life sentences in 2000. It all leads to what one insider described to me as 'the merry-go-round of the mediocre'.

Recent ONS statistics show that 43 NHS patients starved to death last year; 111 died of thirst; 287 people were recorded as malnourished, and 558 dehydrated, when they died; 78 were killed by bedsores and 21,696 were suffering from septicaemia (a condition associated with infected wounds) at their death.[135] Of course, such statistics are ambiguous. People can die *with* something or *of* it; they can die dehydrated because further life support has been deemed pointless or cruel. In a system in which millions of people are treated, some will die of almost anything. But, whether it's the elderly and infirm being overlooked or wrongly diagnosed, or people who have gone to hospital for simple, routine operations only for them to go wrong in some way, often mortally – neglect is too commonplace.

Other common complaints include: waiting times are too long; the bureaucracy is burdensome and inflexible; there is a shortage of beds; the NHS is too slow to react to problems (e.g. the swift spread of bacterium such as MRSA and *C. difficile*); turnover of staff is such that it is difficult to build up any kind of personal relationship; morale among staff is low; drugs companies have too much influence on policy and practice; too much money is spent on litigation and tribunals; it's difficult to get to see a doctor outside of normal working hours. And so on.

On the other hand, many who work for the NHS complain about the poor behaviour of patients, who perpetrate all sorts of abuses. Verbal abuse and violence to staff is prevalent and increasing (57,830 incidents of violence in 2010–11 according to statistics from NHS Protect). This is because of the belief that there is an inalienable 'right' to treatment, irrespective of conduct. This can plausibly be linked to the sense-of-entitlement culture.

Good health is famously difficult to quantify, but the most commonly used measures are life expectancy and infant mortality. The most compelling failure of the NHS is simply this: since the founding of the NHS in 1948, the difference between the life expectancy of the richest and poorest people in Britain has kept increasing. It accelerated at precisely the time (1997–2007) when most money was spent on the health service.[136] Whatever else it might have done, the NHS has not equalized life chances, as it set out to do. The opposite has happened. Health inequality has risen. In this regard, the NHS must be considered a failure.

The Doctors Whose Mouths Are Stuffed With Gold

In 2011, government spending on health care was around £120 billion – 20% of its outgoings.[137] That works out at just under £2,000 per head of the population, or £5,600 per full-time worker – more than on welfare and education, but a little less than on pensions.[138] In 1997 the figure was about £44 billion, so spending has almost tripled in 15 years. This is considerably higher than the government's stated inflation rates which averaged below three per cent during this period.[139] A chairman of an NHS trust, who prefers to remain anonymous, calculates that 'inflation in the NHS has been running at 14% per year for the last 18 years.' In other industries, better technology and other forms of progress have led to lower prices. Why has this not happened in health care? As P. J. O'Rourke said, 'If you think health care is expensive now, wait until you see what it costs when it's free.'[140]

Part of the problem of public health systems is their sheer size. In *The Tipping Point*, Malcolm Gladwell shows how, once a company employs more than 150 people, its productivity sharply declines until it finds a way of dividing the entities within it into smaller groups.[141] A study conducted by consultancy firm QSM in 2005 showed how communication and coordination costs rise with size. In an IT project where everyone needs to communicate and coordinate with each other, the cost actually rises as the square of the number of people in the team. In other words, if you double the size of a team, you need to have four times as many conversations. QSM also found that the error rate for large teams is five times greater than for the small teams. It then takes time and resources to discover, document and repair errors. The defection rate is higher too. New staff then take time to train and acclimatize. In short, error, waste and inefficiency are almost inevitable in government systems simply because of their size.

But the issue goes beyond size. Walmart is big, Tesco is big, but they work well and provide things cheaply. The difference is that the state is not involved in Walmart and Tesco. Things the government provides – health care and education – tend to rise in price; things it doesn't – clothes and food – fall.

The problem, as I see it, is this loss of a natural market dynamic. On the one hand, if something is free, it breeds an irresponsible and wasteful attitude – if you don't have to pay for something, you don't value it. On the comedy circuit, we dread 'free gigs', when the audience hasn't had to pay: audiences are always more difficult. If people had to pay for doctors' appointments, they would be less likely to miss them. Missed appointments are, of course, yet another form of waste. But it goes beyond that to the way some value their entire health: if you offer all motorists free breakdown cover, people are less likely to service and maintain their car. If people had to pay for the upkeep of their own health, many would look after themselves better.

When costs are not felt by the paying customer, the power of the supplier grows out of balance. There is no better example of this than the general practitioner's (GP's) contract. In the words of my anonymous NHS trust chairman:

> In Primary Care, GPs are, bar a handful, self-employed. Each practice is a small business. Through the British Medical Associ-ation (BMA) they block-negotiate with the government and it's a totally closed shop. The contract GPs have is endless, as in it is theirs forever. No, not for life – forever. When they wish to retire they hand that contract to someone of their choice, if they are qualified. It is a guaranteed income forever. The contract also guarantees them rent on a building they buy – nice earner. The NHS also supplies their computers and IT support. How many other businesses get a deal like that? By working the system GPs can earn huge sums and do as few hours as they wish. And the GPs with the worst health outcomes always seem to be the ones making the most money. Consultant clinicians and those in acute care have similarly ridiculous contracts. Look on the halo above the head of doctors that work in the NHS with extreme scepticism. This has been going on since the NHS was founded. The most telling quote of all was Bevan explaining how he got the clinicians to sign up to the NHS in the first place and how he silenced the BMA's criticism: 'I stuffed their mouths with gold'. The latest round of GP contracts awarded by the last government was even more absurdly generous.

This contract is rent-seeking of the worst kind – something that is rife throughout the NHS. Doctors now enjoy privileges beyond even the loathed, titled aristocracy of yesteryear. A simple dynamic is missing: the NHS is run to suit its suppliers; it should be run to suit its customers. Only when control is returned to the paying customer can the proper balance be restored.

US Health Care – A Rent-Seeker's Paradise

Congress and the White House are working out their scheme for pushing through a health care reform bill that has more pages than the US Constitution has words. I guarantee you that not a single member of the House or Senate has a complete understanding of that legislation any more than they understood all the implications of the USA Patriot Act back in 2001.

'Butch' Otter, 32nd Governor of Idaho[142]

When at dinner parties with my centre- or left-leaning friends, if somebody moans about some recent experience with the NHS, most just shrug their shoulders as if to say, 'Well, you just have to take it.' Somebody usually pipes up with an anecdote about how they had a really good experience at a hospital. And somebody else goes, 'Well, what's the alternative? The American system?'

The idea that health care in the US is private is misplaced. Though hospitals and other health care facilities in the US are, broadly speaking, owned privately, they are paid for by insurance – a Health Maintenance Organization (HMO) – and the government is the largest health care insurer. If you work in the public sector, government provides your insurance through Medicare and Medicaid; otherwise your employer provides it – or you have to buy it on your own, which many people don't. According to the US Census Bureau around 16% of the population is uninsured, though that number may change as a result of Obama's health care reforms. So the government still pays for health care – just not for everyone and not directly. Shot through with mandates, regulation and other forms of government intervention, the system is in many ways the worst of all worlds, where private companies exploit government-created monopolies. As with the NHS, the fundamental failing is that it is not run for the benefit of the patient-customer, but for the supplier, and costs are not directly felt by the paying customer.

Health care spending in the US is the highest in the world – about 17.5% of GDP, against a global average of 9% (10% in the UK). It is growing at twice the rate of the US economy. Despite the fact that under this system not everyone gets 'free' health care, the US still has the fifth highest government spending per capita – (*c.* $4,000) – on health care in the world[143] – after Monaco, Luxembourg, the Netherlands and Norway, all of which have higher levels of GDP per capita. (And Monaco and Luxembourg are both so small, their figures are bound to be anomalous.) 2013 government spending on health care will be about $1.1 trillion, with most of it funding insurance or subsidies.[144]

Do Americans get value for money? Though paying twice as much, the US has a higher infant mortality rate than most industrialized nations and lies in 42nd place in the life expectancy leagues, behind the other G5 nations – Japan, France, Germany and the UK – as well as, notably, Cuba, in 37th.[145] Even with high government spending, health care costs are the most common cause of personal bankruptcy in the US. In fact, health care is so expensive as to be unaffordable to most people if they had to pay for it themselves (i.e. without insurance). This system clearly does not deliver value for money. Prices are out of proportion with earnings. Given that health care is a basic necessity, this is a gross economic distortion. In fact health care has become so expensive that HMOs and Medicare, in order to lower their bills, often deny treatment for various drugs, treatments and procedures. As a result, doctors and patients cannot always choose which treatment is appropriate, instead that decision can fall to an accountants or bureaucrat somewhere.

How has it become so expensive? There's the sheer size; the layers of bureaucracy. There's also the way it is structured. When you have a system in which 'somebody else is paying' – whether it's the government or an insurer – there is not the same onus to deliver as good a service as efficiently as possible. In fact, when a third party is paying the bills and malpractice lawsuits loom, as they so often do in the US, doctors are incentivized to do quite the opposite, to order all possible tests and treatments and charge the maximum insurers will allow. As he was leaving his job in December 2011, the Administrator of the Centers for Medicare & Medicaid Services Dr Donald Berwick asserted that 20% to 30% of health care spending is waste. He listed five causes for the waste: overtreatment of patients, the failure to coordinate care, the administrative complexity of the health care system, burdensome rules and fraud.[146]

The cost of health care – health care inflation – began to rise disproportionately with the introduction of Medicare and Medicaid under the Lyndon B. Johnson government of the 1960s. In 1960 health expenditure was just over 5% of GDP. It began rising in 1965, and reached 17.5% last year. In other words, the more involved government has been, the more costs have risen. But, despite the higher spending per capita, more people are not getting care. The American doctor-turned-politician Ron Paul writes in *The Revolution*:

> In the days before Medicare and Medicaid, the poor and elderly were admitted to hospitals at the same rate they are now and received good care. As a physician I never accepted Medicare or Medicaid money from the government and instead offered cut-rate or free services to those who could not afford care. Before those programmes came into existence every physician understood that he or she had a responsibility towards the less fortunate, and free medical care for the poor was the norm. Hardly anyone is aware of this today . . . Laws and regulations that inflated the cost of medical services and imposed unreasonable liability standards on medical professionals even when they were acting in a volunteer capacity later made offering free care cost prohibitive, but free care for the poor was common at a time when America wasn't so 'governmentish' (to borrow a word from William Penn).[147]

The role of insurance is to protect against unforeseen and potentially catastrophic events or grave illnesses, not for routine visits and check-ups, which are an inevitable and entirely predictable part of our lives. To pay for these through insurance is a distortion of insurance's natural function.

Both in the UK and the US, there's something better, simpler and cheaper waiting to happen, but it can't happen while the current systems are in place, continuing to drain resources.

What Happens When People Have to Look After Themselves

No society can legitimately call itself civilized if a sick person is denied medical aid because of lack of means.

Nye Bevan[148]

The NHS and the American health system are full of brilliant, able, caring, competent people. It is these very same people who will be working in and running health care in our brave new world. However, they will be doing so without the confines of government and its systems, in an environment in which rent-seeking is not given incentive.

The sentiment behind the 'free health care' idea at the heart of the NHS and behind Obama's reforms is that those who cannot afford it still get care – I couldn't agree more with this sentiment. But all they have done is make health care expensive and not particularly good. Perhaps the issue at the heart of health organizations should be that health care is cheap, as cheap as possible – so that people can actually afford it for themselves and for others. Then health care can easily be provided – by families, friends, communities, charities and other organizations – to those who can't afford it, just as food is. There is an instinctive fear that in a free market rapacious organizations will exploit the weak and infirm. But we already have a system where rapacious exploitation takes place! The medical industry is full of rent-seekers because a large, inefficient, overly regulated, heavily subsidized environment is not only the optimum environment in which they can thrive, it actually incentivizes rent-seeking. It may not be apparent or directly felt, because insurance or the NHS pays. That does not mean it isn't there.

The only way to eliminate all this is through transparency. If the customer actually pays, costs are seen and felt directly. The customer, quite naturally, becomes the regulator; he enforces lower costs and better practice. At present a doctor or a hospital can't go bust through bad practice. They are, effectively, protected by government. They have to get struck off or shut down, both of which are rare. There has to be a genuine risk of failure. Costs, waste, inefficiency and rent-seeking will continue to spiral, until control is returned to the paying customer and the market is opened up the market to the forces of competition. This notion of competition in health care will, I'm sure, fill many with horror.

I don't pretend for a second that I know enough to be planning a health service. I would have thought a simple market system where one pays cash for everyday doctor or nurse appointments, with insurance for catastrophe and more serious occurrences, is the most natural system and the one that is least open to abuse, either by the medical industry or by patients. It seems to me that, at present, doctors are paid too much and nurses too little, that medicines and equipment are too expensive and that current systems of practice and administration are cumbersome and inflexible. But what I think means nothing. It should be the market – patients and doctors between them – that determines what health care costs, not me, not any central planner, politician, bureaucrat or anyone else. A free market would keep costs in line with what local people earn, and thus can actually afford. This is natural and efficient. It wouldn't surprise me if – without any state or government involvement – something akin to what used to be would return. Let me explain.

The UK's story is told in David Green's book *Working-class Patients and the Medical Establishment* (1985). There is a similar story to tell in the US, which David Beito outlines in *From Mutual Aid to Welfare State*. Both describe how, in the 1800s and early 1900s, welfare – and, in particular, health care – was provided by what were known in the UK as 'The Friendly Societies'. People grouped together, usually locally, to form these voluntary societies, which arose quite organically.[149]

In the UK, their peak came in the early 1900s. According to Green, they had branches in almost every town and city district, they employed doctors to treat their members and provided sick pay for them too. In 1877 registered membership was 2.75 million, by

1887 it was 3.6 million – increasing at 90,000 per year. This increase accelerated to 120,000 a year, and by 1897 membership was 4.8 million. This accelerated again to 140,000 per year and by 1910 membership was 6.6 million – some three-quarters of Britain's manual workers.[150] These were just the societies that had registered; many others chose not to. In 1892 the Chief Registrar of Friendly Societies, when asked what proportion of the working classes were insured against sickness through a building society or trade union, replied that 'of seven million male industrial workers 3.86 million belonged to registered societies and another three million to unregistered societies.'[151]

There was competition among societies for members, which meant that they were motivated to get standards up, and costs down. But there was also cooperation with other societies, which, from a bigger-picture perspective, allowed for the mobility of labour. You could pay into your insurance fund and, if you moved, it could move with you. Parents could also buy membership for their children.

The societies tended to be small and local. They held events and meetings, so members would get to know each other – and thus they had a social, communal function too. In such an environment, monitoring becomes more efficient. Dodgy sick-pay claims, theft by management and other such crimes become less likely: you're less likely to steal if the chances of being caught are higher; you're also less likely to steal when the consequences of your theft are right in front of you, unlike the defrauding of an invisible organization that happens with the modern insurance scam.

There was usually a flat subscription fee for membership (a lower percentage of earnings than now goes towards the NHS or Medicare) though you could pay in extra. The more you paid in, the more you could receive, should you fall on hard times. Thus, there was self-reliance and responsibility. Members could also vote for extra care to be given to those in need or whose premiums fell short.

Doctors were often elected, societies negotiated contracts directly with them and they were answerable to the committee of the society. They would win and lose contracts for the same reason anyone lands or loses a job – cost, experience, the 19th-century equivalent of 'good team player', track record and so on. Thus, under this system, unlike now, doctors were accountable to their patients, who were also their employers – the hands that fed them. Competition for patients (i.e. work) kept doctors' salaries at levels that the majority of working-class people could actually afford. In other words, the market – not central planners – set the price.

I'm not pretending there weren't faults. There are bound to have been. There is bound to have been malpractice and all the other failures of which humans are forever guilty. The medical profession was nothing like as advanced then as it is now. But none of this changes what I am trying to demonstrate, which is that a health care system emerged quite organically and voluntarily without the state; by the standards of the times, it was more efficient than the NHS is today and it gave considerably better value for money. It also shows how ordinary people, despite the considerably more difficult circumstances that were present in the 19th century, can act with great dignity and consideration for each other. Human beings aren't necessarily, rabidly exploitative, but in fact quite the opposite when they have responsibility for their own lives. This was a freely chosen, private welfare state.

It seems the success of the Friendly Societies led to their decline. With the National Insurance Act in 1911, it became compulsory to pay insurance into a national pot. The intention of David Lloyd George – who piloted the bill – was to provide Friendly Society-type membership to those who could not afford it. But the Friendly Societies had two enemies, and those enemies effectively destroyed them through concessions to the 1911 Act.

First, there were the commercial insurance companies. They disliked the competition that the societies had given them and had formed themselves into an association known as the 'Combine'. The second threat was a vocal and influential faction of the British Medical Association (BMA) – effectively the doctors' union. They loathed the fact that, under the Friendly Society system, the customer, or patient, had control and doctors were accountable to them. There is some old-fashioned snobbery at work here: a doctor should not be given orders and held to account by proletarian workers. Not only this, but sometimes these workers did not pay their doctors the salaries the BMA thought they deserved, and on occasion they even had the impertinence to vote them out of a job.

These two enemies formed an alliance to lobby the government, and, in particular, Lloyd George. They argued successfully, somehow, that a doctor couldn't give a patient a 'full, unbiased, professional service' if he was being paid by a society.[152] They also argued that if doctors undercut other doctors to get individual subscriptions it was 'bad for the provision of medical care'.[153] The result saw a doubling of the minimum wage for doctors. A doubling! This was to be paid for by so-called National Insurance – a tax, basically, which was compulsory and deducted at source. People had no choice but to pay it. If you were a manual worker, you could not spare your three shillings per annum to the Friendly Society on top of the three shillings that the government was now taking directly from your pay. If you were a doctor, you went where the wages were highest, which was *not* working for the Friendly Societies. The result was that the Friendly Societies were crowded out and replaced by something inferior.

Green says:

> The essence of working-class social insurance was democratic self-organization: amendments to the Bill obtained by the BMA and the Combine undermined it. Doctors' pay had to be kept within limits that ordinary manual workers could afford: under pressure, the government doubled doctors' incomes and financed this transfer of wealth from insured workers to the medical profession by means of regressive poll tax, flat-rate National Insurance contributions.
>
> The unhappy outcome of this legislation initially intended to extend to all citizens the benefits of friendly society membership, already freely chosen by the vast majority, was a victory for the political muscle of the Combine and the BMA. They achieved a very considerable transfer of wealth and power from the relatively poor working class to the professional class.[154]

In the years that followed, the Friendly Societies disappeared. With them went the communities they had developed. With them too went the free-market model of welfare in which people got together quite voluntarily and formed groups to look after themselves. In their place came the state – something altogether uglier, more expensive, more inefficient, more inhuman and more incompetent.

Lloyd George and others may have started with good intentions, but they were perverted by powerful, rent-seeking vested interests. Such are the risks of state intervention. The state, through National Insurance, undermined not only the ability of people to organize themselves, but also the desire for them to try. Affordable, voluntarily funded health care was no more.

After 1948 doctors were paid by the state via the National Health Service, which is beholden to the BMA. As we know, Bevan 'stuffed their mouths with gold'. Their mouths were stuffed with gold once again when Labour health minister Alan Milburn sought doctors' consent for his reforms – hence the sudden inflation in GPs' earnings towards the end of the New Labour years.

'The history of workers' cooperatives, the friendly societies and the unions from which the Labour Party sprang is one of individuals coming together for self-improvement and to improve people's potential through collective action. We need to recreate for the 21st century the civil society to which these movements gave birth,' said young Tony Blair in 1994 to the IEA.[155]

What went wrong, Tony?

From National Health to Rude Health

In my opinion, our health care system has failed
when a doctor fails to treat an illness that is treatable.
Kevin Alan Lee, author[156]

It is not as simple as just going back to the friendly societies, of course. When these groups were in their prime, medicine was comparatively primitive and low tech. Mostly you went to a GP who gave you medicine with full authority. Occasionally you might need surgery, staying in hospital for a few days, or weeks, but not needing very intensive care. That has changed enormously. Many procedures might now be best done in specialized centres, perhaps one for a whole district or region. There is always going to be the problem of insurance driving up costs. Procedures such as liver transplants, which can cost over £250,000 ($400,000), will probably remain beyond most people's pockets for a long time to come. A national bureaucracy of transplant organs might be more efficient than a local one. But these are all issues that a free market can address and solve.

In both the NHS and the American system of insurance we have a huge organization – a voracious government monster – that consumes tremendous amounts of resources. It is unstoppable. It keeps on feeding. As it does so, through lack of accountability, subsidy and waste, it pushes up the price of everything. We then have to tax people more to feed it. The more we tax people, the less money people have, and they become dependent on government. And the monster that is the state gets bigger and more expensive.

The amount of capital that would be freed by an efficient system of health care is breathtaking. It would make for the most tremendous opportunities elsewhere. And it would happen on both sides: on the one hand individuals would pay less; on the other they would have more money, as the state would take less from them.

At present, choice in services is limited. Patient or consumer control of the medical provider is limited. Until we have patient control, our service will be a long way short of what it can be. Meanwhile, I bet there are a figurative million things GPs, nurses and others who work in the NHS don't like about it and would change, if they could. In a free market, under their own auspices, they can make those changes – and be properly rewarded for them.

Both in the UK and the US, health care was better in *relative* terms and more affordable, before the government got involved and turned it into a political tool. Health care would be better and cheaper without government now.

But how do you do this? How do you make the transition? How

do you get consumer control and patient power back to Britain? No politician who wants a career will ever recommend abandoning the NHS, even if the numbers are compelling. It would be political suicide. 'The National Health Service is the closest thing the English have to a religion,' said former Chancellor of the Exchequer, Nigel Lawson, in his memoirs.[157] The same goes for the US – which politician is going to announce, 'We're abandoning Medicare and Medicaid and opening up health care to the free market'? Thanks to the way the words 'free market' have been corrupted, there's just too much sentiment against the idea. And should a politician actually win on this mandate, the logistics would be nightmarish. The media would have a frenzy. Lawsuits would start flying. Unions would get militant. How do you terminate the contracts of 1.7 million people?

Perhaps some kind of voucher system could help the transition. People receive vouchers in exchange for their tax and can spend these where they choose. Doctors and medical practices are, meanwhile, given the option of opting out of the system and into the open market. Many might do so for the opportunity to escape the burdens of government bureaucracy and regulation, as well as the opportunity for greater profit in return for better practice.

Another possibility is medical savings accounts. Instead of your tax going to the government, you have the option to open your own medical savings account and your tax is paid into that. This money is then used to pay for health care, and the patient has the ability to negotiate directly with the doctor of his choice for the care he chooses without intervention. Perhaps handing over hospitals to charitable trusts or making them independent not-for-profit companies would break that monopoly.

But the ultimate solution has to be devoid of government altogether. It cannot be a halfway house. A mix between public and private can be the most toxic of all worlds. It creates a fertile environment for rent-seeking and monopolies. It's what has happened to US health care and it's what we have on UK railways, where certain for-profit organizations enjoy monopolies and push up prices, without giving any discernible improvement in service. It's what happened in banking, where risk was socialized and profits privatized.

Without wishing to sound too negative, my outlook is that the NHS will more likely collapse in on itself, along with the rest of the welfare state, just as Soviet Russia did, before any group can end it democratically. One look at the debts and deficits Western governments have run up suggests this collapse is nearer than most realize.

But don't despair. Have trust in the generous, communal spirit of man. The end of the NHS does not mean the end of 'free' health care. It means the beginning of better, cheaper health care.

Points to Consider:

1　Health care is currently expensive, wasteful and inefficient. It could be much better and much cheaper.
2　Health care will not disappear just because the government stops providing it. It is a basic human need. The market will provide it as cheaply as it can be provided, just as it does with other basic human needs such as food and clothing.
3　Without government provision, there will be greater health equality. The more government has spent on health care, the greater health inequality has risen.
4　There are many recipients of health care who see it as 'their right', regardless of comportment.
5　Health care has become a political tool.

13   The State: Looking After Your First Breath

The knowledge of how to give birth without outside interventions lies deep within each woman. Successful childbirth depends on an acceptance of the process.

Suzanne Arms, author[158]

There is no single experience that puts you more in touch with the meaning of life than birth. A birth should be a happy, healthy, wonderful experience for everyone involved. Too often it isn't.

Broadly speaking, there are three places a mother can give birth: at home, in hospital or – half-way house – at a birthing centre. Over the course of the 20th century we have moved birth from the home to the hospital. In the UK in the 1920s something like 80% of births took place at home. In the 1960s it was one in three. By 1991 it was 1%. In Japan the home-birth rate was 95% in 1950 falling to 1.2% in 1975. In the US home-birth went from 50% in 1938 to 1% in 1955.[159] In the UK now 2.7% of births take place at home. In Scotland, 1.2% of births take place at home, and in Northern Ireland this drops to fewer than 0.4%.[160] Home-birth is now the anomaly. But for several thousand years, it was the norm.

The two key words here are 'happy' and 'healthy'. The two tend to come hand in hand. But let's look, first, at 'healthy'. Let me stress, I am looking at planned home-birth; not a home-birth where mum didn't get to the hospital in time.

My initial assumption when I looked at this subject was that hospital would be more healthy. The hospital is full of trained personnel, medicine and medical equipment. My first instinct against home-birth, it turned out, echoed the numerous arguments against it, which come from many parts of the medical establishment. They more or less run along the lines of this statement from the American

College of Obstetrics and Gynaecology: 'Unless a woman is in a hospital, an accredited free-standing birthing centre or a birthing centre within a hospital complex, with physicians ready to intervene quickly if necessary, she puts herself and her baby's health and life at unnecessary risk.'[161]

Actually, the risk of death for babies born at home is almost half that of babies born at hospital (0.35 per 1,000 compared to 0.64), according to a 2009 study by the *Canadian Medical Association Journal*. The National Institute for Health and Clinical Excellence reports that mortality rates are the same in booked home-birth as in hospitals.[162] In November 2011 a study of 65,000 mothers by the National Perinatal Epidemiology Unit (NPEU) was published in the *British Medical Journal*. The overall rate of negative birth outcomes (death or serious complications) was 4.3 per 1,000 births, with no difference in outcome between non-obstetric and obstetric (hospital) settings. The study did find that the rate of complications rose for first-time mums, 5.3 per 1,000 (0.53%) for hospitals and 9.5 per 1,000 (0.95%) for home-birth. I suspect the number of complications falls with later births because, with experience, the process becomes easier – and because mothers who had problems are less likely to have more children than those who didn't. The *Daily Mail* managed to twist this into: 'First-time mothers who opt for home birth face triple the risk of death or brain damage in child.' Don't you just love newspapers? Whether at home or in the hospital there were 250 negative events seen in the study: early neonatal deaths accounted for 13%; brain damage 46%; meconium aspiration syndrome 20%; traumatic nerve damage 4% and fractured bones 4%. Not all of these were treatable.

There are so many variables in birth that raw comparative statistics are not always enough. And, without wishing to get into an ethical argument, there are other factors apart from safety. There are things – comfort, happiness, for example – for which people are prepared to sacrifice a little safety. The overriding statistic to take away from that part of the study is that less than 1% of births in the UK, whether at hospital or at home, lead to serious complications.

But when you look at rates of satisfaction with their birth experience, the numbers are staggering. According to a 1999 study by *Midwifery Today* researching women who have experienced both home and hospital birth, over 99% said that they would prefer to have a home-birth in the future!

What, then, is so unsatisfying about the hospital birth experience?

I'm going to walk through the birthing process now, comparing what goes on at home to hospital. Of course, no two births are the same, no two homes are the same, no two hospitals are the same, but, broadly speaking, it seems women prefer the home-birth experience because: they have more autonomy at home, they suffer less intervention at home and, yes, it appears they actually suffer less pain at home.[163]

When mum goes into labour, the journey to the hospital, sometimes rushed, the alien setting when she gets there, the array of doctors and nurses who she may never have met before, but are about to get intimate, can all upset her rhythm and the production of her labour hormones. These aren't always problems, but they have the potential to be; they add to stress and detract from comfort.

At home, mum is in a familiar environment, she can get comfortable and settled, go where she likes and do what she likes. Often getting on with something else can take her mind off the pain of the contractions, while in hospital there is little else to focus on. She can choose where she wants to give birth – and she can change her mind, if she likes. She is in her own domain, without someone she doesn't know telling her what she can and can't do. She can change the light, the heating, the music; she can decide exactly who she wants at the birth and who 'catches' her baby. She can choose what she wants to eat. She will have interviewed and chosen her midwife many months before, and built up a relationship over that time. But in hospitals she is attended by whoever is on duty, she has to eat hospital food, there might be interruptions, doctors' pagers, alarms, screams from next door, whirrs of machinery, tube lighting, overworked, resentful staff to deal with, internal hospital politics, people coming in, waking her up, and checking her vitals, sticking in pins or needles, putting on monitor belts, checking her cervix mid-contraction – any number of things over which mum has no control.

Mums who move about freely during labour complain less of back pain. Many authorities feel that the motion of walking and changing positions can even enhance the effectiveness of the contractions, but such active birth is not as possible in the confines of many hospitals. Many use intravenous fluids and electronic foetal monitors to ensure she stays hydrated and to record each contraction and beat of the baby's heart. This all dampens mum's ability to move about and adds to any feelings of claustrophobia.

In hospital the tendency is to give birth on your back, though this is often not the best position – the coccyx cannot bend to help the baby's head pass through. There are many other positions – on your hands and knees for example – where you don't have to work against gravity and where the baby's head is not impeded. On your back, pushing is less effective and metal forceps are sometimes used to pull the baby out of the vagina, but forceps are less commonly used when mum assumes a position of comfort during the bearing-down stage.

This brings us to the next issue: intervention. The NPEU study of 2011 found that 58% of women in hospital had a natural birth without any intervention, compared to 88% of women at home and 80% of women at a midwife-led unit. Of course, there are frequent occasions when medical technology saves lives, but the likelihood of medical intervention increases in hospitals. I suggest it can actually cause as many problems as it alleviates because it is interruptive. Even routine technology can interrupt the normal birth process. Once derailed from the birthing tracks, it is hard to get back on. Once intervention starts, it's hard to stop. The medical industry is built on providing cures, but if you are a mother giving birth, you are not sick, there is nothing wrong with you, what you are going through is natural and normal. As author Sheila Stubbs writes, 'the midwife considers the miracle of childbirth as normal, and leaves it alone unless there's trouble. The obstetrician normally sees childbirth as trouble; if he leaves it alone, it's a miracle.'[164]

Here are just some of the other interventions that occur. If a mum arrives at hospital and the production of her labour hormones has been interrupted, as can happen as a result of the journey, she will sometimes be given syntocinon, a synthetic version of the hormone oxytocin, which occurs naturally and causes the muscle of the uterus to contract during labour so baby can be pushed out. The dose of syntocinon is increased until contractions are deemed normal. It's sometimes given after birth as well to stimulate the contractions that help push out the placenta and prevent bleeding. But there are allegations that syntocinon increases the risk of baby going into distress, and of mum finding labour too painful and needing an epidural. This is one of the reasons why women also find home-birth less painful.[165]

Obstetricians sometimes rupture the bag of waters surrounding the baby in order to speed up the birthing process. This places a time limit on the labour, as the likelihood of a uterine infection increases after the water is broken. Indeed in a hospital – no matter how clean – you are exposed to more pathogens than at home. The rate of post-partum infection to women who give birth in hospital is a terrifying 25%, compared to just 4% in home-birth mothers.[166] Once the protective cushion of water surrounding the baby's head is removed (that is to say, once the waters are broken) there are more possibilities for intervention. A scalp electrode, a tiny probe, might be attached to baby's scalp, to continue monitoring its heart rate and to gather information about its blood.

There are these and a whole host of other 'just in case' interventions in hospital that you just don't meet at home. As childbirth author Margaret Jowitt, says – and here we are back to our theme of Natural Law – 'Natural childbirth has evolved to suit the species, and if mankind chooses to ignore her advice and interfere with her workings we must not complain about the consequences.'[167]

At home, if necessary, in the 1% of cases where serious complications *do* ensue, you can still be taken to hospital – assuming you live in reasonable distance of one.

'My mother groaned, my father wept,' wrote William Blake, 'into the dangerous world I leapt.' We come now to the afterbirth. Many new mothers say they physically ache for their babies when they are separated. Nature, it seems, gives new mothers a strong attachment desire, a physical yearning that, if allowed to be satisfied, starts a process with results beneficial to both mother and baby. There are all sorts of natural forces at work, many of which we don't even know about. 'Incomplete bonding,' on the other hand, in the words of Judith Goldsmith, author of *Childbirth Wisdom from the World's Oldest Societies*, 'can lead to confusion, depression, incompetence, and even rejection of the child by the mother.'[168] Yet in hospitals, even today with all we know, the baby is often taken away from the mother for weighing and other tests – or to keep it warm, though there is no warmer place for it that in its mother's arms (nature has planned for skin-to-skin contact).

Separation of mother from baby is more likely if some kind of medical intervention or operation has occurred, or if mum is recovering from drugs taken during labour. (Women who have taken drugs in labour also report decreased maternal feelings towards their babies and increased post-natal depression). At home, after birth, baby is not taken from its mother's side unless there is an emergency.

As child development author Joseph Chilton Pearce writes, 'Bonding is a psychological-biological state, a vital physical link that coordinates and unifies the entire biological system . . . We are never conscious of being bonded; we are conscious only of our acute disease when we are not bonded.'[169] The breaking of the bond results in higher rates of postpartum depression and child rejection. Nature gives new parents and babies the desire to bond, because bonding is beneficial to our species. Not only does it encourage breastfeeding and speed the recovery of the mother, but the emotional bonding in the magical moments after birth between mother and child, between the entire family, cements the unity of the family. The hospital institution has no such agenda.

The cutting of the umbilical cord is an area of contention.[170] Hospitals, say home-birth advocates, cut it too soon. In *Birth Without Violence*, the classic 1975 text advocating gentle birthing techniques, Frederick Leboyer – also an advocate of bonding and immediate skin-to-skin contact between mother and baby after birth – writes:

[Nature] has arranged it so that during the dangerous passage of birth, the child is receiving oxygen from two sources rather than one: from the lungs and from the umbilicus. Two systems functioning simultaneously, one relieving the other: the old one, the umbilicus, continues to supply oxygen to the baby until the new one, the lungs, has fully taken its place. However, once the infant has been born and delivered from the mother, it remains bound to her by this umbilicus, which continues to beat for several long minutes: four, five, sometimes more. Oxygenated by the umbilicus, sheltered from anoxia, the baby can settle into breathing without danger and without shock. In addition, the blood has plenty of time to abandon its old route (which leads to the placenta) and progressively to fill the pulmonary circulatory system. During this time, in parallel fashion, an orifice closes in the heart, which seals off the old route forever. In short, for an average of four or five minutes, the newborn infant straddles two worlds. Drawing oxygen from two sources, it switches gradually from the one to the other, without a brutal transition. One scarcely hears a cry. What is required for this miracle to take place? Only a little patience.

Patience is not something you associate with hospital birth. There are simply not the resources, even if, as the sixth US president John Quincy Adams said, 'patience and perseverance have a magical effect before which difficulties disappear and obstacles vanish'. The arguments to delay the early cutting of the cord (something not as frequent in hospitals as it once was) are that, even though blood going back to the placenta stops flowing – or pulsing – non-pulsing blood going from the placenta into baby *is* still flowing. After birth, 25–35% of baby's oxygenated blood remains in the placenta for up to ten minutes. With the cord cut early, baby is less likely to receive this blood, making cold stress, infant jaundice, anaemia, Rh disease and even a delayed maternal placental expulsion more likely. There is also the risk of oxygen deprivation and circulatory shock, as baby gasps for breath before his nasal passages have naturally drained their mucus and amniotic fluid. Scientist W. F. Windle has even argued that, starved of blood and oxygen, brain cells will die, so cutting the cord too early even sets the stage for brain damage.[171]

Natural birth advocates say it is vital for the baby's feeding to be put to the breast as soon as possible after birth, while his sucking instincts are strongest. Bathing, measuring and temperature-taking can wait. Babies are most alert during the first hour after birth, so it's important to take advantage of this before they settle into that sleepy stage that can last for hours or even days.

Colostrum, the yellow fluid that breasts start producing during pregnancy, is nature's first food. This substance performs many roles we know about and probably many we don't as well. Known as 'baby's first vaccine', it is full of antibodies and protects against many different viruses and bacteria. It has a laxative effect that clears meconium – baby's black and tarry first stool – out of the system. If this isn't done, baby can be vulnerable to jaundice. Colostrum lines baby's stomach ready for its mother's milk, which comes two or three days later, and it meets baby's nutritional needs with a naturally occurring balance of fat, protein and carbohydrate. Again, with the various medical interventions that go on in hospitals, from operations to drug-taking to simply separating mother and baby, this early breast-feeding process can easily be derailed. Once derailed, as I've said, it's often hard to get back on track. I am no scientist and cannot speak with any authority on the science behind it all, but I *do* know that nature, very often, plans for things that science has yet to discover.

Once upon a time, when families lived closer together and people had more children at a younger age, there was an immediate family infrastructure around you. People were experienced with young. If mum was tired, nan or auntie could feed the baby. Many of us are less fortunate in this regard today. With a hospital, you are sent home and, suddenly, you and your partner are on your own with a baby in your life, and very little aftercare. When my first son was born I was 30. I suddenly realized I had only held a baby once before. I was an only child so I had never looked after a younger brother or sister; my cousins, who had had children, lived abroad. Suddenly there was this living thing in my life, and I didn't know what to do. But, having had a home-birth, the midwife, who you already know, can you give you aftercare. She comes and visits, helps with the early breastfeeding process and generally supports and keeps you on the right tracks.

It's so important to get the birthing process right. There are all sorts of consequences to our health and happiness to not doing so. And in the West, with the process riddled as it is with intervention, we don't. We need to get birth out of the hospital and into an environment where women experience less pain, lower levels of intervention, greater autonomy and increased satisfaction.

A 2011 study by a team from Peking University and the London School of Hygiene found that, of 1.5 million births in China between 1996 and 2008, babies born in hospitals were two to three times *less* likely to die. China is at a similar stage in its evolutionary cycle to the developed world at the beginning of the 20th century. The move to hospitals there looks inevitable.

Something similar is happening in Bolivia. In 2009 the Evo Morales government created 'Juana Azurduy', a child social payments programme whereby mums who give birth and then take their children for regular check-ups receive payments that will total 1,500 Bolivianos (about $220). In the five years since the programme began, the rate of Bolivian women having hospital births has risen from 55% to 76%. Malnutrition in children has fallen 43% from 27% to 15.5%. Infant mortality rates have fallen from 5.5% to 4.6%.[172]

In his book *A History of Women's Bodies*, Edward Shorter quotes a doctor describing a birth in a working-class home in the 1920s:

> You find a bed that has been slept on by the husband, wife and one or two children; it has frequently been soaked with urine, the sheets are dirty, and the patient's garments are soiled, she has not had a bath. Instead of sterile dressings you have a few old rags or the discharges are allowed to soak into a nightdress which is not changed for days.

For comparison, he describes a 1920s *hospital* birth:

The mother lies in a well-aired disinfected room, light and sunlight stream unhindered through a high window and you can make it light as day electrically too. She is well bathed and freshly clothed on linen sheets of blinding whiteness . . . You have a staff of assistants who respond to every signal . . . Only those who have to repair a perineum in a cottars's house in a cottar's bed with the poor light and help at hand can realize the joy.[173]

Most homes in the developed world are no longer as he describes, if they ever were, except in slums. It would seem the evolution in the way we give birth as a country develops passes from the home to the hospital. It is time to take it away from the hospital.

Why am I spending so much time on birth in a book about economics? The process of giving birth is yet another manifestation of this culture of pervasive state intervention. (Hospitals, of course, are mostly state run.) It's another example of something that feels safer, if provided by the state in a hospital, even if the evidence is to the contrary. And it's another example of the state destroying for so many something that is beautiful and wonderful.

What's more, like so many things that are state-run, hospital birth is needlessly expensive. The November 2011 study of 65,000 mothers by the National Perinatal Epidemiology Unit looked at the average costs of birth in the NHS. They were highest for planned obstetric unit births and lowest for planned home-births. Here they are:

- £1,631 (c. $2,600) for a planned birth in an obstetric unit
- £1,461 (c. $2,340 for a planned birth in an alongside midwifery unit (AMU)
- £1,435 (c. $2,300) for a planned birth in a free-standing midwifery unit (FMU)
- £1,067 (c. $1,700) for a planned home-birth.[174]

Not only is it as safe; not only are people more satisfied by it; not only do the recipients receive more one-to-one – i.e. better – care; home-birth is also 35% cheaper. Intervention is expensive.

So I return to this theme of non-intervention, whether in hospitals or economies. It often looks cruel, callous and hard-hearted; it often looks unsafe, but, counter-intuitively perhaps, in the end it is more human and more humane.

When you look at the cost of private birth, the argument for home-birth is even more compelling. Private maternity care is expensive. For example, in summer 2012, a first birth at the Portland Hospital in London costs £2,880 (about $4,400) for a normal delivery and £3,790 (*about* $5,685) for an elective caesarean and for the first 24 hours of care. Additional nights in a standard room cost around £1,000 (about $1,500). You also have to allow for the fees charged by your private consultant obstetrician, which might be £3,000–£4,000 ($4,500–$6,000). So, in total, a private birth at a hospital such as the Portland could cost £7,500–£10,000 ($10–$15,000). There will be some saving if you opt for a 'midwife-led delivery service' or 'midwife-led care'. In this instance, you will still have a named obstetrician, but he or she will see you less often, and the birth may be 'supported by an on-call Consultant Obstetrician'. London midwives charge £2,500–£4,000 (*c.* $4–6,000) for about *six months* of care from early pregnancy to a month after birth. The comparative value is astounding, I would say.

To have a planned home-birth on the NHS is possible, but can be problematic to arrange, depending on where you are based. Most people, after they have paid taxes, do not now have the funds to buy a private home-birth, so they are forced into the arms of government health care, such is the cycle at work.

I was first introduced to the idea of home-birth by my ex-wife, Louisa, God bless her. She hated hospitals due to an earlier experience in her life and only found out about alternatives thanks to the internet. I, as well as my friends and family, thought Louisa was insane. But she insisted. And she was right to.

Our first son was actually two weeks and six days late. We were obliged to go to the hospital, which we did, after two weeks and five days. We were kept waiting so long in there, and eventually persuaded an overworked nurse that we were fine to go and we left. The confused nurse was glad to have one less thing to think about.

The next day Samuel was born: a beautiful and wonderful experience that I will never forget, one of the happiest days of my life – exactly as nature intended.

Simply talking to people that have experienced both home-birth and hospital birth, or reading about their experiences, the anecdotal evidence is compelling. Home-birth may not be for everyone – I'm not suggesting it is. Birthing centres seem a good way forward. But a hospital birth should only be for emergencies. Childbirth is a natural process that no longer requires hospitalization, except in those 1% of situations where something goes seriously wrong. If it does go wrong and there is an emergency, call an ambulance and be taken to hospital – that is what they are for.

Returning to the original premise of Natural and Positive Law, it's pretty clear which category hospital birth falls into. Hospitals do things in the way that they do because of the pressures they are under, not least the threat of legal action should some procedural failure occur. Taking birth back home and away from the state reduces the burden of us on it and of it on us.

14   We Don't Need No Education?

*No man who worships education has got the best out of
education . . . Without a gentle contempt for education
no man's education is complete.*

G. K. Chesterton, author[175]

How to Make Your Child Five Times More Likely
to Win an Olympic Medal

Over the last decade the cost of private school fees has been rising
at almost twice the official rate of inflation.[176] Indeed, many feel
that school fees better reflect the true rate of inflation than official
government measures such as RPI or CPI. I would agree, but it
also reflects the desperation that many parents feel to secure a good
education for their children. With that rising cost of school fees in
mind, consider the following: in 2012, the total UK government
spending on education (excluding tertiary, i.e. universities and so on)
was about £90 billion ($128 billion).[177] There are currently more than
9.6 million pupils in pre-primary, primary and secondary education,
of which about 620,000 attend private school.[178] Let's use simple
round numbers. If you divide the £90 billion spent by the 9 million
pupils in state education, you arrive at the figure £10,000 ($16,000)
per year per child. According to Independent School Fees Advice,
the average cost of private school fees in the UK is £10,200 (lower up
north, higher down south).[179] The Independent Schools Council 2012
Census has it a little higher at around £11,000.[180] In other words, for
almost the same money it spends, the government could send every
child in the UK to private school – even with the terrifying inflation
in fees that has taken place. I know I'm over simplifying the numbers
– but even so, that is a telling statistic.

Currently, about 7% of UK children go to independent (private) schools, and around 93% are educated in the state sector. It would be overly simplistic to try to argue which is better. 'What makes a good education' is subjective. Dealing, generally, with the poorer end of society, state education is operating in a more difficult context, so any evaluation, somehow, needs to reflect that. It all makes the quality of education notoriously hard to measure.

As it happens, the most successful pupils of all, at least until the age of 14, come from an educational sector that is the cheapest of all to fund, costing considerably less than the £10,000 figure stated above. It is also the simplest to administrate. Though cheap, this sector makes up less than 1% of pupils. I'm talking, of course, about home education. A doctoral thesis by Dr Paula Rothermel from Durham University found that children of primary school age who are taught at home learn more than those in schools, whether state or private. In national literacy project assessments, the level reached by the top 16% of school-educated children was attained by 80% of home-educated children.[181] We'll look at this in more detail later in the chapter.

There are some who intensely dislike those who went to private school, feeling them to be blinkered, arrogant, privileged, and not in touch with the so-called 'real world'. There are others who are ashamed of their own private school background and try to conceal it. The state education sector is packed with talented, passionate people who have dedicated their lives to it. But, for all this and more, you cannot argue with the results.

At private school you are six times more likely to achieve top A* grades at GCSE and three times more likely to get top grades at A level.[182] Even with all the incentives – sometimes forced by law – to get more state-educated children into Oxbridge, other universities and into major corporations, private-school children still dominate top universities and, eventually, the elites positions in politics, law, business and the media. The London 2012 Olympic Games was a bonanza of state spending and statist propaganda if ever there was one, yet 37% of the British medallists went to private school.[183] In other words, private school children were more than five times as represented on the winners' podia. In the Beijing Olympics, four years earlier, the discrepancy was even greater: 50% of British gold medallists came from that 7% of the population who are privately educated.[184]

A 2010 study by Sheffield University found that some 22% of 16- to 19-year-olds at state school in England are functionally innumerate – their maths skills are limited to basic arithmetic and their numeracy levels are at or below an 11-year-old's;[185] while 17% are functionally illiterate – they cannot handle more than 'straightforward questions, do not understand allusion and irony and their reading standard is below an 11-year-old's'. In a world where words and numbers flood our lives through TV, computers, the internet, phones, iPads, emails, texting, newspapers, magazines, books and goodness knows what else, I am amazed that one-fifth of 16- to 19-year-olds are functionally illiterate and innumerate. Official statistics say Britain's overall literacy rate is 99%.

In the summer of 2013 around 25,000 children will leave school without a single qualification to show for their ten or more years of education.

My own experience in the London Borough of Wandsworth is that the state primary schools are better than the state secondary. That may or may not be so, it's just my 'on the street' view and nothing more than that. The Head of History at King's College, Wimbledon, a leading private school, told me, 'We get our best kids from state primary school.' But even primary schools in the UK are disappointing, according to Sir Michael Wilshaw, the chief schools inspector, who recently declared, 'one in five children – about 100,000 – were not reaching the standard expected at the end of primary school every year'.[186]

On an international scale, the UK is falling too. The international league table compiled by the Organization for Economic Cooperation and Development saw us fall from 17th to 25th last year in reading skills and from 24th to 28th in maths.

Yes, successful education is notoriously difficult to measure, statistics are easy to manipulate, it's easy to use only the ones that suit your argument, yet for all the thinking, passion and energy, for all the reforms, for all the investments of capital, it's hard to deny that state education in most cases languishes behind that of the independent sector and other European nations.

But some of the UK's independent schools – the likes of Eton, Harrow and St Paul's – are the envy of the world. The global super-rich send their children to school here. Why such discrepancy? The failure may not be admitted, but parents know it. Poll after poll shows the majority would send their children to independent, private schools, if they could only afford to do so.

Where does the blame for our lagging state sector lie? With parents? Students? Teachers? The government? Society? With practices and methods – too much assessment, targeting or focus on exams, for instance? Perhaps it's the schools themselves? Or lack of funding, maybe? All sorts of different explanations get offered.

Writing in the *Daily Telegraph*, Dr John H. Newton, headmaster of Taunton School, says: 'It seems to be a constant assumption by the state that it knows best. In education, it does not and never has. In fact the meddling in education we have seen over the past 50 years explains our fast decline into world education's Division Two'.[187] Is he right?

Perhaps it's not the UK government that is the problem, but, simply, government. In his paper for the Cato Institute, 'Markets vs. Monopolies in Education', the author and educationalist Andrew J. Coulson surveyed 25 years of international research comparing market- and state-provided education systems, and made 'over a hundred statistical comparisons involving eight different educational outcomes'. He found that, 'Across time, countries, and outcome measures, private provision of education outshines public provision according to the overwhelming majority of econometric studies.'[188] In short, state education lags behind private just about everywhere you go.

As it happens, I think private schools also fall short in many ways. They can be too big and bloated, arrogant, and slow to react to change. There are many things they fail to teach. They are, in my view, too expensive for what they are. The scope of this chapter on education is, simply, to highlight some of the current failings in education and show that something much better can be had for a fraction of the price. That something can satisfy all the differing, but passionate ideologies that accompany the subject of education.

All most people want is this: the best possible education for all, at the cheapest possible price. That is what is best for children, it's what is best for families, communities and nations. It's what is best for mankind.

Ten and More Ways in Which State Education Gives Parents Nightmares

In the first place, God made idiots. That was for practice.
Then he made school boards.
Mark Twain[189]

Talking to parents and teachers, trawling through chat boards and blogs, and drawing on my own experiences, here are just some of some of the frustrations that many have with state education in the UK, as it now stands. Similar complaints abound abroad.

Class sizes are too big. In the UK the average of 26.1 pupils per class is the third highest in the developed world. We are beaten only by Turkey and Mexico. The developed world average is 22.[190] These large class sizes are in spite of the fact that in the UK we spend more on primary and secondary schools as a percentage of GDP than 26 of the 32 OECD countries, including France, Germany, Japan, Canada, the USA and Australia.[191]

Lack of discipline is rife. Some blamed the 2011 London riots on poor schooling. Teachers complain that they are not given enough power to deal with discipline issues, and are left unsupported and open to abuse.

Despite restricted powers, teachers are burdened with un-reasonable expectation – something independent schools complain of too. They are required to be parents, psychologists, social workers, administrators, crowd controllers and disciplinarians, as well as teachers. As with health, free education is perceived as a right, regardless of comportment. This has all led to a lack of morale among teachers. Data from the Department of Education (DoE) in 2012 showed that there are 232,000 qualified experienced teachers under the age of 60 no longer working in schools. As many as 8,880 – an increase of 1,560 on the previous year – took early retirement, compared to 2,370 in 1997–98. The number of teachers as a whole dropped by 2% in 2012.[192]

Bad teaching is exonerated. According to a recent BBC *Panorama* documentary, just 18 teachers have been struck off in the last 40 years. This in spite of former chief schools inspector Chris Woodhead suggesting that as many as 15,000 bad teachers are at large – a figure disputed, as you would expect, by teachers' unions. This 'unsackableness' breeds complacency and mediocrity. It has the very opposite effect of competition. Schools are not accountable to parents – their customers – but to the office which sets their targets and budgets.

There are insufficient sports facilities. The removal of competition from within the classroom and from sports means that the clever and the slow are lumped together, while teaching is aimed at the middle ground – boring the intelligent and alienating those who can't keep up. It makes fertile ground for mediocrity. (As an aside, I remember being amazed at my elder son's sports day at his local state primary in 2006. The kids lined up for the 'running race'. There were lanes, a start line, a ribbon was held up over the finishing line and, through a megaphone, a teacher called, 'On your marks, get set, go'. The children all dashed the 40 yards; there was a clear winner. But there was no mention of it. The outcome was ignored, as though it had never happened. 'Are we', I wondered, 'teaching kids to ignore what's right in front of their eyes in the name of some dictum that no one must win and no one must lose?' It is not a race, if there is no winner, it's just a class run, so why not call it that? It was as though some ridiculous sub-Orwellian bureaucratic compromise had been reached to try and have the fun of a race without the pain. Still, it was an opportunity for those children to experience state obfuscation at an early age.)

The system is not flexible enough to meet the differing needs of different children. Learning by rote suits some, for example; un-structured learning suits others. Neither does the curriculum have enough relevance to the outside world. Simple personal finance, for example, should be taught. Mandarin, Hindustani, Russian or Arabic are four of the six most-spoken languages in the world, yet barely a school teaches them.

In London, thanks to the huge immigration that has taken place over the last half a generation, there are many pupils who do not have English as a first language. When grouped in classes with pupils whose mother tongue is English, either the former are left behind, or the latter are overlooked.

The 'dumbing down' of exam standards, something the current Education Secretary Michael Gove is trying to address, means that qualifications have been devalued. Though standards of education have slipped, exam results have got better. This is simple fiddling of the figures by successive governments so they can then say, 'Look how successful our policies have been. Students are all getting top grades.' It's the same process of devaluation that has happened with money. Education has now become a political tool. It should be about teaching and learning, not the ambitions of political parties.

These are arguments that, in many cases, have been going on for years and attempts are forever being made to address them. Some point to the recent emergence of free schools, academies, chartered schools and so on, all of which involve more specialization, if wanted, and greater autonomy. The system is becoming less monolithic and more fragmented, they say, with communities given a greater say in curriculums and competition returning. But the whole process of change is so slow and expensive. All attempts to reform and evolve meet with resistance; there are bureaucrats and unions and politicians to persuade; negotiations and arguments to be had, often with people with opposing ideologies and agendas; research reports have to be undertaken to prove things that are often obvious; there is in-fighting between the various schools of thought, sometimes one has the upper hand, sometimes another. There are just so many layers to get through to effect any real change that many just give up. Then of course there's the possibility that changes will make things worse.

The author Toby Young has founded a state free school in West London. Free schools are a new development whereby they are free to attend, funded by taxpayers but outside of local authority control. Despite the support of the government and the funding he has received, his struggle to do this is staggering. There are many within education who despise what he is doing, saying it will come at the expense of other schools in the area, and waiting for the moment when they can 'bring him down'. The same goes for Michael Gove, who, rightly or wrongly, is meeting with barrier after barrier, as well as having to put up with the most terrible slander, as he attempts to implement his proposed reforms. It just takes so long to get anything done. By the time they are done, another generation of children has passed through and a whole new raft of changes is now sought to meet the new conditions. Why waste so many resources attempting to fix a model that is broken?

Similar frustrations abound in the US. 'The US public school monopoly is guilty of seven deadly sins,' writes economic consultant Mark Harrison. 'It wastes resources, discourages good teaching, inhibits parental involvement, suppresses information, stifles innovation, creates conflict and harms the poor.'[193]

If a family decides it doesn't want its children to go to a school where standards are low, discipline is poor and so on, there's not a lot they can do about it – places in good schools are so limited – unless they move to a different area or somehow raise the funds to send their kids to private school. This means they have to pay for their education twice – once through taxes – which gives them in return an education service that is unsatisfactory (but they can't ask for their money back) – and then again through school fees. Most cannot afford to do this and so they find themselves relying on the state.

Perhaps the most common reason given for failing state schools is lack of funding. 'Education costs money, but then so does ignorance,' said statistician Sir Claus Moser.[194] We must spend more, runs the thinking. But I have already shown how similar amounts – around

£10,000 – get spent as at private schools with quite different results. In certain parts of London state spending per pupil reaches £33,000 per pupil: that's more than Eton. It is a lucky pupil who receives such support.[195]

One primary pupil referral unit (PPRU) that I looked at in North London has 12 pupils and 20 staff. The annual budget per pupil is £40,000. This budget is justified on the grounds that, later in life, these children are likely to act in a harmful and potentially expensive way. It is better to try to prevent this now through education.

The 2010 Sheffield University study on literacy and numeracy also examined levels of attainment of 13- to 19-year-olds in England from 1948 to 2009. Average reading scores rose between 1948 and 1960 and remained 'remarkably constant' between 1960 and 1988. Between 1997 and 2004, scores 'gently' rose and then plateaued. There was little improvement in teenagers' writing between 1979 and 2004. Government spending on all education in the period from 1948 to 2012 has risen 20,800%, going from £432 million to £90 billion (including tertiary).[196]

Of course, this rise is in part a consequence of the systematic debasement of money that has taken place, so let's consider spending as a percentage age of GDP. State spending on education began the 20th century at 2% of GDP. In 1946 it reached 3%, rising to 4% in 1960 and 6.5% in 1975. It then slipped to 4.33% in 1998 and is now back above 6%.[197] So, in relative terms, we're spending as much on education as ever, if not more.

One problem is, of course, that not enough of this spending reaches the pupil – too much gets lost in the great government machine, most of it in some kind of bureaucracy. According to a November 2011 report by the DoE, entitled 'School Workforce in England', there are more education officials than there are teachers. Large independent schools have also been dragged into the great regulatory web. King's College Wimbledon, for example, also has more administrative staff than teachers. It even has its own HR department.

The problem, as I see it, is not so much lack of funding; it is, simply, that the state makes everything expensive. Education is just another example. It need not cost so much. We do need to run such a big, bloated system. Just as health care would fall in price and improve in quality with zero state involvement, so would education.

A free market in education? The very idea would make many weep.

How People Learned Before the State

I don't believe in colleges and universities. I believe in libraries because most students don't have any money. When I graduated from high school, it was during the Depression and we had no money. I couldn't go to college, so I went to the library three days a week for ten years.

Ray Bradbury, author[198]

As my father keeps saying to me, we have the state to thank for pulling so many people in the late 19th–early 20th century out of illiteracy and into learning. Without the state, there would be an underclass of illiterates. This is a compelling argument. Except that it isn't true. There is a great deal of false assumption about education – dogma – and I want to correct some of it.

By 1818 about 478,000 pupils were being schooled. This was the finding of the Henry Brougham Select Committee in 1820, and it revealed a considerable improvement since the first estimates were made 20 years earlier. Brougham was a polymath – a politician, lawyer and scientist – who fought passionately (and successfully) for the abolition of the slave trade. He was also a firm believer in education and called for a public education act to make it available for all. In 1828, he conducted his own study into the education system, using the same sources (the parochial clergy). He found that, in the ten years since 1818, the number of children in schools had doubled.

R. K. Webb, a specialist historian of literacy, describes Britain's literacy in the late 1830s thus: 'in so far as one dare generalize about a national average in an extraordinarily varied situation, the figure would seem to run between two-thirds and three-quarters of the working classes as literate, a group which included most of the respectable poor who were the great political potential in English life'.[199] By

1834, the number of children at schools had increased to 1,294,000. Within 24 years, the number had doubled again to 2,535,462 – about 13% of the population and 95.5% of all children.[200] In other words, there was an explosion of schooling. It happened quite naturally and without the involvement of the state. That 95.5% attendance is perhaps better than today, if you factor in modern delinquency rates.

By 1855, 99% of men recruited to the navy and marines could read.[201] The education historian E. G. West calculated that by 1880, the year compulsion came, 'over 95% of fifteen-year-olds were literate'.[202] Compare that to today. It depends on how you define literate, of course, as we have already seen; it has been estimated that today 17% of boys aged 16–19 are 'functionally illiterate'.[203] The 19th-century levels were achieved without the state, in a time when man was considerably less advanced and when less was available to him. They were achieved before education was free and compulsory by statute.

Compulsion came in 1880, though the process towards this began in 1870 with Forster's Education Act. State schooling did not become free until 1891. In other words, since the government got involved in education in the UK standards have actually slipped in relative terms, despite the advances man has made over the same time period.

As incomes rose from the turn of the 19th century onwards, parents could afford increasing amounts of education for their children. In other words, the vigorous growth in schooling was a response to rising income, which is entirely natural. Self-improvement is one of the main priorities of most families, if not the main priority, once food, clothing and shelter needs are met. Income per head was rising between 1801 and 1871 at the rate of about 1% per year; yet, says E. G. West, 'the average annual growth rate of day scholars was well over 2%'.[204] The 'largest contributors to education revenues' – the biggest spenders, in other words – were working parents; the second largest was the Church of England.

Despite the fact that education depended almost completely on private funds, the supply of it was substantial, varied and flexible; it went beyond everyday schools. E. G. West tells us that there was also:

the adult education movement, the mutual improvement societies, the literary and philosophical institutes, the mechanics' institutes, the Owenite halls of science, the freelance lecturers who travelled the towns and stimulated self-study among the poor . . . In part-time formal education the Sunday schools and adult evening schools were obvious examples. Simultaneously also, there were the factory schools . . .[205]

This, says West, was the 'fluid, flexible, heterogeneous and competitive educational scenario of the pre-1870s'. He continues:

The post-1870 era without the Forster Act provided precisely the setting necessary for the emergence of a truly dynamic and innovative education market in the 1990s. It is unfortunate that this market was destroyed by the combined action of politicians, bureaucrats and rent-seekers, action that not only reduced the potential quality of education but also imposed on citizens enormous financial burdens, especially in the deadweight costs of taxation.[206]

Of course, the 19th century is not some idyll to which we all should nostalgically hope to return. Less schooling per child was available than there is now. There was less of everything. GDP was lower; mankind was considerably less productive. But it is proof that the ordinary people were successfully educating themselves and their children before education became compulsory, supplied by government and 'free'. As people grew richer, they bought more and more of it.

If education was so good, we must ask, why then did the state need to get involved? The reason it did was not unlike the thinking behind the introduction of National Insurance. There was still delinquency at the bottom of society – that 5% of illiterates. It was believed compulsory education would help them and prevent them from entering a criminal lifestyle. It was also an argued principle that state education could help to form the thinking of the young. Imagine if such an admission were to happen now.

Compulsory, uniform provision of education for the majority, I suggest, is not the way to deal with the problem that a minority of parents cannot be trusted to educate or choose an education for their children. It's one of those situations where the many suffer because of the few. When we think of 19th-century schools, many of us imagine the depictions of Charles Dickens. Portrayals such as Dotheboys Hall in *Nicholas Nickleby* have come to be seen as how things were. But, being fiction, his depiction of schools in the early 19th century will have been coloured by exaggeration. He was profoundly affected by his experiences with, and sometimes in, the underclasses of Britain. He was horrified by what he experienced and was adamant that conditions should improve. As prosperity grew, they did.

Unsurprisingly, given his experiences in the working-class slums, Charles Dickens was among those in favour of public education for all. But were he alive today, writing stories, there would be many set in the world of grim council estates with illiterate slum kids dealing drugs and leading hopeless lives. From the houses they live in to their illiteracy and the illegality of the drugs they deal, this is a world that is largely the creation of the state – the very thing for more of which he was campaigning.

How Untrained Sub-Saharan Seven-Year-Olds Became Computer Hackers

But to go to school in a summer morn,
Oh, it drives all joy away!
Under a cruel eye outworn,
The little ones spend the day –
In sighing and dismay.

William Blake, *The Schoolboy*

State schools are expensive. Private schools are expensive. Education doesn't have to be expensive. Lack of competition, rent-seeking, government intervention, regulatory requirements, institutional size, land prices and building restrictions – these have all conspired to drive up prices. Just as state health care has pushed up the cost of private health care, so has state education inflated the price of private education.

Almost anywhere can be a schoolroom. Thanks to the internet and the app – both the most wonderful resources for learning – you often don't even need a teacher. You can teach yourself anything from chemistry to carpentry to Classical Greek and it costs as little as nothing. Compare that to the huge costs of building and running schools. Big buildings with lots of facilities and employees are impressive, and some people like the status they bring, but they do not necessarily improve learning. In some ways having large premises that somebody has to maintain and that students have to get to and from every day is inefficient and inelastic. They can be as big a curse as they are a boon, particularly now that the electronic age has brought so much to our homes. I'm not saying fantastic premises and facilities are not a boon – they can be – but they are not essential.

I commented before on how few state schools teach Mandarin, Hindustani, Russian or Arabic. To get a school to make a subject such as this a mainstream part of their syllabus you would need to persuade the head teacher, or whoever decides these things within a school, that it's a good idea and that it's worth allocating some of his budget to, which will mean doing away with something else. He or she probably wouldn't be able to do anything until the next academic year. You need to find and hire a teacher with the necessary qualifications – there are fewer than 100 qualified teachers in these subjects. You need to arrange a classroom and pay for its upkeep. It's all do-able, but it takes time and costs money. Yet you can download apps that can take students to basic levels of proficiency – never as good as immersing yourself in the country itself, of course, but a basic level of proficiency nonetheless – for nothing. You don't need a classroom or a teacher.

Far more important, I suggest, than facilities, buildings, administrators, targets or even exams, is attitude – that 'little thing that makes a big difference' as Churchill once said. The student has to want to learn. He/she has to be curious. A student is not going to learn a language via a computer app, unless they have the right attitude. If they are not interested, it will become boring, and they will not learn. They will be no more successful in a classroom, if they don't have the right attitude. 'I think the big mistake in schools,' said film-maker Stanley Kubrick in 1975, 'is trying to teach children anything, and by using fear as the basic motivation. Fear of getting failing grades, fear of not staying with your class . . . Interest can produce learning on a scale compared to fear as a nuclear explosion to a firecracker.'[207]

The more I have read and thought about this subject, and the more I have considered the words of high achievers, the more this theme seems to occur. A child – anyone – will pursue knowledge insatiably if he/she has the right attitude – if he/she is interested. That attitude, that interest, can be fostered by parents. Disciplinarians argue that it can be instilled – and, in some cases, it probably can. Teachers, certainly, can inspire and engender it. But without the right attitude, education is almost pointless. 'A teacher,' said the 19th-century American education reformer, Horace Mann, 'who is attempting to teach without inspiring the pupil with a desire to learn is hammering on cold iron'.[208] 'The best teacher,' said novelist Edward Bulwer-Lytton, 'is the one who suggests rather than dogmatizes, and inspires his listener with the wish to teach himself.'[209]

The curricula and systems of education that have, largely, been in place for many decades do not engender this attitude. In fact, they often do the very opposite. 'It is, in fact, nothing short of a miracle,' said Albert Einstein, 'that the modern methods of instruction have not yet entirely strangled the holy curiosity of inquiry; for this delicate little plant, aside from stimulation, stands mainly in need of freedom. Without this it goes to wrack and ruin without fail.'[210] Compulsion – by state or otherwise – goes against this 'need of freedom', it is a dangerous thing. Learning is and should be a pleasure. This passage is taken from T. H. White's classic children's novel, *The Once And Future King*:

'The best thing for being sad,' replied Merlin, beginning to puff and blow, 'is to learn something. That's the only thing that never fails. You may grow old and trembling in your anatomies, you may lie awake at night listening to the disorder of your veins, you may miss your only love, you may see the world about you devastated by evil lunatics, or know your honour trampled in the sewers of baser minds. There is only one thing for it then – to learn. Learn why the world wags and what wags it. That is the only thing which the mind can never exhaust, never alienate, never be tortured by, never fear or distrust, and never dream of regretting. Learning is the only thing for you. Look what a lot of things there are to learn.'[211]

Mankind – and children, in particular – have a natural instinct to learn, voluntarily, for their own ends. They do not need to be compelled. If you learn things when you want to, you'll understand them better, you'll have more fun, and you'll develop a love of learning. Schools, bizarrely, can often kill that instinct. 'Just as eating against one's will is injurious to health,' said Leonardo Da Vinci, 'so studying without a liking for it spoils the memory, and it retains nothing it takes in.'[212] 'Bodily exercise when compulsory', said Plato in *The Republic*, 'does no harm to the body; but knowledge which is acquired under compulsion obtains no hold on the mind.' He continues, 'Do not train children to learning by force and harshness, but direct them to it by what amuses their minds, so that you may be better able to discover with accuracy the peculiar bent of the genius of each.'[213]

Even learning by rote, of which I am a believer, works better when the student has the right attitude. Latin declensions have been notoriously loathed by students through the centuries. I will never forget mine, simply because my Latin teacher, when I was 11, Mr Bayon, was such an inspiring man. He led me to fall in love with classical mythology, brilliantly acting out each story, and turned learning declensions into an exciting competition that we all wanted to do well at. Sadly, he was too 'characterful' for the school and left, discreetly, to become a gardener.

If you'd asked me to learn the part of Romeo when I was 16, I wonder how well I could have done it, even if I could have done it at all. Aged 22, I was word perfect in three days because I got the part in a professional production. I *wanted* to learn it. I am not saying that discipline has no place in learning; it does, absolutely. Nor am I suggesting that teaching is a waste of time. I am saying that *compulsory* learning, without first engendering the right attitude, is dangerous. It can have the very opposite effect to that which is intended: it makes people uninterested, rather than interested; it gives them the wrong attitude. 'Drop out of school,' advises rock star Frank Zappa, 'before your mind rots from exposure to our mediocre educational system. Forget about the Senior Prom and go to the library and educate yourself, if you've got any guts.'[214]

Early in 2012 the One Laptop Per Child (OLPC) organization left 20 tablets loaded with apps with seven-year-olds in two remote Ethiopian villages. The children were given no instruction. Within four minutes some children had opened the boxes and switched them on. After five days they were using an average of 47 apps per child per day. After two weeks several had learned the alphabet song (in English) – and one child was already starting to use a paint programme. After just five months some of them had learned to hack Android, something many in the West can't even do, including your author, and how to freeze the software that had been installed by OLPC. Those children taught themselves, as Zappa recommends. The Chinese proverb runs, 'Teachers open the door, but you must enter by yourself.' By leaving those laptops in that village, OLPC 'opened the door'. That is good teaching.

Charles Dickens never went to university. He came from humble family origins in an era before compulsory education. He was almost entirely a product of self-education. In Dickens's most autobiographical novel, the main character David Copperfield says: 'I had no advice, no counsel, no encouragement, no consolation, no assistance, no support, of any kind, from anyone, that I can call to mind, as I hope to go to heaven!'[215] Dickens, a believer that the state should do more to educate people, would have done well to consider how he himself achieved what he did.

The responsibility for education does not lie with the state. It lies with the self.

You're Just Another Brick in the Wall

Experience is the teacher of all things.
Julius Caesar[216]

In writing and researching this chapter, in looking at the lives and words of high achiever after high achiever, as well as considering my own life and experiences, another theme keeps recurring alongside that of attitude. It's one that follows on from self-education and dances with it endlessly. It is this: there is no substitute for real world experience. 'Nothing ever becomes real till it is experienced,' said John Keats.[217] 'My works are the issue of pure and simple experience,' said Leonardo Da Vinci.[218] 'All knowledge of reality starts from experience and ends with it,' said Albert Einstein.[219]

Of course, many of us have amazing experiences at school, because of our fellow pupils, and our teachers – and because growing up is, largely, 'amazing' – but this is the experience of school itself and of being young, rather than the actual lessons.

One of the reasons many find what they learn at school dull and un-interesting is that subjects seem to have no relevance to the world around them – to their experience. 'In real life,' says author Fran Lebowitz, 'I assure you, there is no such thing as algebra.'[220] What, indeed, is the point of algebra or Latin or oxbow lakes or copper sulphate crystals or '*Où est la bibliothèque?*', many a student has asked him or herself. In the abstract environment of a classroom, these appear to have little to do with their lives. Schools give you an academic intelligence, which often seems to have little relevance to the world outside. The curriculum, argues author Sir Ken Robinson in his TED Talk on education, and the hierarchy of subjects (with science more highly regarded than the arts, for example) was conceived in a different age, in an industrial age, when needs were different.[221] It develops only certain parts of the brain. It discourages creativity and, as a result, many leave school at 17 *less* creative than they were when they entered at the age of five. Some leave school believing themselves stupid, when in fact they're just not particularly suited to the subjects taught at school, in the way that they're taught.

There is one school of home education that believes you should not have lessons at all. It suggests children should be left to learn 'autonomously' through everyday experience. Primary level maths, for example, can be learned through everyday activities such as cooking, shopping and DIY. This autonomous home-learning process is chaotic. It lacks structure. But it is the very essence of a 'bottom-up' approach, one based on experience, rather than the top-down, planned approach of current education. In many ways it reflects the apparently chaotic, haphazard way of nature – which is, as I have argued, often more structured than we realize. Just because we don't see that order, doesn't mean it isn't there. Just because we can't control or regulate something, doesn't mean we can't trust it. Can you imagine a government or a large institution ever sanctioning or administering 'autonomous learning'?

John Kay convincingly persuades us to embrace this chaos of life in *Obliquity*. He argues that, paradoxically, anything more than simple, transparent goals are more likely to be achieved indirectly, saying:

> The notion of a best solution may itself be misconceived . . . To fit the world into a single model or narrative fails to acknowledge the universality of uncertainty and complexity . . . Good decision making is oblique because it is iterative and experimental: it constantly adapts as new information, of many kinds, becomes available.

This line of thinking does not just apply to education, but to entire economies. As Kay says, 'Soviet planners managed their economies far less successfully than the adaptive, disorganized processes of market economies.'[222] It is the very essence of Natural Law. Education doesn't stop when you leave school or university. It is, as teacher and author Bel Kaufman wrote in 1967, 'a never-ending' process. Nevertheless there is a definite plan to formal education. You go to school to go to university to get a job. It's not so much about learning, but about getting the right qualification – a Positive Law – which secures you a safe, steady path in the future. Kids are being put on this conveyor belt as young as five. But I suggest this grand plan is not what it was. A degree no longer makes you special, unless you are a graduate of one of the top few universities. Yet thousands upon thousands of students are now encouraged by some of the craziest government lending schemes ever conceived to get into debt in order to get the tertiary education that ends with this qualification of dubious practical value. The freshers who began university in 2012 are likely to finish their degrees with an average debt of £53,000 ($85,000) that will take over 14 years to pay back.[223] In his viral TED Talk, Ken Robinson said:

> Suddenly, degrees aren't worth anything. Isn't that true? When I was a student, if you had a degree, you had a job ... But now you need an MA where the previous job required a BA, and now you need a PhD for the other. It's a process of academic inflation. And it indicates the whole structure of education is shifting beneath our feet. We need to radically rethink our view of intelligence. Our education system has mined our minds in the way that we strip-mine the earth: for a particular commodity. And for the future, it won't serve us.[224]

There are plenty of examples of geniuses who were never formally educated and who never had 'proper' qualifications: Shakespeare, Da Vinci, Dickens, Eddison, Ford, Carnegie, for example. There are plenty more who dropped out of formal education early to do their own thing: Bill Gates, Albert Einstein, Walt Disney, Elton John, Steve Jobs, Michael Dell (Dell), Larry Ellison (Oracle), Simon Cowell, Coco Chanel, Mark Zuckerberg (Facebook), Ray Kroc (McDonald's), Ingvar Kamprad (Ikea), Richard Branson (Virgin). These are all people who got out into the world and gained experience. They are all examples of what the motivational speaker, Jim Rohn, meant when he said, 'Formal education will make you a living; self-education will make you a fortune.'

We are forever hearing that diversity is something Britain celebrates and encourages, but the uniformity of schools does not do this – it encourages homogeneity. 'Thank goodness my education was neglected, I was never sent to school', said artist and author Beatrix Potter, who was educated at home. 'It would have rubbed off some of the originality.'[225]

In an environment of regulation, supervision, and bureaucracy, people lean away from the colourful and characterful towards the beige and the bland. They take the safe option. I have spoken to some of the people who set curricula in the course of writing this chapter. They have been, at least by my judgement, intelligent, caring people, but they are operating in just such an environment that engenders this bland line of least resistance. And there is a moral issue here. Extremely pleasant though they were, who are these unelected, unknown people to be setting curricula and thereby determining what our children do or don't learn?

In his essay 'On Liberty', the 19th-century philosopher John Stuart Mill – who was a proponent of state schools (although he perhaps would not have supported the system we have today) – wrote:

> A general State education is a mere contrivance for moulding people to be exactly like one another: and as the mould in which it casts them is that which pleases the predominant power in the government, whether this be a monarch, a priesthood, an aristocracy, or the majority of the existing generation; in proportion as it is efficient and successful, it establishes a despotism over the mind, leading by natural tendency to one over the body.[226]

This is a view echoed by the political philosopher Isabel Patterson, who writes in *The God of the Machine* that, 'A tax-supported, compulsory educational system is the complete model of the totalitarian state.'[227]

Economic philosopher Noam Chomsky seems to endorse a similar view. In *Understanding Power* he says: 'The whole educational and professional training system is a very elaborate filter, which just weeds out people who are too independent, and who think for themselves, and who don't know how to be submissive, and so on – because they're dysfunctional to the institutions'.[228] I put this line of thinking to one teacher who sets curricula. He thought I was verging on the delusional. 'Such a thing simply does not happen', he said. I'm not so sure. I'm not suggesting there is some kind of Orwellian conspiracy to brainwash and suppress people, which is something you might read into Chomsky's quote above; but compulsory mass education, when that education is, largely, uniform, cultivates the homogenous, the beige and the bland. This isn't a conspiracy, just an accident or a consequence of our system. You have to get out of it somehow to be original. It is the people who drop out of school that are different.

As well as cultivating homogeneity, the ideologies and dogma that exist within the state educational sector – which tend to be statist – will inevitably be perpetuated by it. If you want your child to go to a school with a certain ideology, then fine, that is your choice. If you don't, that is your choice too. Except that it isn't, as things stand, unless you are wealthy. My children, for example, were taught at their state school that the NHS is a 'good thing'. I hope I have demonstrated to you that this is not necessarily so. They are taught that so-called 'multiculturalism' is 'a good thing'. 'Multiculturalism' may well be 'a good thing' but that is an opinion, not necessarily fact. (My view, for what it's worth, is that if multiculturalism leads to more exchange, then great; if it leads to more rent-seeking and more state, then it is not). Some things that are taught in schools – the 'money-multiplier theory' on fractional reserve banking, for example, are plain wrong.

But without state education, runs the counter-argument, we would see the emergence of, for example, creationist or Islamic Fundamentalist schools. We need the state to prevent such extremism from rising. Neither Fundamental Islamic nor creationist thinking is in line with my own, I should say, but if people want their children to learn those views and be indoctrinated by them, as long as they do not infringe upon the life, liberty and happiness of others, it is, in my view, their business. It is not the business of a toe-the-line bureaucrat or policy-maker to make a moral judgement about the way people should or shouldn't be taught. Anyhow, I dare say that, given a few years of unrestrained free markets, and the innovation, discoveries and prosperity that would ensue, extreme Fundamentalist Islamic and Creationist views would fairly rapidly dissipate.

This passage from Doris Lessing rang very true to me:

Ideally, what should be said to every child, repeatedly, throughout his or her school life is something like this: 'You are in the process of being indoctrinated. We have not yet evolved a system of education that is not a system of indoctrination. We are sorry, but it is the best we can do. What you are being taught here is an amalgam of current prejudice and the choices of this particular culture. The slightest look at history will show how impermanent these must be. You are being taught by people who have been able to accommodate themselves to a regime of thought laid down by their predecessors. It is a self-perpetuating system. Those of you who are more robust and individual than others will be encouraged to leave and find ways of educating yourself — educating your own judgements. Those that stay must remember, always, and all the time, that they are being moulded and patterned to fit into the narrow and particular needs of this particular society.'[229]

Perhaps we must accept that, as Ezra Pound says, 'Real education must ultimately be limited to men who insist on knowing – the rest is mere sheep-herding.'[230] But if you want character, diversity, free will and curiosity, if you want attitude and experience, you won't find it in the grey domain of the state, but somewhere in the free world.

You're More Likely To Be a Genius If You Don't Go to School

From my grandfather's father, [I learned] to dispense with attendance at public schools, and to enjoy good teachers at home, and to recognize that on such things money should be eagerly spent.

Marcus Aurelius Antoninus, Roman emperor[231]

My children are all educated at schools – for the time being, at least. It takes a great deal of courage, I believe, to take the decision to home-educate your children and go through with it – even if you don't go down the autonomous route, but teach your kids formally. People who home-educate are often considered odd. 'Why is it that millions of children who are push-outs or drop-outs amount to business as usual in the public schools, while one family educating a child at home becomes a major threat to universal public education and the survival of democracy?' asks Professor Stephen Arons.[232] It's because home-educated children are unusual. Less than 1% of the population chose to home-educate. But, in many ways, it is the most natural option. Home is a natural place to learn and to be, particularly at a young age. School is a far more artificial environment. At home the child is experiencing 'real life', whatever that is.

In many families home education isn't even an option, due to the parents' work commitments. But, remember, in my minimum tax, low debt, small government world full of constant exchange, families are going to have a lot more disposable income and a lot more time to home-educate – if they want it. There won't be that same financial pressure to work, if one parent doesn't want to.

The arguments for home education are many. It makes the most efficient use of time. In a normal school day, kids go to school from about 8.30/9 a.m. until about 3.30 p.m. But, as numerous studies have demonstrated, in those six or seven hours, only two or three are actually spent learning. Time is wasted on moving about, changing classes, on discipline issues, administrative duties, getting changed, and all the other activities, non-activities and distractions that go on. Plus there's the time spent getting to and from school.

At home you might give your child two or three hours of classes in the morning. The child has the rest of the day to play (where, as many argue, they learn the most anyway) or do whatever else he/she wants (self-educate, perhaps?). As the French priest and author of *The Art of Thinking* Ernest Dimnet said, 'Children have to be educated, but they have also to be left to educate themselves'.[233] There are many things that could be done with that extra time, all of them potentially instructive in some way.

With the extra attention at home, a child can get through the national curriculum much quicker than if at school. No teacher can instruct a class of 20 or 30 kids as fast as one child can go alone. As the 19th-century philosopher Henry Thoreau famously said, 'The man who goes alone can start today; but he who travels with another must wait till that other is ready.'[234] If interested, a child can do two years' curriculum in just a few months. Every few years in the UK, a child, often a genius in mathematics or physics, hits the news as he/she manages to get into Oxford or Cambridge at the age of 13 or 14. It turns out as often as not that this child is home-educated.

Home education is cheaper. There are not all those buildings and facilities to pay for. Even if you hire tutors it can work out less expensive, particularly if you get together other like-minded parents who have children of a similar age. A part-time teacher or tutor costs around £25 ($40) per hour. At this cost, tutoring for 25 hours per week, 34 weeks a year equals £21,250 ($34,000) per annum. Divide that by the number of children – let's say there are five between you and your like-minded neighbours. It works out at about £4,250 ($6,800) per child – less than half the ten grand the government now spends.

Home education is more flexible than school. If you want to change the curriculum, or teaching practices, or do something spontaneous or left-field, you just do it. There's no need for forms or regulation or permission.

At home, parents have greater control of the influences children come under in their formative years. Children can't come home with some bad behaviour or language they learned at school. The children need not undergo testing, if it isn't wanted. Bullying is less likely to be an issue. There isn't the problem of being segregated into classes with people the same age, and being constantly compared to them, even though they might be developing at a different pace. They can come into regular contact with older children to look up to, and younger children to look up to them, as well as a range of adults.

Home schooling bonds parent and child. They get to know each other better. The act of being teacher, even if only part time, forces parents to behave in a more exemplary fashion. Parents learn through the process as well.

Perhaps the most compelling reason of all is that, as well as it being a more efficient use of time, money and resources, home-educated children actually perform better. I remind you of that doctoral thesis by Dr Paula Rothermel that I mentioned at the beginning of the chapter, 'Home-Education: Rationales, Practices and Outcomes'.[235] In national literacy project assessments, the level reached by the top

16% of school-educated children was attained by 80% of home-educated children. This was the largest study of home education ever undertaken in the UK. Rothermel found, simply, that children of primary school age who are taught at home learn more than those in schools. And it's not just at primary level where they outperform.

Home schooling methods vary enormously. Some imitate schools and even ring a bell in the morning; others go down the autonomous learning route, allowing their children to do as they please. Some parents hire teachers, others teach themselves, others do a bit of both. *How Children Learn at Home* by Alan Thomas and Harriet Pattison, two academics from the Institute of Education at the University Of London, concludes that informal home education is 'an astonishingly efficient way to learn'; as good, if not better than school. 'The ease, naturalness and immense intellectual potential of informal learning up to the age of middle secondary school means they can learn certainly as much if not more'.[236]

The pair interviewed and observed 26 families who, between them, home-educated over 70 children. Most were British; all were English-speaking. They discovered that children absorb information by 'doing nothing, observing, having conversations, exploring, and through self-directed learning'. Thomas and Pattison compare this to the thought patterns and processes one might go through in the act of composing music, sketching out a novel or story, coming up with a solution to a problem, or even a scientific breakthrough. 'Its products are often intangible, its processes obscure, its progress piecemeal,' they say. 'There are false starts, unrelated bits and pieces picked up, interests followed and discarded, sometimes to be taken up again, sometimes not . . . Yet the chaotic nature of the informal curriculum does not appear to be a barrier to children organising it into a coherent body of knowledge.' Even the possibility that children may be taught inaccurate information is not a problem, they say. 'In some ways, it may be an advantage because, rather than presenting knowledge in neat packages, the informal curriculum forces learners to become actively engaged with their information – to work with it, move it around, juggle ideas and resolve contradictions . . . It is not a static thing contained in a series of educational folders. It is alive and dynamic.'[237]

Thomas and Pattison endorse home education for children to the age of 14. At this age, perhaps contrary to expectations, the home-educated child does not have difficulty entering formal education, they found. 'The young people had the personal skills to make the transition with apparent ease.'

Rothermel's study also found that children taught at home to be more confident, with better social skills than those taught at school. At home, she explains, more emphasis is put on learning 'life skills' – communication, interpersonal skills, as well as self-esteem and responsibility. She says:

> If you look at these children in comparison with school-taught children, they are very different. They seem to develop more responsibility, they are far more involved in what is happening in the family. That's very different from children who are out of the house during the daytime. Because inspectors are used to seeing schoolchildren, they are judging by school standards – they might find these children very different indeed.[238]

My argument is not that all children should be educated at home or anything so simplistic. My argument is this: *it is your responsibility to educate your children, not the state's, and however you want to do it is up to you* (unless, of course, cruelty is involved). I am not suggesting that 'schools are bad' and 'schools don't work'. Many are excellent. I am just highlighting the fact that there are legitimate, cheaper alternatives to schools – alternatives that are increasingly compelling in this fast-changing age of electronic communication and shared knowledge, by which children might more easily find the areas in which they want to specialize.

Getting the State Out of Education

*The real cost of this dysfunctional system is not measured in
dollars and cents but in the hopes and futures it has destroyed . . .
our inner-city school districts have become slaughterhouses of dreams.*

Andrew J. Coulson, educationalist[239]

It's easy to hold court and say the world should be run a certain way
and that the long-term strategy should be for the state to stay away
from education, so that individual choice can be restored and costs
can come down. The apparently insurmountable problem is how we
get there from where we are now.

After the 1870 Forster Act, people's direct spending on education
was replaced by indirect spending by government on their behalf.
To do this, government had to increase taxes, which meant people
now had less much capital to spend on education themselves. So,
just as compulsory National Insurance killed the Friendly Societies,
so did compulsory education force many educational establishments
that were emerging at the time into dependence on the state for their
funding. The effect of compulsion was to strengthen the monopoly of
government and weaken the power of those wanting to buy education
for themselves, bringing us eventually to the imbalance we have
today. Any transition has to have the reverse effect, it has to weaken
state control and strengthen the person who wants education – the
customer. The appropriate strategy should be to put more money in
people's pockets – to tax them less, in other words.

One relatively simple transformation that would at least nudge us
in the right direction is the introduction of vouchers. Families could
be given a voucher per child for, say, £10,000 ($15,000) – perhaps
more in some regions, less in others – to spend on their child's
education. Alternatively, parents could apply to pay £10,000 less in
tax per child and receive no voucher at all. Schools would then be
given autonomy and control over themselves. There has already been
a small step towards this in the UK with the 'free schools' movement,
which, in the words of their own PR, 'are all-ability state-funded
schools set up in response to what local people say they want and

need in order to improve education for children in their community'. Head teachers and their teams make their own decisions about what they want their schools to be – places of excellence, places catering for local children, for under-achievers, whatever the Head decides. Independent schools can specialize if they so desire. There'll be more opportunities for specific vocational training – practical rather than academic, if that's what's wanted, more opportunities for sport, drama, music, computing, Latin – whatever it is that parents and pupils want. This process of independence takes government *out* of schools and makes things smaller – remember our size versus efficiency argument. Independent schools are then in a better position to shrink or expand according to local demand.

With its voucher, a family can pick and choose where it likes – home school, local school, boarding school. It has been found that parents who make their own choice and investment work harder for their children and make more of a contribution to the school. They will have aims for their children, which are united with the aims of other parents. The quality of parenting improves. Parents will make for better regulators of good practice in schools than government inspectors and referrals. This way you are returning control to the consumer, the parent/child. You are giving them back the power of choice. Schools will have to deliver a desirable service or face the penalty of declining revenue. This market reality will force better practice on them, instead of forever acting in the interests of the supplier or regulator.

Schools that only the rich can afford suddenly become more affordable with the help of a voucher. More independent schools are likely to spring up as there will be a much greater market for them – especially if planning laws on where you can and cannot have an education institution, as well as other regulations, can be eased. There will be a more effective market-led balance between competition for pupils and competition for places, which force both schools and parents to keep up standards.

Any form of subsidy, however, will push up prices. I'd rather we were not taxed in the first place, but a voucher system is considerably better than what we have now because, at least, it would bring back choice.

But what happens to those few children – that 5% – at the very bottom? If the aim of the state is to ensure that the poorest in society have access to education, the answer is not necessarily the universal, compulsory provision we have now. The morals of 'selective compulsion' are also hazardous. I remind you of my scenario: without the burdensome cost of government, everyone will be richer, costs will be lower, restrictions will be fewer. Communities will be in a much stronger position to come together and provide aid, if required; there will be scope for cooperatives and new Friendly Societies to reappear; all sorts of other institutions could spring up, funded by the philanthropic, to help those at the very bottom – if, indeed, they even want to be helped. It is a natural human instinct to give. A free market is the optimum environment in which to do it. The free market is a better provider of care than government – and we'll have more on this in the final chapter. It's hard to see how the plight of that bottom few per cent can be much worse than it is now, but the other 95 or 99% should not be sacrificed for the few.

If the government wants to offer schooling, let it. If people want to go to them, let them. But the taxpayer should not have to pay; those who go to them should, with their vouchers, if necessary. As long as the playing field is level, and the government is operating by the same rules as everybody else, I am happy. As John Stuart Mill said, 'Though a government, therefore, may, and in many cases ought to, establish schools and colleges, it must neither compel nor bribe any person to come to them.'[240] Mill advocated that a state school should exist, 'if it exist at all, as one among many competing experiments, carried on for the purpose of example and stimulus, to keep the others up to a certain standard of excellence.'[241] State schools will 'keep up the others up to a certain standard of excellence?' How wrong could you be?

The 12 Takeaways:

1 If the government does not provide education, there will still be education.
2 Public education is expensive, homogenous and often counter-productive.

3   People do not need to be compelled to learn by the state – they instinctively want to learn anyway.

4   The free market can provide better education at lower cost.

5   State involvement has pushed up the cost of education for all, be it private or public.

6   The sheer size of the state, the layers of bureaucracy and the opposing views within it, make it very difficult to get anything done. Mediocrity flourishes.

7   State compulsion has not made the underclass any more literate. If anything, the state has just increased the size of the underclass.

8   The free market is the only environment flexible enough to evolve quickly to meet changing needs.

9   The free market is the only supplier adaptable enough to meet niche and minority needs.

10   The most important thing in education is the attitude of the student.

11   Experience is the greatest educator.

12   There is more to education than schools.

15   27,000 Words to Sell a Cabbage

Corruptissima republica plurimae leges.
(The more laws there are the more corrupt the state)
Tacitus, Roman historian[242]

The Blair and Brown government, which took office in 1997, created new laws every day of the week. I'm not exaggerating. In the 13 years that Labour was in power over 4,300 new crimes were invented. Twenty-seven per month. But Brown took it over the one-per-day mark with 33 per month.[243] These crimes include 'disturbing a pack of eggs when instructed not to by an authorized officer' – that is, eggs that may hatch – and 'swimming in the hull of the *Titanic* without a cabinet minister's permission'. I'd love to know the penalties for these offences. I'm no diving expert, but I dare say that Natural Law will take care of the worrying swimming-in-the-hull-of-the-*Titanic* problem. Labour also illegalized 'causing a nuclear explosion'. Thank goodness.

The same goes for American law. There is one school of legal thinking, known as Declarationism, which holds that the (extremely noble, in my view) principles on which the US is founded – the Declaration of Independence and the US Constitution – are based on Natural Law. But that was before various administrations started making amendments.

Now, the US government doesn't seem to be bothered by making amendments. Whether it's changing the debt ceiling, appointing unelected city Czars, obliging people or companies to buy health insurance or the American Recovery and Reinvestment Act (economic stimulus), these directives pretty much ignore the Constitution altogether. If not through money and taxation, government is at its most intrusive through the legal system.

The British legal system, once the envy of the world, is too complicated. It's rife with regulation, subsidy, distortion and intervention of all kinds. Those who work in it and exploit it become rich. It is a rent-seeker's paradise. But legal costs mean that justice is often out of reach for most people.

One problem seems to be that it is easier to make new laws and legislation than repeal those already in existence, so every year the system gets ever bigger and more complicated. For example, at 11,520 pages, the 2009 UK handbook of tax legislation is estimated to comprise more than 4.6 million words!

The EU, however, trumps almost all. I came across this at Mike Shedlock's blog, 'Global Economic Analysis':

- Pythagoras' theorem – 24 words.
- Lord's Prayer – 66 words.
- Archimedes' Principle – 67 words.
- Ten Commandments – 179 words.
- Gettysburg address – 286 words.
- US Declaration of Independence – 1,300 words.
- US Constitution (with all 27 Amendments) – 7,818 words.
- **EU regulations on the sale of cabbage – 26,911 words.**[244]

How *did* we ever manage to sell cabbage before the EU, one wonders? Or, rather, how do we manage to sell it now?

Legislation creates barriers to exchange. The more legislation, the more scope for error and the greater the possibilities to game the system. Legislation can have far-reaching, unintended consequences – from forcing businesses to act wastefully for fear of being sued, to the proverbial health-and-safety officer getting in the way of productive endeavour, to laws that actually harm where they were supposed to protect. As with money, education and health care, the legal system has become a political tool, by which politicians try and win votes.

Each new piece of legislation is an erosion of freedom in that it entails the removal of a choice. 'The more you limit people's choices, even in the name of helping them,' says Russell Roberts in his economic romance, *The Invisible Heart*, 'the more responsibility you take away from them.'[245] Legislation erodes responsibility.

I want to consider an example next – a law that has unimagined and devastating consequences – our drugs laws.

The Inane Laws That Gave a Bad Trip to Millions

I'm glad mushrooms are against the law, because I took them one time, and you know what happened to me? I lay in a field of green grass for four hours going, 'My God! I love everything.' Yeah, now if that isn't a hazard to our country . . . how are we gonna justify arms dealing when we realize that we're all one?

Bill Hicks, comedian[246]

Drugs are bad for you. They're dangerous. They damage your brain. You can get addicted. They can kill you, even. If you legalize drugs, more people will take them and we'll have an even bigger problem. Therefore drugs should be illegal. That's a rather facile summary of the argument for anti-drugs legislation.

I live in South London. I work in Soho a great deal. I see the damage drugs can do every day, just going to work in the morning. Twenty-five-year-old heroin addicts whose skin is in such disrepair they look 20 years older, so skinny their trousers look several sizes too big; dirty, smelly, sleeping rough; begging for money, pretending it's for a cup of tea or for a room for the night; shoplifting, offering their bodies for sex. Theirs is a grim existence, with a future that looks bleak and short.

Heroin is indiscriminate. It claims victims from all sections of society. It doesn't matter if you're rich or poor, black or white, from a broken or settled home. A heroin addict needs to find something like £200 a day to fund his habit. Most heroin addicts don't earn that kind of money, so they usually turn to crime. In Wales in 2008 a child of ten was arrested for supplying heroin.[247]

According to a 2006 ICM/BBC survey, 75% of people think that illegal drug taking is a problem in their area. But it doesn't take a survey to see that something needs to be done. However, the more governments pursue the 'War on Drugs', the more money that is spent, the more manpower and resources that go into it, the worse the situation seems to get. The illegalization of drugs was touted as a cure for a problem. It hasn't been. If anything it's been the opposite. It's created more problems.

In 1960, there were 94 registered heroin users in the UK.[248] Eight years later there were 2,240. In 1971 heroin was formally made illegal with the Misuse of Drugs Act. By 1990 the number was 18,000; by 1996 it reached almost 45,000.[249] Even though the number of young addicts has fallen since 2008, estimates suggest that the number of problem heroin users, registered and unregistered, is still above 300,000. The reason that heroin use has seen a slight decline is the proliferation of other drugs that are now available. Prohibition has failed to cut the supply of illicit drugs and failed to cut drug use. In fact, if anything, it has cemented the businesses of those selling and trafficking drugs, and protected them from the forces of legitimate competition.

Rulers have forever been trying to regulate drug consumption amongst their people – and without success. Passages in the Koran, dating from the 7th century, led to the prohibition of alcohol under Islamic law. Islamic law now prohibits all intoxicants, not only alcohol, but let's not beat about the bush. Ever been to Morocco, Egypt, Lebanon, Afghanistan, Pakistan or South-West Thailand? The ancient practice of hashish smoking is – as it has always been throughout the Islamic world – widespread. As for Orthodox Christianity, at one stage it even tried to ban coffee.

What is recognized as the first prohibition of the modern era came from Napoleon, who was worried about the widespread use of cannabis by his occupying troops in Egypt. My views on occupation and wars are that the French army shouldn't have been in Egypt at all, but now that they were, I think the troops got it right. I went backpacking round Egypt when I was 19 – probably the same age as many of his troops – and I can vouch that one of the most pleasurable ways of spending the day there is with cannabis as your companion. Napoleon would not have approved: 'It is forbidden,' came his ordinance to his troops in 1800, 'in all of Egypt to use certain Moslem beverages made with hashish, or likewise to inhale the smoke from seeds of hashish. Habitual drinkers and smokers of this plant lose their reason and are victims of violent delirium which is the lot of those who give themselves full to excesses of all sorts'.[250] This quote is a good example of the kind of scaremongering that always seems to go on and the misinformation that gets spread. Violent delirium? They were stoned. The reason Napoleon didn't want his troops smoking the 'seeds of hashish' is, I suspect, for no other reason than he wanted his army sober. Stoned soldiers don't make good soldiers.

One of my close friends is the comedian James Dowdeswell. His dad is a publican who runs a country pub in a village just outside Bristol. He gave James his first pint aged 13 or 14, even though it was below the legal age limit, not because he wanted his son to be a drinker, but because he wanted his son to learn how to drink, what his limits would be, what can happen and so on. He knew it was inevitable that his son *would* drink, so he wanted to make sure he could do it properly.

A similar attitude would be very welcome in the world of drugs. There is no point saying that drug-taking must remain illegal because it is bad, wrong and leads to 'violent delirium', when drug-taking is inevitable. The cultivation, use and trade of psychoactive drugs goes back as far as civilization itself. There is evidence that the opium poppy was cultivated in lower Mesopotamia in 3,400 BC, and the Sumerians called it 'Hul Gil', the 'joy plant'. Even under the most totalitarian, oppressive, controlling, '*1984*-type-Sauron-evil-Emperor-Palpatine' regime, it will go on. Mankind's desire to 'get out of it' is normal, natural and has existed for as long as we have. It is part of the rituals of almost every small-scale society. Rather than regulate against human nature, a better attitude, I suggest, is to be open and upfront. That way knowledge and information will be shared, rather than buried. Users are less likely to be guarded about their experiences. There is less scope for dishonesty, fear and cover-up, for misinformation, ignorance and falsehood. That way drugs can at least be taken safely.

According to the Crime Survey for England and Wales 2011–12, about one in three 16- to 59-year-olds have used one or more illicit drugs in their lifetime – that's 12.5 million people. Nothing like that number have had their lives ruined by the experience. Drugscope, the UK's leading centre of expertise on drugs and drug use, estimate that of those 12.5 million who have used drugs, 130,000 – a little over 1% – have become addicts. Compare that figure with alcohol. The NHS has published these figures from the Office of National Statistics. Of the 65 million or so people in the UK, about 50 million drink. One million are 'problem drinkers', but 200,000 are dependent – government-speak for 'alcoholic' or 'addict'. In other words, if you use drugs there's only a 1% you'll become an addict. If you drink, there's somewhere between a 0.4 and 2% chance you'll go on and become an alcoholic. Drug use doesn't inevitably lead to addiction, just as drinking doesn't necessarily lead to alcoholism.

They could of course make alcohol totally illegal and then spend billions enforcing and policing this law. They tried that in the US with Prohibition. Instead of being supplied by breweries, vineyards, bars, clubs and shops, alcohol was supplied by criminals – thereby putting money and power in their hands. Alcohol and other content was unknown. Alcohol poisoning became prevalent. This is the precisely problem we have today with drugs. They are supplied by criminals. *Water* would be dangerous, if it was supplied by criminals.

Drugs would be safer, for example, if we knew the narcotic content of each dose, where it's from, what the ingredients are, what the effects are; if we knew the reputation of that farm or that laboratory. The biggest causes of heroin fatalities are overdosing and the impurities with which heroin is cut. But if dosages are marked and content is pure, death via impurity would be dramatically reduced, while the risk of overdose would be minimized. At present drug laws actually increase the likelihood of fatality because they suppress clear information. Abolition of these laws could save lives.

Looking at my own experience, I tried all sorts of things in my teens and early twenties, more than I ought to have. By my late twenties I was an occasional user. Now I'm 43, it's so occasional it's verging on the non-existent. I have since found out that this is the normal progression. According to both the British Crime Survey and the UK Drug Policy Commission, the highest level of drug use takes place among the 16–19 and 20–24 year age groups.[251] Most young people moderate or completely stop using illegal drugs and moderate their alcohol use by their mid–late twenties, as they start to take on adult responsibilities.

Instead of arresting young people for doing what they will inevitably do, instead of driving them underground and into the unscrupulous hands of criminals, let's make drug-taking as safe as we can for them. Some will go on and become addicts, yes, but they do not have to be driven onto the streets and into petty crime.

Privately, many politicians agree that the laws are counter-productive, yet no politician of influence in the UK will campaign with any great passion to have the drug laws repealed, despite the great historical example that is the failure of Prohibition, for fear of the media reaction and the false perception that by legalizing drugs you are somehow promoting their use.

Then there's the expense. I wonder how much money has been spent enforcing the unenforceable – all the military, policing, legal, prison and hospital costs that have compounded over the years – as well as how much has been stolen in petty crime.

And there are the moral issues. Is it not the right of an individual, rather than a government, to decide what he or she puts into their body? And is it right to penalize a drug user? Most likely he or she will be someone aged between 16 and 24, for whom drug taking is not only natural, but socially normal. Incarceration and a criminal record will most likely have a negative effect on his life and career prospects. If the drug user has a genuine problem and is some kind of addict, then arresting and criminalizing him will not help him. And in many cases drug-use actually continues while in prison. 'Now here's somebody who wants to smoke a marijuana cigarette,' said Milton Friedman in his 1991 America's Drug Forum interview. 'If he's caught, he goes to jail. Now is that moral? Is that proper? I think it's absolutely disgraceful that our government ... should be in the position of converting people who are not harming others into criminals, of destroying their lives, putting them in jail. That's the issue to me ... Most of the harm that comes from drugs is because they are illegal.'

The numbers in the US are particularly terrifying. It has the highest incarceration rate in the world, ten times more per 100,000 citizens than other 'First World' nations.[252] Indeed, a quarter of the world's inmates are locked up in the US.[253] One-fifth of them are for drug offences, and 80% of drug incarcerations are merely for possession.[254] As many as 58% of the women incarcerated in the US, a disproportionately high number of which are black, have been put away for drug-related offences.[255] In 1985 there were 41,000 drug offenders in federal prisons; by 2010 this had risen to 500,000. Since Richard Nixon began the 'War on Drugs' in 1970, some 31 million people have been imprisoned on drug related charges![256] Has this made society any safer? I doubt it.

I haven't even begun to consider the consequences of Western drug laws on other countries. American drug laws have been a curse on Mexico, for example, which in 2011 experienced as many as 47 drug-related killings per day.[257] There have been all sorts of adverse consequences to countries all across the world, from Bolivia and Colombia in South America to Afghanistan and Thailand in Asia.

In my view the answer to the drugs problem lies, yet again, in the free market. Costs will fall, quality will rise, education and information will improve, individual responsibility will grow. Current drugs laws are a classic example of Positive Law replacing Natural Law. The laws have had terrible and unintended consequences on people's lives, yet the inflexibility of the state means they are taking decades to reverse. Government inaction, rather than action, would have been so much more preferable. Who now mourns the demise of Prohibition?

Drugs laws are by no means not the only legislation that needs reform. Our whole legal system has become a haven of obsfuscation, rent-seeking and abuse. It's too easy to make a law or a regulation, and too problematic to repeal or remove it. That's why our legal and bureaucratic systems become so increasingly bloated. I once read a proposal on the website HousePriceCrash that laws should expire after five years, unless voted by the House of Commons or Congress to continue for another five. That's a quick way to get rid of legislation that doesn't work, while keeping that which does. It forces improvement rather than expansion.

Part IV

Towards Life After the State

16 Why the Poor and Endangered Should Fear the State

Lack of money is the root of all evil.
Mark Twain[258]

Without some kind of state protection, run common fears, the earth's resources will be exhausted, pollution will increase, climate change will worsen and poverty will become even more extreme. I'm not so sure.

You might argue that what we are experiencing with the three most pressing environmental issues – climate change, the depletion of the world's resources and the destruction of natural habitats and species – is part of natural evolution, 'survival of the fittest' and so on. But it all appears to be unravelling at too great a speed and on too big a scale. We rely on nature to sustain us. If we destroy nature, we destroy ourselves. Recalling the free market transaction of earlier, where both parties benefit, man's current attitude seems to be one where we take, but don't seem to give in return – more theft or rape than symbiosis and cooperation. We are not living harmoniously with nature.

Every time a new building is built, every time we drive our car or switch on a light – some small part of nature gets consumed. Are we to stop living modern lifestyles altogether, as some, such as the *Guardian*'s George Monbiot, would have us do? Must we somehow try to prevent emerging nations from enjoying the same luxuries we take for granted in the West? No amount of regulation, propaganda, summits, protocols, treaties, incentives, subsidies or whatever else will stop this inevitable tide. In fact, such measures may even make it worse in that they hinder exchange and thus impede progress. It is *progress*, surely – discoveries and inventions leading to improved efficiency, technological advances, new sources of food and energy and so on – that is going to solve our environmental problems.

Take modern farming methods, for example. In 2005 worldwide we produced twice as much grain from the same acreage of land as we did in 1968, according to Indur Goklany.[259] The idea of intensive farming appals many. To an extent it appals me. But if the average crop yields of the 1960s prevailed now, it would mean instead of ploughing around 3.7 billion acres as we do, we would have had to plough almost 8 billion. The entire landmass of Central and North America is only 6 billion acres. Intensive methods may actually have saved wilderness that might otherwise have been turned to farmland – 44% of it, according to Goklany. The argument has been made that such farming practices – a form of progress – are actually environmentally *friendly*.

The issues of whether climate change is man-made, whether it poses a genuine threat to mankind, and whether we need alternative sources of energy to fossil fuels oil, are incendiary. I've read quite a lot of material on the subjects – I was particularly persuaded by the work of Matt Simmons on Peak Oil – however, I'm not a scientist and I cannot possibly make any judgement.[260] But I suggest that nobody can, because nobody is cognisant of all the facts, particularly regarding climate. There is too much we don't know, especially relating to the sun, and so most discourse inevitably involves at least a little theory and supposition. At present some compelling and well researched scientific arguments declare there is a need to cut carbon emissions and develop alternative energy sources, but since the work of Thomas Malthus in the 18th century – and even earlier – there have been well-researched and compelling arguments that some kind of crisis is around the corner, only for said crisis not to materialize. I tend to fall back on the cliché: if there is a need, the market will provide. If we run out of oil, the oil price will rise, alternative energy sources will become economic and necessity will give birth to invention. And, yes, profit will be the motive. If the ozone layer becomes desperately depleted, there could be horrible problems, yes, but I do not see how any government or league of governments can avert them. The answer will lie in improved practice enforced by circumstance, migration perhaps and invention.

Private property rights, one of the mainstays of free markets, are also key to conservation. 'If no one owns something,' say William J. Boyes and Michael Melvin in *Macroeconomics*, 'no one has the incentive to take care of it.' They continue:

> Consider the fish in the ocean. No one owns the fish, and hence, no one has the incentive to protect them, raise them, and ensure that future generations of fish exist. Someone has to own an item for someone to take care of it. Also, it is private property rights that count, not public property rights. If no one owns something, no one takes care of it. But equally, if everyone owns something no one has the incentive to take care of it. In the former Soviet Union, the government owned virtually everything. No one had an incentive to take care of anything. As a result, housing was decrepit and dingy, industries were inefficient and run down, chemicals were dumped in the rivers and on the land, the air was polluted, and, in general, standards of living were very poor.[261]

Boyes and Melvin are describing what is known as the 'tragedy of the commons' and it applies to the environment. If people own their land and resources, they tend to exploit them in a sustainable way. If they don't, or if land and resources are protected by a distant regulation – as in the case of the Amazon or the African wilderness, for example – people exploit them for the 'now', with no thought of the future.

*

Most of us in the West have more things in our lives than we probably need. Yes, things can be fun, but surely in the West we consume too much: we eat too much, we drive too much, we work too hard, we spend too much time on our computers – all of these things. But, above all, *we waste too much*. And the biggest offender of all is big government. We live in a world obsessed with economic growth, but at what cost? I'm all for growth in knowledge, for growth in efficiency and quality, but not growth for the sake of some target somewhere. As the American author Edward Abbey once wrote, 'Growth for the sake of growth is the ideology of the cancer cell'.[262] In Japan in the 1990s they built roads to nowhere to try and boost the flagging economy. In China they have built entire cities that now sit empty. Look on Google Earth at Erenhot, Zhengzhou New District, Kangbashi, Dantu, the north-east of Xinyang and you will see huge cities, in some cases built to boost growth in the wake of the 2008 financial crisis, almost without life. You'll see six-lane highways in huge metropolises with barely a car on them. They have been dubbed China's 'ghost cities'. Meanwhile, in the UK we have a propped-up housing market, unaffordable housing and almost a million homes sitting unoccupied.[263] Huge inefficient government institutions, bailed-out businesses and bloated rent-seeking corporations carry on gorging themselves on capital, energy and resources for years. As much as two billion tonnes of food – half of global production – is thrown away each year.[264] Wars around the world have done almost unquantifiable damage to the environment. Our inflationary system of money has created terrifying malinvestment in needless projects.

None of these would exist to anything like the same extent in a free market environment, because a free market enforces efficiency in a way that the state simply cannot. Only that which is actually wanted is produced. I'm not suggesting that private enterprise has never damaged the environment – of course it has – but it does not create waste on a scale that governments, or enterprises in collusion with governments, do. Empty cities are not built. Existing cities are not bombed.

Many of us do live efficiently, but government and other large corporate machines do not. Let them operate without privilege, unsubsidized, in the same free market as the rest of us, and they will quickly be forced to stop their needless waste. Which brings us to the next subject: food and Third World poverty.

An eighth of the global population – some 870 million people, most of them in Asia or sub-Saharan Africa – is 'chronically undernourished'.[265] Meanwhile, in the West we enjoy an unprecedented abundance of cheap food. In Britain, 60% of adults are overweight and 26% are obese; 30% of children aged 2–15 years are either overweight or obese.[266] Yet the UK ranks behind the US in the global obesity stakes. And there are some new fat kids on the block. Almost 50% of Brazilians are now either overweight or obese.[267]

Worse, perhaps, than our over-eating, is our habit of throwing food away – I'm not referring to food we have bought but not got around to consuming, though this might make our thrifty grandparents despair, but the industrial quantities discarded by supermarkets and the catering trade, often simply because it has not sold by its sell-by date or because its appearance is not deemed good enough to sell. Regulation and the threat of legal action mean they can't, or daren't, risk even *giving* it away. Elsewhere, subsidy – to farmers in Europe – for example, means that proverbial mountains of butter and lakes of milk sit unconsumed. As much as half of global food production goes unconsumed, yet even with this excess supply, more and more rainforest is being cut down to make farmland, in particular grazing for cattle. So much of this waste is, simply, an unintended consequence of regulatory systems.

There has been a 70% increase in world population since 1970, yet agriculture produces 17% more calories per person today than it did then. There is enough food, according to the World Hunger Education Service, to provide everyone with 2,720 kilocalories per day.[268] In other words, the world already produces more than enough food to feed everyone. However, many people do not have the means to buy it, or grow it.

The World Bank has estimated that there are an estimated 1,345 million (1.34 billion) poor people in developing countries who live on $1.25 a day or less. The World Hunger Education Service (WHES) blames this poverty on faulty economic and political systems. A minority, who live well, control resources and power, while those at the bottom struggle. (Oh, for land value tax!)

How can people escape poverty? At the 1996 World Food Summit a target was set to halve the number of undernourished people by 2015 from their number in 1990–92 (the FAO uses three-year averages). There were 824 million in 1990–92. In 2010, the number had not fallen – but risen to 925 million. The 2015 target looks unlikely to be met. For all the government aid, subsidy and other funds that have gone into this problem, the number of hungry people has actually risen.

Aid, as is widely starting to be agreed, in the form it currently takes, does not work. It often fails to reach its target, money is embezzled, wrong decisions are made, capital injections are sporadic and do not have the intended effect. Zambian economist Dambisa Moyo declares, 'Aid doesn't work, hasn't worked, and won't work . . . no longer part of the potential solution, it's part of the problem – in fact, aid is the problem.'[269]

Remember my money-supply chain, where those furthest from the issuance of money suffer while those closest to it benefit? Part of the problem is that those in sub-Saharan Africa and other impoverished parts of the world are the very end of the money-supply chain. But an even greater problem is that they face too many barriers to Matt Ridley's magic 'exchange': location; topography; crime, corruption, war and oppressive regimes; European farming subsidy making farming produce, potentially one of Africa's greatest exports, uncompetitive (who would have thought a well-intentioned subsidy in Europe would turn distant African farmers into Mr Loss and Miss Doubt?); ill-health; lack of capital to invest; lack of access to education and modern technology; rotten systems of money; the monopolization of Africa's huge natural resource wealth; aid and its unintended consequences; and onerous bureaucracy. In Cairo, for example, to acquire and register a piece of state-owned land it can take 14 years and 77 bureaucratic processes through 31 different agencies.[270]

Another barrier to exchange comes in the failure to recognize private property rights. Botswana, which also operates a land value tax, does recognize them. When it became independent from the UK in 1966 it had a per capita GDP of just $70. That $70 now sits above $14,000, the third highest in Africa, higher than all its neighbours – South Africa, Zimbabwe, Angola, Zambia and Namibia – higher even than China (though China's large population makes this comparison dubious), with no wars, coups, dictators or hyperinflations. This is despite being landlocked. Yes, its population (two million) is small, but it also has secure, enforceable property rights. People can operate knowing that what they own is theirs, and will not be taken from them. Meanwhile, windfalls from its diamond mining, thanks to its land value tax, have been, to an extent, shared.

But property rights are not enshrined elsewhere in Africa. 'The existence of such massive exclusion generates two parallel economies legal and extra legal,' says Peruvian economist Hernando de Soto. 'An elite minority enjoys the economic benefits of the law and globalization, while the majority of entrepreneurs are stuck in poverty, where their assets – adding up to more than US$10 trillion worldwide – languish as dead capital in the shadows of the law.'[271] The thrust of de Soto's work is that a strong market economy is not possible without framework that records ownership of property. In Tanzania, for example, he says that something like 98% of business operates outside the law. This doesn't mean it is lawless. There are many local rules; contracts are agreed and drafted, but with no official recognition or registration it is hard for businesses to obtain credit, to be valued, bought and sold, to expand beyond their immediate vicinity or to resolve conflicts in court. I've travelled a fair bit in Africa. Everywhere I've been, but particularly in the Arab north, I've found myself bombarded by people trying to sell me stuff. I am not alone in this experience, it happens to everyone who goes there. There is no shortage of entrepreneurial spirit. There are, simply, too many barriers to exchange.

Technology is already having a role to pay fixing this. Now almost 70% of Kenyans, for example, use mobile phone technology to make and receive payments (the M-PESA is the market leader). Africa actually leads the world in this field of mobile phone payment and it is proving to be a facilitator for exchange. The number of people with internet access trebled in Kenya between 2009 and 2011, and Nairobi is fast becoming an internationally significant tech hub.[272] It's not Bangalore yet, but it is developing rapidly.

Africa is no poorer than China was in 1978. A similar transformation can occur. The way for it to happen is through exchange, not through aid or any other government involvement. In fact, it needs government devolvement. Individuals in the West who are so inclined should find ways to exchange with these people where possible. The One Laptop Per Child initiative is a great example; microfinancing – providing finance for small businesses that lack access to banking – might be another. The more we exchange, the more we will all progress. The freer the market, the more this becomes possible.

17 How a Rubbish Tip Became Slumdog Millionaires' Row

*A major source of objection to a free economy is precisely that it . . .
gives people what they want instead of what a particular group thinks
they ought to want. Underlying most arguments against the free market
is a lack of belief in freedom itself.*

Milton Friedman[273]

Perhaps, more than anywhere, Friedman's paradox applies to India's largest slum. Dharavi sits right in the heart of Mumbai, one of Asia's most expensive cities, next to Bollywood mansions and the grand new towers of the Bandra Kurla financial district. Its most famous resident is probably Jamal Malik, the fictional character who made his fortune in the story *Slumdog Millionaire*. Conditions in Dharavi – by the standards to which even the poorest of us in the 21st-century West are accustomed – are worse than appalling.

Though just one square mile (about the size of Hyde Park and Kensington Gardens; or two-thirds the size of Central Park), it is home to about one million people. They live on top of each other crammed into some 60,000 one- or two-storey shacks. There isn't room for cars or gardens. At prayer times the street doubles as a mosque. Space is so cramped and compressed that every room has several functions. What is a factory by day becomes a kitchen at meal times, then a living room, then a bedroom with as many as fifteen people sleeping side by side in a space barely bigger than a UK university student's digs; 25% of workers sleep on the floors of the factories where they work.[274]

Open sewers carrying the excrement of Mumbai pass through. Kids play beside them, crossing streams and rivers polluted with toxic waste on perilous rotting bridges barely a foot across. Rats scuttle by underneath. Diphtheria, TB and typhoid are ever-present, and as many as 4,000 cases of disease are reported each day.[275] This is at its worst during the monsoon season when there is regular flooding.

Pipes pass through the sewers. If they crack, the water they carry to Dharavi is contaminated. Water is rationed, being turned on for just a few hours per day, with many households sharing each tap. Up to a third of residents don't even have access to a communal tap.[276] As many as 1,000 people share each toilet, which is just a hole in some boards in a small shed on stilts over the river. Visitors find the smell alone overpowering.

Dharavi sprang up on a swamp and a rubbish tip that nobody wanted. Workers began to come here in the 1980s and '90s, first from Tamil Nadu in the south, then Bihar and Uttar Pradesh in the north, fleeing poor rural communities in a virtual mirror of the emigration from rural to urban that took place in Industrial Revolution Britain. In both cases, they came of their own volition.

Mohammad Wazair, says the *New York Times*, earns roughly 6,000 rupees a month (£80/$120) as a labourer in a workshop. He sends about half home to support his wife and two children. Though he is illiterate, he is now paying for his children to attend a private school in their rural village.[277] He visits them twice a year. He has chosen to endure near sweatshop conditions, so that his children have the chance to go to school and enjoy a better future than he had. The lack of space, the poor hygiene and so on, are all part of the price people are prepared to pay for the opportunities Dharavi offers; opportunities to work and earn money. What a Westerner might see and deplore is, for a Dharavian, preferable to the rural poverty that many leave behind.

Many children come here to work too; there is no age restriction. If kids want to come here and work, they can. This is a thought that will horrify many. Mohammad Mustaqueem arrived aged 13. He recalls having rubbish tossed on top of him as he slept in the streets. Now, aged 57, he is in charge of 300 employees in 12 garment workshops with a turnover of $2.5 million per year. He is worth over $20 million.[278]

The land, the houses – shacks is a better term – are mostly unregistered. This is a place that has grown up ignored by the Indian government. The businesses that operate here are outside the law, unregulated and also unregistered – they don't pay tax. And they are thriving. Pottery, textiles, leather works, embroidery, print makers, foods and recycling. There are 15,000 one-room factories, at least 500 large garment workshops (50 or more sewing machines) and about 3,000 smaller ones.[279] There are 5,000 leather shops. Food processors make snacks for the rest of India. The 300 bakeries, unwatched by food standards authorities, supply most of Mumbai's bread (and delicious it is, declares Kevin McCloud) though they are careful not to put the name Dharavi on their packaging, such are the prejudices against the place.[280]

Outside, there is discrimination against Dharavi's 'untouchable' caste. People with a Dharavi address complain that they are rejected for credit cards. Banks have been reluctant to open branches in Dharavi or make loans to businesses there. Children are often not welcomed at schools outside the slums. Yet 85% of Dharavi's population is employed. Yes, 85%! To put that phenomenal number in some kind of context, US and UK employment is about 45%–50%.

One of Dharavi's biggest businesses is recycling. In the US about 25% of waste is recovered for recycling. In the UK, with heavy subsidy, we recycle about 40% of household waste, and 50% of industrial. Dharavi, with no directive from government, recycles 80% of *all Mumbai's* waste. Every day 35,000 people walk through the streets and sift the dumps of Mumbai looking for rubbish, which they then sell to the armies of recyclers in Dharavi. It shows that recycling will happen, if there is profit to be made from it.[281] The absence of the cost of government suddenly makes it so.

On the other hand, slopping barefoot through the mud and liquid waste of Mumbai landfill sites looking for rubbish to sell to recyclers is not something you would wish on any human. But there is the contradiction at the heart of the concept of freedom. The rubbish is collected voluntarily. Those who do it feel they stand to gain by it. Without their endeavour, nothing would be recycled, and Mumbai, it is said, 'would choke on its waste'. Should they be stopped from doing this? Who has the right to make that moral call?

Unlike other parts of India, Hindus and Muslims live side by side, able to cooperate and exchange, echoing Milton Friedman's assertion that: 'The great virtue of a free market system is that it does not care what colour people are; it does not care what their religion is; it only cares whether they can produce something you want to buy. It is the most effective system we have discovered to enable people who hate one another to deal with one another and help one another.'[282] There are no police here, yet crime rates are lower than elsewhere in Mumbai. Children walk the streets quite safely at night. The community is self-policing.

On a personal level, there is no privacy. With so little space, emotions, ideas, entire lives become communal. Even the daily drudgery of washing and cleaning becomes a shared, social affair. The consequence is that there are low levels of depression and loneliness.

Despite the realities of being in a vile slum, the Dharavians' appearance is immaculate. The television presenter Kevin McCloud, in his documentary *Slumming It*, described the residents as, 'The best dressed people on the planet'. So the people of Dharavi are proud too.

The unemployed of the West are vastly better off in material terms than many of the employed people here, yet they are not happy or proud in the way that Dharavians are. What can we learn from this?

Perhaps I have exaggerated the idyllic qualities of Dharavi. It is, of course, a slum with no proper sanitation. There is bound to be misery, just as there is everywhere. If it was so perfect, perhaps I should be joining the people moving there to escape their rural poverty. But I wanted to write about it for two reasons. Firstly, because, from its astonishing use of space and limited resources to its recycling, it demonstrates the overwhelming efficiency of a free market. And secondly, because it shows what humans can achieve when they are not subsidized, but free. Being desperately poor need not necessarily cause people to surrender and do nothing; to turn to crime or demand handouts. Even the poorest of poor people find peaceful and productive ways to make themselves and their children better off – as long as there is the opportunity for them to exchange.

Within just two decades, people with nothing, if left to their own devices, can turn a swamp and a rubbish dump into a booming and growing economy with an annual turnover of more than $1 billion; into a community in which people are social, proud and, dare I say it, happy.

The sanitation issues could quickly be fixed, just as they were in 19th-century London when the engineer Joseph Bazalgette built the sewers (which are still functioning 150 years on). The parallels between London then and Dharavi now are uncanny: so bad was the stench emanating from the Thames in 1858 – then an open sewer – that the summer became known as 'the Great Stink'. The problem Dharavi faces is the Mumbai government authorities and recognized property ownership. Who owns Dharavi? It emerged on a dump and a marsh that nobody wanted and the land and houses are, largely, unregistered. Now that land is wanted. It is near the airport, it is near the financial district, it is near railway stations. Mumbai is enjoying a property boom. There are – and this is desperately sad – plans to raze the place to build so-called 'prime' real estate.

The Dharavians do not have the paperwork to defend themselves against government and big business in the law courts of India. They cannot embark on a multi-year, multi-million-dollar venture to bring sanitation, if there is no assurance of ownership at the end of it. Offers are being made to rehouse those Dharavians who can prove they have been there for a certain period, but whatever they are given will not be the same. The intangible qualities of somewhere like Dharavi cannot be planned. They will not be found in some bland splurge of replacement blocks. It has to spring up organically, over time, through need.

In the 1960s, Harold Wilson's Labour government knocked down many thousands of back-to-back terraced houses with outdoor lavatories, deeming them not good enough for people. The clearances were at the time hailed as a great achievement, but they also broke up communities. They were replaced by magnificent, gleaming tower blocks. These blocks went on to become the sink estates that are the root of so many social problems today, and many of them are now being knocked down. It's yet another example of government planning gone wrong. May the authorities of Mumbai be warned.

There is a magic to Dharavi that exists nowhere else. With 'proper' modern appraisal and regulatory procedures, it wouldn't exist (and nor, for that matter, would the mighty sewers of London, argues John Kay[283]). Leave it alone and let it thrive.

Dharavians have chosen to come to a slum to escape the poverty of the countryside and attempt to build a better future for themselves and their children. If you were given such an option, which would you choose? Or would you rather government razed the place, deeming it inhumane, perhaps gave you some welfare and left you with no decision at all?

Dharavi is a terrible, terrifying and wonderful example of freedom.

18   Why the European Union Is a Lesson in Folly

People are talking about immigration, emigration and the rest of the fucking thing. It's all fucking crap. We're all human beings, we're all mammals, we're all rocks, plants, rivers. Fucking borders are just such a pain in the fucking arse.

Shane MacGowan, songwriter[284]

Throughout history it has been the freest countries with wide dispersal of power that have not only been the most prosperous, but also the most innovative. In AD 1000, Europeans had a per capita income below the average of the rest of the world.[285] China, India and the Muslim world were richer and had superior technology: China had already had the printing press for 400 years. Its navy 'ruled the waves'. Even as late as 1400 the highest standards of living were found in China, in the robust economies of places like Nanjing. But the empires of the East became centralized and burdened with bureaucracy and taxes. In Western Europe, however, made up of many tiny nation states, power was spread. There was no single ruling body except for the Roman Catholic Church. If people, ideas or innovation were suppressed in one state, they could quickly move to another, so there was competition. The city-states of Italy – such as Genoa and Florence – are a good example. They became immensely prosperous. Venice in particular showed great innovation in turning apparently useless marsh and islands into a unique, thriving city – the key hub between East and West.

The Renaissance came. People thrived, and the period saw many of the greatest individuals that ever lived: Da Vinci, Galileo, Michelangelo. I suggest there are not only potential Da Vincis, Galileos and Michelangelos, but Watts, Bairds, Trevithicks, Bells and Eddisons in every society. But they need the right circumstances – a confluence of liberty, knowledge, social attitude and prosperity – to emerge.

In the 16th century the repressive forces of Roman Catholicism, increasingly viewed as a corrupt power, began to be overturned in Northern Europe. The Bible was translated into local vernacular. The Protestant movement saw deregulation and liberalization. Gutenberg's printing press, invented a century earlier, was furthering the spread of knowledge and new ideas – and thus the decentralization of power. Over the next two centuries northern Europe caught up with Catholic Southern Europe, in terms of both progress and prosperity, and then overtook it. The pace was set by Holland, also made up of many small states. Then, in the 18th and 19th centuries, Britain led the pack. In spite of its union with Scotland and its later empire building, England had further dispersed centralized power by reducing the authorities of the monarch after the Civil War of 1642–51, and by linking its currency to gold.

Meanwhile, out East, the Ottoman Empire and China went into a relative dark age, centrally governed by autocratic or imperial elites, slow to react and unable to cope with the plagues and wars that befell them. By 1950 the average Chinese, according to Douglas Carswell, was as poor, if not poorer than someone living there a thousand years before.[286]

The success of the small nation state continues even today. If you look at the World Bank's list of the richest nations in the world (as measured by GPD per capita at purchasing power parity), you see Luxembourg, Qatar, Macau, Singapore, Norway, Kuwait, Brunei, Switzerland and Hong Kong. Perhaps Macau and Hong Kong, as part of China, should not be included, in which case you add the US and the United Arab Emirates (similar nations appear on the International Monetary Fund's list). The US excepted, the common characteristic of all these nations is that they are small. Switzerland (7.9 million) and Hong Kong (7 million) have the largest populations; Singapore and Norway both have around 5 million. The rest are below 3 million.

Of course, many of these nations – Qatar, Norway, Brunei, the

UAE, and the US – appear because of their oil. But why then do other oil-producing nations such as Saudi Arabia, Russia, Iran, China, Nigeria or Venezuela not feature? Other small nations – Luxembourg and Switzerland, for example – appear on the list because of their competitive tax rates and banking. But these are legislative options that are open to other countries in the world. In 1950 and 1970 the US, with its currency tied to gold, freedoms, low taxes, property rights and semi-autonomous states, topped the list. As its government has grown, its ranking has fallen.

In a small state there is a smaller gap between those at the top and bottom, there is more transparency and accountability, it is harder for the state to hide things, there is more monitoring, less waste and more dynamism. Small is flexible, small is competitive, small really is, as economist E. F. Schumacher said, beautiful.[287]

In that case, a large, centrally planned Europe is *precisely* the opposite destination to which we should be heading. It is already bringing poverty to its people. What suits Germany clearly does not suit southern Europe, yet the model is inflexible. If the goal really is innovation, prosperity and progress, not only should Europe break up, but so too should the nations within it.

Italy has twice been the global centre of innovation and invention – once under the Romans (until their state grew bloated), then again during the Renaissance. No other part of the world can claim such an emphatic double. You cannot doubt the potential of the Italian people, nor their talent. Yet since unification in 1870 (actually total unification did finally not come until after WWI) Italy has been a cradle of infighting, bureaucracy, organized crime, corruption, rent-seeking, inflations, division, fascism and communism. Its state is bloated, its political system dysfunctional. The country might be nominally unified, but in reality it is anything but. Italy would be much better off if it broke up into some modern equivalent of its old city states.

Belgium went without a government for 541 days between 2010 and 2011. Many businesses thrived through the government inaction. Now it has a *six-party* coalition. It's hard to see what a six-party coalition can achieve beyond negotiating and compromising into waffle and nothingness. A much more natural way of things is for the country to separate along the roughly linguistic lines of the Flemish-speaking north and French-speaking south. But a country breaking up into smaller entities does not mean there need be barriers between the two: there can still be trade; there's no need for border checkpoints and tariffs. There can still be exchange; it just means the disintegration of large, unnecessary, overruling bureaucratic bodies.

A similar argument could be made for Catalonia. It could even be joined by the Catalan regions of south-west France, if it so wanted – or was allowed. The same even applies to the United Kingdom. Not just the partition of Scotland, but a much more fluid, adaptable (albeit unlikely) model for modern times would be for the whole country to divide – London and the home counties; the South-West; the Midlands; Manchester and Lancashire; Leeds and Yorkshire; Liverpool, Cheshire and north-east Wales; and so on – it separates quite naturally. One solution to the 'Irish problem' – which, amazingly, still goes on – might be a simple return to the four kingdoms of Ireland – Munster, Leinster, Ulster and Connacht. This is all unlikely to happen in the short term, I know, but that doesn't mean it wouldn't work.

If a region wants a large expansive government and welfare state, it can vote for it. If it wants low, transparent taxes, it can vote for that. In such a small environment, political change can actually happen. People can get the government they want. New parties can spring up. Welfare becomes easier to administrate. It's easier to change or adapt laws. Competition between states will improve governance and productivity. Each region would benefit from increased pride, flexibility, dynamism and responsibility. It would be a return to diversity.

Scandinavian countries all have expansive welfare states, high levels of taxation and big government. Those who argue in favour of the large government-expansive-welfare-state-heavy-regulation-and-taxation model often cite the Scandinavian countries as proof that this model can work, and they have a point. These countries enjoy high standards of living, comparatively good education and health care, and their people are productive, industrial and entrepreneurial. Denmark, Finland, Norway, Sweden and, even now, Iceland, as well as Holland, are all in the top 25 richest countries in the world on a GDP (PPP) per capita basis (the UK, by the way, comes 22nd). Elsewhere such large welfare states have become corrupt and inefficient.

One factor in that relative success might be that, despite large welfare states, much of that welfare is delivered and administered by commercial and private providers, which are usually able, as author Toby Young puts it, 'to deliver more for less'.[288] I suggest a larger part of the Nordic success lies in the fact that their populations are small (Sweden 9.5 million, Norway 5 million, Denmark 5.5 million). This caps the size to which their welfare state is able to grow. Possibilities for abuse either by incompetence or corruption increase the more people there are. The sheer inefficiencies of size mean that, if a large welfare state is to work, the nation has to be small.

Of course, such talk of small nations is little short of fantastic as far as the UK and US are concerned. Our systems of politics are so set. They might appear competitive because the two controlling parties fight with each other and compete to 'do more to help us', but the reality is that politics is an industry dominated by two firms. The Republican and Democrat parties have had a stranglehold on American politics since 1853. It took two world wars to fully break the duopoly of British politics – Liberal/Whig and Conservative – that had existed since the 1680s, only for it to be replaced by another duopoly in the form of the Labour and Conservative parties – with a little bit of Liberal Democrat. Occasionally, another party comes along and makes waves. We saw it with the Social Democrat Party in the late 1980s. UKIP is doing something similar now – but it doesn't have a single seat in Parliament.

In both the US and the UK, the party that wins elections is usually the party that best hushes its resident extremists and most occupies the social-democrat middle ground. The UK coalition government of Cameron and Clegg is the first since WWII to actually have more than 50% of the vote – Blair never had it and nor did Thatcher.

Meanwhile the state grows, whichever party is in charge. Only the rate of growth changes. A constant set of lifelong civil servants run the machine. According to Cameron's former policy chief Steve Hilton, the Prime Minister often finds out about policies that are being implemented from the radio, TV or the press. These are often policies he has neither approved or even agrees with. Hilton declared that Cameron and others in his inner circle feel horror, frustration and impotence in the face of the unelected bureaucratic machine. 'The bureaucracy masters the politicians', he says.[289]

It all makes for maintaining the status quo. When an issue comes up that really could bring change and open politics up to competition – Scottish independence, membership of the EU, changing the electoral system – it seems to get deferred and diluted. There has been talk of a vote on Scottish independence ever since I was a child. Only in 2014 is it finally happening. Cameron went back on his promise of a referendum in EU membership, deferring it to the next parliament. Heaven knows what happened to the Lib Dem demands for proportional representation.

I doubt if there is a Greek word for 'government by an unelected civil service and one of two parties (whose policies are largely the same), to the benefit of certain vested interests at the expense of everyone else, through a bureaucracy so opaque that nobody knows what's really going on and, even if they did, there's not a lot they can do, so most just lose interest . . . ?' Let's invent one. We live under an 'obfuscatocracy'.

19   A Monopoly on Compassion

*The state is made for man, not man for the state . . . I regard it as the chief
duty of the state to protect the individual and give him the opportunity to
develop into a creative person. That is to say, the state should be our servant
and not we its slaves.*

Albert Einstein[290]

If the government did not give us health care, the sick would go
untreated. Without its education, ignorance, illiteracy and innumeracy
would prevail. Without its welfare, the poor and infirm would not
be looked after. Without its transport infrastructure, there would be
chaos and disorder. Without its police, we would be overrun with
crime. Without its regulation, fraud and corruption would abound.
Without its laws, there would be confusion and delinquency. Without
its bailouts, the financial system would come crashing down, bringing
riots and mayhem. Without its military and defence, we would be
invaded; terrorism would destroy the fabric of society. Without its
border checks, we would be overrun with immigrants. Without its
planning laws, the countryside would be destroyed. Without its drugs
laws, addiction would be everywhere. Oh, how we need the state.

Governments repeatedly create, foster and play on these fears to
get elected and stay in power. In competing with each other, political
parties make more and more promises. As they strive to meet these
promises, the state grows ever bigger. As it grows, it interferes further
and further into our lives, more and more people fall into its net and
become dependent. It taxes more, it obfuscates more, it inflates more,
it creates more and more paperwork, debt and waste. Mr Loss and
the long-suffering, unaudited Miss Doubt carry on paying the bills
and become poorer and poorer as they do so. We become further
entrapped in this web of never-ending government expansion. The
state has become the greatest expense in our lives. Either through

dependency or taxation, we have all become slaves to it in some way. And it is everywhere. To paraphrase economist Leon MacLaren, it looks after the birth of the baby, educates the child, employs the man, cares for the aged and buries the dead.[291] Do we really need it to do all this? Can we not do most of this perfectly well ourselves? Must it continuously make judgments on our behalf?

The irony at the heart of this book is that in turning to the large state for essentials we are turning to something that is actually a force for harm. It is the large state that is responsible for so many of the ills in the world. With state control of money, we see the spread of debt, the loss of purchasing power, the impoverishing of the young and the widening of the gap between rich and poor. With state control of education and health care, we see costs rise and standards fall. With state control of benefits, we see more and more people slipping into welfare and more and more abuses. With state regulation and legislation, we see more and more rent-seeking and corruption. With state provision of defence, we see wars, military intervention overseas and terrorism. With state control of the economy we see boom and bust, with the few favoured at the expense of the many. With the expansion of the state, we see decline in relative prosperity.

The core belief of those in favour of a large welfare state is that we need it to look after people. I suggest we do not. The 12th-century Jewish philosopher Maimonides argued that the highest form of charity is when the help given enables the receiver to become self-sufficient. State provision of charity – or welfare – has too frequently had the opposite effect. It has actually created dependency.

The provision of care is a delicate, complicated and capricious process. That is why there is so much argument about what forms state care should take. Sometimes giving money might help the recipient towards self-sufficiency, but sometimes not. Giving money might lead to the temporary lessening of suffering, but often it can lead to dependence. Sometimes a proverbial kick up the backside might be more beneficial – sometimes something else is required, perhaps something local or practical. The dignity of the recipient also needs to be considered in the charitable process. It can be demeaning to receive charity – anonymity might be required on occasion. Different circumstances require different forms of care.

A free market can meet these varying requirements. In areas where the state doesn't provide, just about every good or service you could ever conceivably want is on offer. Something similar could happen in the world of welfare. Compassion, the giving of charity and care are essential human functions, they are a part of human nature; people need to give as much as they need to receive. Even perhaps the most ruthless, murderous drug-trafficker that ever drew breath, Pablo Escobar, was a prolific giver – he built houses, churches and schools in the city of Medellin where he grew up, on a scale unmatched by the Colombian government. The market will provide for this need to give, better than the state ever can. Care can thrive in a free market, but not when the state is draining resources.

The giver goes unconsidered in the process of state care. Taxes are taken and that is it. But the giver too has needs. Sometimes the giver needs to be anonymous – sometimes he needs recognition. Sometimes he or she likes to be involved with the recipient in some way, sometimes not. The forced giving that is taxation destroys the satisfaction that altruistic people get from giving voluntarily. To share with others is part of humanity. In a world in which the government takes care of the poor and needy, compassion is removed from life. As a result, the state now has a monopoly on compassion! In fact it is even more bizarrely specific than that: the pro-welfare left wing has a monopoly on compassion. Anyone who doesn't agree with the concept of a large, generous welfare state is deemed heartless and selfish.

While you have to pay the government to provide care, your ability to provide it yourself is reduced. Government provision of care absolves you of the *responsibility* to provide it yourself. But in a world with no or zero state, our greatest expense – the government – is removed. Suddenly we have more capital to spend and invest. Simultaneously, everything we want to buy is dramatically cheaper. We are all empowered. Our ability to help others is increased, as is our responsibility to do so.

With no state, who then looks after those in need? Who looks after the poor, the elderly and the infirm? Who looks after the education of our children? Who makes sure we have money stored away for our retirement? The answer is: you do. You must help those in need. You must educate your children. You must provide for your retirement. If you want to know for sure that something will be done, you must take the necessary steps yourself. With freedom comes responsibility. I'm not suggesting that in a world of minimal government we all become carers. That role does not suit everyone. I am suggesting, however, we all become givers. That role does.

The Conservative MP Steve Baker has on his website the slogan, 'Enjoy freedom responsibly'. Here is the heart of the matter. I suggest that if you give someone responsibility, the surprises are to the upside: they behave responsibly. Take away their responsibility, and irresponsibility soon follows. Part of the contract of being free is that you must face consequences of your actions. If you act badly, you suffer. Thus being free incentivizes good conduct.

*

'*Liberté, égalité, fraternité*', runs the French national motto. Liberty, equality, brotherhood – the three come hand in hand. They cannot exist under a large state. A small erosion of freedom here – a tax, a subsidy, a regulation – means an erosion of responsibility, of brotherhood and equality, somewhere else.

People think we need the state to ensure what we feel is right is implemented, and what is wrong isn't. My argument, of course, is that we need ourselves. Though the sentiment behind any state action may be 'good', too often something unintended occurs that has the very opposite result to that which the initial sentiment intended. When you tamper, things happen that you cannot predict. Let people bloom unmolested. Let us have decentralized power and unplanned decision-making by individuals. Let us have independent money and small government. Let us have transparency. There are many ways to make the world a better place without relying on laws or political processes or governments. Legislation is as likely to harm as to help.

With legislation you can discourage the private impulse to do the job that might be able to do it in a more effective way. Social pressure can be far more effective.

The fear is that, left to their own devices, given freedom and choice, people will do terrible things. This is a fear of freedom itself. It shows a lack of faith and trust in mankind.

In electing a government, people show faith in it. In return the government should show faith in its people. The sole aim of a government should be that its people thrive and prosper. All it need do, therefore, is lay the foundations for them to do so. That simply means protecting people's private property rights so that they can then exchange goods, ideas, knowledge and services as freely and easily as possible. *That is all a government need do.* People's exchange will take care of the rest. Exchange leads to progress and prosperity.

In *Capitalism and Freedom* Friedman sums up the view of the classical liberals (now known as libertarians or 'minarchists' – in favour of minimal state): 'Government has three primary functions. It should provide for military defence of the nation. It should enforce contracts between individuals. It should protect citizens from crimes against themselves or their property . . . Government should be a referee, not an active player.'[292] But even within this limited scope, abuses occur. In protecting property, enforcing contracts and being 'a referee', the legal system has grown to onerous levels of complication and become a rent-seeker's paradise. The same can be said of defence. How much of government policy, particularly in the US, is determined by military lobbying? The US Department of Defence, with 3.2 million employees, not to mention suppliers, is now the biggest employer in the world. Does the US need such a big army? Does it need forces in some 150 different countries?[293] The unintended consequences of overseas intervention and the cost to Mr Loss and Miss Doubt do not bear thinking about.

So I lean to the more extreme, but less realistic (in the sense that it is less likely to occur) anarcho-capitalist viewpoint and say we don't need a government at all. You can't plan an economy – events always get in the way – nor can you plan a government and consign it to limited tasks. People who reject prescriptivism for economic life, if they are consistent, ought to reject the same principle for politics, and thereby conclude we don't need government at all.

Sadly, no party standing on an anarcho-capitalist platform is ever going to get elected. A party proposing to do nothing for anyone is never going to win the popular vote. Therein lies the flaw in the way modern democracy currently works. It actually incentivizes governments to do more. But, just because we are unlikely to see it, that does not mean we should not advocate it. As I quoted in the preface, 'Find the right answer, realize you'll never see it in your lifetime, and then advocate it anyway because it's the right answer.'[294]

I began this book suggesting that the state and its institutions are crumbling. If you measure US debt by the generally accepted accounting principles (GAAP) by which any corporation is expected to account, the US deficit for 2012 is not $1 trillion, but $7 trillion. Its national debt is not $16 trillion, but over $70 trillion.[295] Debt is not growing four or five times as fast as GDP, but 20 times. Equally horrendous multiples apply to the UK. But the government is not a corporation. Maybe, as the neo-classical economists suggest, debt doesn't matter. Japan has muddled on in a mire of it for 23 years. Perhaps bankruptcy won't trigger some kind of collapse.

But there is more to it than the financials. There is a tide of social feeling, of anger. More and more young people growing into adulthood with reduced opportunity and debt, all as a result of the profligacy of their forebears. Both Greece and Spain have over 50% youth unemployment. More and more people are demanding change. We are seeing riot after riot the world over. As the internet spreads and disperses more and more knowledge and information, the tide will get stronger. It feels as though we are approaching some kind of tipping point. But an explosive conflict can be pre-empted with a little tweak – a tweak that will go almost unnoticed. The train can be re-routed in a very English, understated, un-confrontational way.

With their 'People's Budget' and other small steps towards government care, little did those politicians at the beginning of the 20th century know the path they were putting us on: the path to this huge, ever-growing and expanding, invasive state we have today. My simple steps to introduce independent, competing currencies, as outlined in Part II, stealthily re-route the train in a way that nobody will realize at the time – in just the way that People's Budget did, only in reverse. Everything else can happen from there quite organically and without planning. Once it loses control of money, the large state's days are numbered. It will be thrust back into the free market where it will have to operate by the same rules as the rest of us – and tighten its belt. Power will devolve and freedom will ensue.

Let the free market determine what government's role should be!

A bold leader would simplify tax as well, starting with a transparent flat-rate income and corporation tax of 15% and then introducing land value tax to replace all other taxes. The effect of the reduction in tax will be: firstly, that people will have a lot more money in their pockets, which they can then save, spend or invest as they see fit; secondly, that overseas investment will flood in, as it does wherever there is low tax; third, that there will be less evasion and avoidance of tax. We will see markets re-capitalized, investment stimulated and exchange increase.

A third means – for the boldest of leaders – to trim the state and liberate exchange is to introduce the system whereby legislation expires after five years, unless voted to continue. Legislation that doesn't work will disappear, that which does will remain. This calls forth improvement, instead of expansion and bloating. The constant pressure of having to re-vote laws would also force simplicity.

Almost everything the state currently provides is needlessly expensive, the costs are concealed and their natural purpose distorted: health, education, money – they're no longer 'about what they're about' – instead they have become political tools, liable to obfuscation, manipulation, and devaluation. The costs come in lack of progress, lack of motivation, loss of freedom, inefficiency and worse. In many cases government help – from foreign aid to domestic welfare – has had terrible, unintended consequences. People want large government to protect us from ourselves. But large government doesn't do that. So many of the ills in the world can be traced back to some misguided action by some government somewhere. The state makes wars. The state carries out the thoughtless orders of tyrants and despots. The state creates waste. The state takes from people against their will and forces them into debt and dependency. The state creates barriers and hinders progress and innovation. The state creates poverty. Let it, as Einstein says, serve us, not demand that we serve it. Let us abandon its money and so remove its power. Let us indeed have 'power to the people'.

What can replace it is truly wonderful. I am so optimistic for my children and their future, once this bankrupted state has imploded. If the right decisions are made now, a glorious age could be coming. We must not fear freedom; we must show faith in it. In doing so, we show faith in ourselves and in mankind. Let us trust, not fear. With freedom comes responsibility. With responsibility comes happiness.

20   34 Things to Look for in
Life After the State

The State is the curse of the individual. With what is Prussia's political strength bought? With the absorption of the individual in the political and geographical idea . . . Take the Jewish people, the aristocracy of the human race – how is it they have kept their place apart, their poetical halo, amid surroundings of coarse cruelty? By having no State to burden them. Had they remained in Palestine, they would long ago have lost their individuality in the process of their State's construction, like all other nations. Away with the State! I will take part in that revolution. Undermine the whole conception of a State, declare free choice and spiritual kinship to be the only all-important conditions of any union, and you will have the commencement of a liberty that is worth something. Changes in forms of government are pettifogging affairs – a degree less or a degree more, mere foolishness.

Henrik Ibsen, playwright, in a letter to Georg Brandes, 17 February 1871[296]

When I was doodling around ideas for the cover of this book, I sketched a mind map: a ship, HMS *State*, is sinking, as a volcano, Mount Freedom, is rising up and erupting. As HMS *State* sinks down to the depths of the ocean, with it go wars, taxation, paperwork, passports, waste, zombies, rent-seeking, debt, inflation and obfuscation. Meanwhile, Mount Freedom, as it erupts, spews forth progress, invention, innovation, health, knowledge, prosperity, truth, harmony, fulfilment and responsibility.

So what would 'life after the state' be like? Here's a list of some of things I would expect – presented without argument or explanation.

In Life After the State:

- Wealth and power are not concentrated in the hands of a few, but spread. We are all richer.
- There is less paperwork, form-filling and needless regulation. The tyranny of the bureaucrat is no more.
- There are no trade restrictions, customs, duty and other barriers to trade.

- There are fewer taxes, simpler taxes and lower taxes.
- Without pressure of tax, more businesses thrive, leading to more employment.
- There is more trade and exchange, leading to greater prosperity.
- Greater prosperity will lead to more exchange and greater innovation, invention and progress. Amazing things are invented.
- Not only are we all richer, everything is cheaper.
- Without the pressure to fund government, people do not have to work so hard if they do not wish. There will be more time for other endeavours.
- People decide for themselves what they spend their earnings on.
- Those who work hard are rewarded. Those who don't are not.
- There is less waste.
- There are fewer wars. Wars that do happen are of a smaller magnitude.
- There is no government snooping, no storing of internet data, no MI5, no CIA, no NSA, no foreign military bases, no interference in the affairs of other countries, no support of dictatorships, no foreign aid, no invasions and occupations, no torture or assassination.
- Education is no longer standardized and homogenous.
- You are responsible for the education of your children. You decide what you want them to learn.
- Health care is cheaper and better.
- Responsible for ourselves, we take better care of ourselves. We are thus healthier.
- Money, banking and the state separate. Independent currencies compete freely.
- Government and the economy separate. There are no more bail-outs, subsidies or artificial booms created by government inflation of the money supply in order to get re-elected.
- Houses are affordable.

- Official measures, numbers and statistics become honest again as obfuscation is no longer incentivized.
- Truth, integrity and good conduct follow.
- There are fewer laws and fewer regulations. Individual responsibility grows, as does a sense of responsibility to the collective.
- Through being responsible for themselves, communities bond and are more harmonious.
- The institution of the family gets stronger.
- The young are not alienated and priced out.
- The cost of essential services such as health care and education will be in line with what local people earn.
- There is more character, colour and variety.
- There are no zombies.
- The state is not responsible for welfare. Communities, families – people – are. Welfare is therefore more effective and cheaper.
- The decision on whether to help out others is voluntary. There are no more schemes by which government forcibly takes money from people and gives it to others.
- Sink estates are not built.
- There is no more war on drugs and no more laws ruining drug-users' lives.

As a consequence of these libertarian principles, the way that people think and act is transformed. Societies are motivated and incentivized in an entirely different, natural way. This is mass behavioural change. What could result is the most prosperous, peaceful, harmonious, safe, responsible, caring, compassionate, educated, healthy, innovative, inventive, happy, fulfilled, truthful, honourable and free society in history.

– FIN –

Lexicon

There are a number of economic terms which recur throughout the book, and I have tried to make sure they are explained in context. But here, in addition, is a simple lexicon, which you may find useful.

anarcho-capitalism – An extreme form of libertarianism (see below), which advocates that there is no need for government at all. If there is genuine need for something a government typically provides, such as military defence or health care, the market is the most efficient means to provide it to the highest possible standard at the cheapest possible price. In an anarcho-capitalist society individual responsibility plays an important role.

capitalism – An economic system in which prices, production, and the distribution of goods and services are determined by market demand. Resources and the means of production (factories, tools and so on) are not owned by the state, but privately. A business's success or failure is, thus, determined by the market.

crony capitalism – A system by which business success is not determined by the market, but instead by the privileges given to it by the government in the form of tax breaks, subsidies, legislation, regulation and so on.

deficit – When you spend more money than you earn you run up a 'deficit'. If you earn £5 per year, but spend £10, you are running a deficit of £5. Running deficits usually leaves you in debt.

deflation – This has two meanings, which often get confused. One: falling prices. Two: a contraction in the supply of money and credit leading to falling prices.

free market – An idealized economy in which buyers and sellers transact freely, based on a mutual agreement of price, without state intervention in the form of taxes, subsidies, regulation or anything else.

government/state – The organization which administers a nation and makes its rules and laws. I use these words fairly interchangeably in the book.

inflation – This has two meanings. One: rising prices. Two: growth in the supply of money and credit with rising prices being the result.

libertarian (classical liberal) – A political philosophy that advocates limited government, minimal coercion by the state, low tax, individual responsibility, freedom, and laissez-faire economic policy.

rent-seeker – Somebody who does not himself create new wealth, but appropriates that wealth from other people after it has already been created. A rent-seeker exploits some sort of privilege or legislation that has been made by government. He/she will often lobby for more of said privilege. The banking sector leaning on governments to bail it out in 2008, using money generated by taxpayers, is an example of rent-seeking. I have to say 'rent-seeker' is not a great term. It's not self-explanatory, and its meaning does not stick in people's minds. Perhaps 'privilege-chaser' is better or privilegeer.

socialism – There are many different definitions of socialism. In this book I use it to mean a political philosophy that advocates a large state, high levels of taxation, government-provided education, health care, welfare and transport and high levels of regulation, legislation and market intervention. 'From each according to their means, to those according to their needs', is the saying. (Ironically, capitalists, socialists and libertarian philosophies *all* see their systems as the means to achieve equality of opportunity).

Bibliography

In *Life After the State* I have drawn on ideas that have been around a lot longer than I have, as well as, I hope, adding a few of my own.

I would like to mention in particular certain people whose work has had great influence on me. These are: Matt Ridley, James Turk and John Rubino, Douglas Carswell, Ron Paul and Michael Hampton (aka Dr Bubb).

'A Bit of History', Glasgow2018.com. Accessed 1 June 2013. Available: http://www.glasgow2018.com/why-glasgow/guide-to-glasgow/a-bit-of-history/

Abbey, Edward. *The Journey Home: Some Words in Defense of the American West*. New York: Plume, 1991.

Adams, Charles. *For Good and Evil: The Impact of Taxes on the Course of Civilization*. London: Madison Books, 1992.

Ahamed, Liaquat. *Lords of Finance*. London: William Heinemann, 2009.

Alexander, Michelle. *The New Jim Crow: Mass Incarceration in the Age of Colorblindness*. New York: The New Press, 2010.

Alexander, Ruth. 'Which is the world's biggest employer?', *BBC News*, 20 March 2012 [Online]. Available at: http://www.bbc.co.uk/news/magazine-17429786

Arons, Stephen. *Compelling Belief: The Culture of American Schooling*. New York: McGraw-Hill, 1983.

Bank of England statistical releases for notes and coin, central bank reserves, and M4.

Baumeister, Roy F. and John Tierney. *Willpower: Rediscovering Our Greatest Strength*. London: Allen Lane, 2011.

Baxendale, Toby. 'Working class patients and the medical establishment', *The Cobden Centre*, 27 August 2010 [Online]. Accessed 1 June 2013. Available at: http://www.cobdencentre.org/2010/08/working-class-patients-and-the-medical-establishment/

BBC News. 'Heroin use among young rising', 21 April 2008. Accessed 1 June 2013. Available at: http://news.bbc.co.uk/1/hi/wales/south_west/7358152.stm

BBC News. 'Literacy progress has stalled, Ofsted's chief inspector says', 15

March 2012. Accessed 1 June 2013. Available at: http://www.bbc.co.uk/
news/education-17368311

Beito, David T. *From Mutual Aid to the Welfare State: Fraternal Societies
and Social Services, 1890–1967*. Chapel Hill: The University of North
Carolina Press, 2000.

Benes, Jaromir, and Michael Kumhof. *The Chicago Plan Revisited*.
Washington: International Monetary Fund, 2012.

Bernanke, Ben S. 'Deflation: Making Sure "It" Doesn't Happen Here',
speech presented to the National Economists Club, Washington, D.C.
21 November 21 2002. Available at: http://www.federalreserve.gov/
boarddocs/speeches/2002/20021121/

Bernstein, Peter L. *A Primer on Money, Banking, and Gold*. New Jersey: John
Wiley, 1965.

Bevan, Aneurin. *In Place of Fear*. London: Quartet, 1990.

Bolton, Paul. 'Education spending in the UK'. House of Commons Library,
July 2012 [Online]. Available at: http://www.parliament.uk/briefing-
papers/SN01078

Boyes, William J., and Michael Melvin. *Macroeconomics*. Boston: Houghton
Mifflin, 1991.

Brandes, Georg. *Henrik Ibsen and Bjornstjerne Bjornson: Critical Studies*.
Whitefish, Mont.: Kessinger, 2004.

BreakThroughGlasgow. *Ending the Costs of Social Breakdown*. London: The
Centre for Social Justice, February 2008.

Bureau of Justice Statistics. Sourcebook of Criminal Justice Statistics, 2002.
Cited in *Words from prison – did you know…?*, American Civil Liberties
Union, 12 June 2006. Accessed 1 June 2013. http://www.aclu.org/
womens-rights/words-prison-did-you-know

Buzan, Tony. *The Mind Map Book*. London: BBC Active, 2010.

Caesar, Julius. *Commentarii de bello civili (Commentaries on the Civil
War)*, trans Thomas Clark (Google eBook). Philadelphia: Thomas,
Cowperthwait & Co., 1838.

Cahill, Kevin. 'The great property swindle', *The New Statesman*, 11
March 2011. Available at: http://www.newstatesman.com/life-and-
society/2011/03/million-acres-land-ownership

Cahill, Kevin. *Who Owns Britain: the Hidden Facts Behind Landownership in
the UK and Ireland*. Edinburgh: Canongate Books Ltd., 2002.

Callinicos, Alex. 'Anti-war protests do make a difference', *Socialist Worker*,
19 March 2005. Available at: http://www.socialistworker.co.uk/art/5932/
Anti-war+protests+do+make+a+difference

Camus, Albert. *The Plague*, trans. Robin Buss. London: Penguin Modern
Classics, 2002.

Carswell Financial Services Bill, 15 September 2010. Available at: http://
www.publications.parliament.uk/pa/cm201011/cmhansrd/cm100915/
debtext/100915-0002.htm#10091526002134

Carswell, Douglas. *The End of Politics and the Birth of iDemocracy*. London: Biteback Publishing, 2012.

Cassidy, Tina. *Birth: the Surprising History of How We are Born*. New York: Atlantic Monthly Press, 2006.

Central Intelligence Agency (CIA). *The World Factbook* [Online]. Accessed 1 June 2013. Available at: https://www.cia.gov/library/publications/the-world-factbook/

Chamberlain, Geoffrey. *Home Births: the Report of the 1994 Confidential Enquiry by the National Birthday Trust Fund*. New York: Parthenon Pub. Group, 1997.

Chantrill, Christopher (comp.). 'UK public spending' [Online]. Available at: http://www.ukpublicspending.co.uk/

Chesterton, G.K., 'The superstition of school', 1923 [Online]. Accessed 1 June 2013. http://grammar.about.com/od/classicessays/a/supschoolessay. htm

Chomsky, Noam, and John Schoeffel. *Understanding Power: The Indispensable Chomsky*. London: Vintage, 2003.

Clancy, Rebecca. 'UK employment hits all-time high'. *Daily Telegraph*, 17 October, 2012.

'Cost of a child from cradle to college, 2011 report'. Bournemouth, England: LV=], 2011

Coulson, Andrew J. 'Markets vs. monopolies in education: a global review of the evidence'. *Cato Institute*, Policy Analysis 620, 10 September 2008.

Coulson, Andrew J. 'The real cost of public schools'. *Cato Institute*, 7 April 2008. Accessed 1 June 2013. Available at: http://www.cato.org/blog/real-cost-public-schools

Crowdy, Terry, and Christa Hook. *French Soldier in Egypt, 1798–1801: The Army of the Orient*. Oxford: Osprey, 2003.

Da Vinci, Leonardo. *The Literary Works of L. da Vinci*. London: S. Low, Marston, Searle & Rivington, 1883.

Da Vinci, Leonardo. *The Notebooks of Leonardo Da Vinci* (trans. Jean Paul Richter). (Digital version). Accessed 1 June 2013. Available at: http://en.wikisource.org/wiki/The_Notebooks_of_Leonardo_Da_Vinci/XIX

Daily Telegraph, 'NHS is fifth biggest employer in world', 20 March 2012. Available at: http://www.telegraph.co.uk/news/uknews/9155130/NHS-is-fifth-biggest-employer-in-world.html?oo=0

Dalyrimple, Theodore. Speech at Property and Freedom Society, Bodrum, Turkey, September 2012. Accessed 1 June 2013. http://www.thelastditch.org/2013/01/everything-that-is-common-knowledge-about-heroin-addiction-is-wrong.html

de Soto, Hernando. *The Mystery of Capital: Why Capitalism Triumphs in the West and Fails Everywhere Else*. London: Black Swan, 2001.

Dimnet, Ernest. *The Art of Thinking*. New York: Simon and Schuster, 1928.

Donnachie, Ian. 'Industry and Technology – Food, drink and tobacco'. *The*

Glasgow Story. 2004. Accessed 1 June 2013. Available at: http://www. theglasgowstory.com/story.php?id=TGSDE03

Donnelly, Laura. 'Patients starve and die of thirst on hospital wards,' *Daily Telegraph,* 6 October 2012.

Doubleday, Jock. *Spontaneous Creation: 101 Reasons Not to Have Your Baby in a Hospital,* Volume 2 [Online]. Available at: http://www.whale.to/a/ doubleday.html

Dostoyevsky, Fyodor. *Crime and Punishment,* trans. Constance Garnett (new ed.). Ware: Wordsworth Classics, 2000.

Einstein, Albert. Address to the Disarmament Conference of 1932. Reprinted in *Ideas And Opinions,* New York: Crown Publishers, 1954.

Einstein, Albert. 'On the method of theoretical physics'. Speech, Herbert Spencer Lecture, 10 June 1933.

Einstein, Albert, and Paul Arthur Schilpp. *Albert Einstein, Autobiographical Notes: A Centennial Edition.* La Salle, Ill.: Open Court Publishing Co., 1979.

Elliott, Matthew and Lee Rotherham. *The Bumper Book of Government Waste: The Scandal of the Squandered Billions.* Petersfield: Harriman House. 2006.

Empty Homes. *New empty homes figures – not good news,* Oct 16. Accessed 1 June 2013. http://www.emptyhomes.com/2009/10/16/new-empty-homes-figures-not-good-news/

England, Jack. *Sword of Marathon.* CreateSpace, 2012.

Esar, Evan. *20,000 Quips & Quotes: A Treasury of Witty Remarks, Comic Proverbs, Wisecracks and Epigrams.* New York: Barnes & Noble Books, 1995.

Fergusson, Adam. *When Money Dies: The Nightmare of the Weimar Hyper-inflation.* London: Old Street Publishing, 2010.

Fischer, Tom. 'The Approximity Gold Price Model: The MZM Equilibrium Gold Price', 25 October 2009 [Online]. Accessed 1 June 2013. Available at: http://gold.approximity.com/gold_price_models.html

Fraser, Hamish W. 'Second city of the empire: 1830s to 1914'. *The Glasgow Story.* Accessed 1 June 2013. Available at: http://www.theglasgowstory. com/story.php?id=TGSD0.

Friedman, Milton. *Capitalism and Freedom.* Chicago: University of Chicago Press, 2002.

Friedman, Milton. *Why Government is the Problem.* Stanford, Calif.: Hoover Institution on War, Revolution, and Peace, Stanford University, 1993.
Friedman, Milton. Interviewed by John Hawkins, 16 September 2003. Accessed 1 June 1 2013. http://www.rightwingnews.com/interviews/an-interview-with-milton-friedman-2/

Friedman, Milton. Interviewed by Phil Donahue. *The Phil Donahue Show,* 11 February 1979.

Friedman, Milton. Interviewed by *The Times Herald,* Norristown,

Pennsylvania. 1 Friday December 1978.

Friedman, Milton. Interviewed by Richard Heffner on *The Open Mind*. 7 December 1975.

Frydman, Robert, Kenneth Murphy and Andrzej Rapaczyński. *Capitalism with a Comrade's Face: Studies in the Postcommunist Transition*. Budapest: Central European University Press, 1998.

Galbraith, John Kenneth. *The Great Crash, 1929* (3rd edn). London: Penguin, 1975.

George, Henry. *Progress and Poverty: An Inquiry into the Cause of Industrial Depressions and of Increase of Want with Increase of Wealth, the Remedy*. New York: Doubleday, Page, & Co., 1912.

Gibson, Owen. 'Olympics 2012: BOA calls for overhaul of school sport', *Guardian*, 2 August 2012.

Gladwell, Malcolm. *The Tipping Point: How Little Things Can Make a Big Difference*. London: Abacus, 2001.

Goklany, Indur M. 'Modern Agriculture: The Pros and Cons of Modern Farming'. *Property and Environment Research Center* 19 (2001).

Goldman, Emma. *Anarchism and Other Essays*. London: Cosimo Classics, 2005.

Goodhart, Charles. *Monetary Policy in Theory and Practice*. London: Macmillan, 1984.

Graeber, David. *Debt: The First 5,000 Years*. Brooklyn, New York: Melville House, 2011.

Grantham, Jeremy, 'People now see it is a system for the rich only', *Financial Times*, 5 February 2012.

Green, David. *Working Class Patients and the Medical Establishment: Self-Help in Britain From the Mid-19th Century to 1948*. Aldershot: Gower, 1985.

Greenspan, Alan. 'Gold and Economic Freedom', 1966 (published in Ayn Rand's 'Objectivist' newsletter in 1966). Available at: http://constitution.org/mon/greenspan_gold.htm

Grignon, Paul. 'Money as Debt'. Moonfire Studio video, 77:00, 2009. Accessed 1 June 2013. http://www.moneyasdebt.net/.

Hammond, John Hays. *The Autobiography of John Hays Hammond*. New York: Farrar & Rinehart, Inc., 1935.

Hanlon, Phil, and David Walsh. *Let Glasgow Flourish: A Comprehensive Report on Health and its Determinants in Glasgow and West Central Scotland*. Glasgow: Glasgow Centre for Population Health, 2006.

Hannaford, Peter, ed. *The Quotable Ronald Reagan*. Washington: Regnery, 1998.

Hannan, Daniel. 'Whom do we trust on the NHS: elected ministers or trade unions?' [Online]. *Daily Telegraph Blog*, 17 January 2011. Accessed 1 June 2013. Available at: http://blogs.telegraph.co.uk/news/danielhannan/100072220/whom-do-we-trust-on-the-nhs-elected-ministers-or-trade-unions/

Harker, Rachael. *NHS Funding and Expenditure*. London: House of Commons Library, 2012.

Harrison, Mark. 'The seven deadly sins of government-funded schools', Cato Institute, Aug 2005. Accessed 1 June 2013. Available at: http://www.cato.org/publications/commentary/seven-deadly-sins-governmentfunded-schools

Hayek, F. A. *Denationalisation of Money: The Argument Refined* (3rd ed.). London: Institute of Economic Affairs, 1990.

Hayek, F. A. 'International Money' (speech, Geneva Gold and Monetary Conference, Lausanne, Switzerland, 25 September 1975).

Hayek, F. A. *The Road to Serfdom* (repr.). London: Routledge, 1976.

Hazlitt, Henry. *Economics in One Lesson*. New York: Three Rivers Press, 1979.

Hill, Adam. 'The cost of living: 1971 v today', *Guardian*, 18 June 2011. Available at: http://www.guardian.co.uk/worklifeuk/cost-of-living-1971-today.

Hill, Amelia. 'Home birth: "What the hell was I thinking?"' *Guardian*, 16 April 2011. Available at: http://www.theguardian.com/lifeandstyle/2011/apr/16/home-birth-trial-or-rewarding

Hodgkinson, Tom. *How To Be Idle*. London: Penguin, 2005.

Hodgkinson, Tom. *How To Be Free*. London: Penguin, 2007.

Hodgkinson, Tom (ed.) *The Idler: Smash the System*. Issue 42, June 2009.

Hollowell J., Puddicombe D, Rowe R., Linsell L., Hardy P., Stewart, M., et al. 'The Birthplace National Prospective Cohort Study: Perinatal and Maternal Outcomes by Planned Place of Birth'. Birthplace in England Research Programme, Final Report Part 4. NIHR Service Delivery and Organisation programme: 2011.

Huff, Darrell, and Mel Calman. *How to Lie with Statistics* (repr.) London: Penguin Books, 1991.

Hülsmann, Jörg Guido. *The Ethics of Money Production*. Auburn, Alabama: Ludwig von Mises Institute, 2008.

Hume, John R. 'Industry and technology, vehicles and locomotives'. *The Glasgow Story* [Online]. Accessed 1 June 2013. Available at: http://www.theglasgowstory.com/story.php?id=TGSDE09

Iacovou, Maria, and Richard Berthoud.*The Economic Position of Large Families*. Leeds: Corporate Documents Services, DWP, 2006.

Institute of Liberty and Democracy (ILD), 'What we believe'. Accessed 1 June 2013. Available at: http://www.ild.org.pe/about-us/what-we-believe

Institute for Truth in Accounting [Online]. Accessed 1 June 2013. Available at: http://www.truthinaccounting.org/

Institution of Mechanical Engineers. 'Global Food: Waste Not, Want Not', January 2013. Available at: http://www.imeche.org/docs/default-source/

reports/Global_Food_Report.pdf

Jackson, Andrew and Ben Dyson. *Modernising Money*. London: Positive Money. 2012.

Jastram, Roy W., and Jill Leyland. *The Golden Constant: The English and American Experience, 1560–2007*. Cheltenham: Edward Elgar Publishing Ltd., 2009.

Jefferson, Thomas, and Philip Sheldon Foner. *Basic Writings of Thomas Jefferson*. New York: Willey Book Co., 1944.

Jefferson, Thomas. 'The Virginia Act for Establishing Religious Freedom', 1779. Accessed 1 June 2013. Available at: http://religiousfreedom.lib. virginia.edu/sacred/vaact.html

Johnson, David S., John M. Rogers and Lucilla Tan. 'A century of family budgets in the United States'. *Monthly Labour Review*, May 2001.

Johnson, Luke. *Start It Up: Why Running Your Business is Easier Than You Think*. London: Portfolio, 2013.

Jowitt, Margaret. *Childbirth Unmasked*. London: Peter Wooller, 1993.

Kay, John. 'London's rise from sewer to spectacle', *Financial Times*, 16 January 2013.

Kay, John. *Obliquity: Why Our Best Goals Are Achieved Indirectly*. London: Profile Books, 2010.

Keats, John. 'The vale of soul-Making', a letter to George and Georgiana Keats, 14 February 1819. Accessed 1 June 2013. Available at: http:// www.mrbauld.com/keatsva.html

Kirkpatrick, Jeane. 'Interview in Action' *Institute, Religion and Liberty*, Volume 2, Number 2, March/April 1992.

Knoller, Mark. 'National debt up $6 trillion since Obama took office'. *CBS News*, 1 March 2013.

LaCascio, Vincent R. *The Monetary Elite vs. Gold's Honest Discipline*. Old Bridge: Weltanschauung Financial Press, 2005.

Law, Henry. 'What Is LVT?' Land Value Tax Campaign [Online]. Accessed 1 June 2013. http://www.landvaluetax.org/what-is-lvt/

Lear, Linda. *Beatrix Potter: The Extraordinary Life of a Victorian Genius*. London: Penguin, 2008.

Lebowitz, Fran. *Social Studies*. London: Random House, 1981.

Leboyer, Frederick. *Birth Without Violence*. London: Pinter & Martin, 2011.

Lee, Kevin. *The Split Mind: Schizophrenia from an Insider's Point of View*. Nottingham: Nottingham University Press, 2011.

Leighton, Tim. 'Are specialists really necessary?' Speech, Royal College of Psychiatrists Faculty of Addictions Conference. Cardiff, May 2012.

Lessing, Doris. *The Golden Notebook*. London: Fourth Estate, 2013.

Lips, Ferdinand. *Gold Wars*. New York: Fame, 2001.

Lloyd George, David. *War Memoirs of David Lloyd George*. London: Nicholson and Watson, 1933.

MacGowan, Shane. Interviewed by Sean O'Driscoll, *Irish Voice*, 1 March

2006.

MacLaren, Leon. *Nature of Society and other essays*. London: School of Economic Science, 1997.

McRaney, David. *You Are Not So Smart*. London: Oneworld Publications, 2012.

Maddison, Angus. 'The West and the rest in the world economy: 1000–2030 Maddisonian and Malthusian interpretations'. *World Economics*, Volume 9, Number 4, 2008.

Maynard Keynes, John. *The Economic Consequences of Peace*. New York: Skyhorse Publishing, 2007.

Mill, John Stuart. *On Liberty*. London: Cosimo Classics, 2006.

Mill, John Stuart, and Jonathan Riley. *Principles of Political Economy*. Oxford: Oxford University Press, 2008.

Mill, John Stuart, and Donald Winch. *Principles of Political Economy, With Some of Their Applications to Social Philosophy: Books IV and V*. Harmondsworth: Penguin, 1970.

Moneyweek, 'End of Britain'. Accessed 1 June 2013. Available at: http://moneyweek.com/endofbritain/

Mora, Edwin. '47,515 drug-war Murders in Mexico in just 5 years'. *CNS News*, 12 January 2012. Accessed 1 June 2013. Available at: http://cnsnews.com/news/article/47515-drug-war-murders-mexico-just-5-years

Morse J. M. and C. Park. 'Home birth and hospital deliveries: a comparison of the perceived painfulness of parturition', *Nursing and Health*, June 1988.

Moser, Claus. 'Schools inquiry plea to halt "Salt into Ignorance"' *Daily Telegraph*, 21 August 1990.

Mounsey, Chris. 'New from old: a friendly society' [Online]. *Devil's Kitchen*. 14 November 2009. Accessed 1 June 2013. http://www.devilskitchen.me.uk/2009

Moyo, Dambisa. *Dead Aid: Why Aid Makes Things Worse and How There is Another Way for Africa*. London: Penguin, 2010.

National Collaborating Centre for Women's and Children's Health. *Intrapartum Care: Care of Healthy Women and Their Babies During Childbirth*. London: Royal College of Obstetricians and Gynaecologists Press, 2007.

New York Times, 'Tax form baffles even Prof. Einstein'. March 11, 1944.

Newton, Isaac. *The Correspondence of Isaac Newton*. Vol. 1. (ed. H. W. Turnbull). Cambridge: Cambridge University Press, 1959.

Newton, John. 'Coalition "should introduce independent school voucher system"', *Daily Telegraph*, 31 January 2011.

O'Rourke, P. J. 'The liberty manifesto', Speech delivered on 6 May 1993. Available at: http://www.cato.org/publications/speeches/liberty-manifesto

Ogus, Anthony. *Corruption and Regulatory Structures*. Berkeley: University of California, 2003.

Orwell, George. *All Art is Propaganda* (comp. George Packer). Boston: Mariner Books, 2009.

Orwell, George. *Politics and the English Language and Other Essays*. S. l.: Oxford City Press, 2009.

Parliamentary Papers, 1861, XXI. p. 293–328; as reprinted in Young and Hancock 1956. (via Gillard, Derek *Education in England: a brief history, 2011*). Accessed 1 June 2011. Available at: www.educationengland.org. uk/history

Paton, Graeme. 'A-level results 2012: private schools "dominate top grades"', *Daily Telegraph,* 18 October 2012.

Paton, Graeme. 'More teachers "quitting the classroom over indiscipline"', *Daily Telegraph*, 26 February 2012.

Paton, Graeme. 'Third of GCSEs taken at private schools graded A*', *Daily Telegraph*, 3 September 2011.

Paul, Ron. 'Legalize competing currencies!', Daily Paul, 13 August 2012. Accessed 1 June 2013. Available at: http://www.dailypaul.com/248698/ ron-pauls-texas-straight-talk-8-13-12-legalize-competing-currencies.

Paul, Ron. *The Revolution: a Manifesto*. New York: Grand Central Publishing, 2008.

Payne, Chris S. 'Expenditure on healthcare in the UK: 2011'. Office National Statistics (ONS), May 8 2012.

Pear, Robert. 'Health official takes parting shot at "waste"'. *New York Times,* 3 December 2011.

Pearce, Joseph Chilton. *Magical child: Rediscovering Nature's Plan for our Children*. New York: Bantam Books, 1980.

Pérez, Wilma. 'Con el bono bajó la desnutrición y subió la cobertura institucional', *La Razón,* 25 May 2013. (H/T Otto Rock).

Plato, *The Republic*, 380 BC Project Gutenberg [Online]. http://www. gutenberg.org/ebooks/1497

Polo, Marco. *The Travels of Marco Polo, a Venetian, in the 13th century: being a description, by that early traveller, of remarkable places and things, in the eastern parts of the world*. (Google ebook.) Edinburgh: Oliver & Boyd, 1848.

Pope, Alexander. *An Essay on Criticism, 1709*. Auckland: The Floating Press, 2010.

PositiveMoney, 'Positive money system – in plain English', 1 March 2013. Accessed 1 June 2013. Available at: http://www.positivemoney. org/2013/03/the-positive-money-system-in-plain-english/

Pound, Ezra. *ABC of Reading*. Norfolk, Conn.: New Directions, 1951.

Pound, Ezra. *Guide to Kulchur*, p. 359. London: Faber & Faber, 1938.

Powell, Chris. 'Gold is limited government, which is more "civilized" than the alternative', GATA, 6 May 2012. Accessed 1 June 2013. Available at:

http://gata.org/node/11330

Preobrazhensky, Eugeny A., *Bumazhnyeden'gi v epokhu proletarskoi dictatury* (Paper Money During the Proletarian Dictatorship). Moscow: State Publishing House, 1920.

'Private school fees rise nearly twice as fast as inflation in the past decade', Lloyds Bank, 27 August 2012.

Public Sector Finances, ONS, February 2013.

Rand, Ayn. *Atlas Shrugged*. London: Penguin Classics, 2007.

Rashid, S. and Brooks, G. *The Levels of Attainment in Literacy and Numeracy of 13- to 19-year-olds in England, 1948–2009*. London: National Research and Development Centre for Adult Literacy and Numeracy, 2010.

'Reducing obesity and improving diet'. Department of Health Policy, 25 March 2013. Accessed 1 June 2013. Available at: https://www.gov.uk/government/policies/reducing-obesity-and-improving-diet

Reinhart, Carmen M. and Kennth S. Rogoff. *This Time is Different: Eight Centuries of Financial Folly*. New Jersey: Princeton University Press, 2009.

Reuter, Peter, and Alex Stevens. *An Analysis of UK Drug Policy: A Monograph Prepared for the UK Drug Policy Commission*. London: UKPDC, 2007.

Ridley, Matt. *The Rational Optimist: How Prosperity Evolves*. London: Fourth Estate, 2011.

Riegel, Edwin C. *The New Approach to Freedom*. San Pedro, CA: The Heather Foundation, 1976.

Riegel, Edwin C. and Spencer Heath MacCallum. *Flight from Inflation: The Monetary Alternative*. Los Angeles: The Heather Foundation, 1978.

Roberts, Russell D. *The Invisible Heart: An Economic Romance*. Cambridge, Mass.: MIT Press, 2002.

Robinson, Ken. Speech, TED, February 2006. Accessed 1 June 2013. Available at: http://www.ted.com/talks/ken_robinson_says_schools_kill_creativity.html

Rock, Otto. 'Incakola news'. Available at: http://incakolanews.blogspot.co.uk/

Rohn, Jim. *Classic Quotes*. Accessed 1 June 2013. http://www.jimrohn.com/index.php?main_page=page&id=550

Rothermel, Paula. *Home-education: Rationales, Practices and Outcomes*. Durham: University of Durham, 2002.

Rothschild, Michael. *Bionomics: Economy as Ecosystem*. London: Owl Books, 1995.

Saving lives: our healthier nation. London: Stationery Office, 1999.

Schiff, Peter D. and Andrew J. Schiff. *How an Economy Grows and Why it Crashes*. New Jersey: Wiley, 2010.

Schumacher, E. F., *Small is Beautiful: A Study of Economics as if People Mattered*. London: Vintage, 1993.

Schwab, Klaus and Xavier Sala-i-Martín. *The Global Competitiveness Report, 2012–2013*. Geneva: World Economic Forum, 2012.

Shanley, Laura Kaplan. *Unassisted Childbirth*. Westport, Conn.: Bergin & Garvey, 1994.

Shaw, George Bernard. *Everybody's Political What's What?* London: Constable and Co., 1944.

Shaw, George Bernard. *The Intelligent Woman's Guide to Socialism and Capitalism*. New Jersey: Transaction Publishers, 1984.

Shedlock, Mike. 'Global Economic Trend Analysis' [Online]. Available at: http://globaleconomicanalysis.blogspot.co.uk/

Shorter, Edward. *Women's Bodies: A Social History of Women's Encounter with Health, Ill Health and Medicine*. New Brunswick: Transaction Publishers, 1990.

Simmons, Matthew R. *Twilight in the Desert: The Coming Saudi Oil Shock and the World Economy*. Hoboken, N.J.: John Wiley & Sons, 2005.

'The Singer strike 1911'. Glasgow Digital Library. Accessed 1 June 2013. Available at: http://gdl.cdlr.strath.ac.uk/redclyde/redclyeve01.htm

Smith, Adam. *The Wealth of Nations* (ed. Edwin Cannan) (5th ed). London: Methuen, 1904. (Online edition). Available at: http://www.econlib.org/library/Smith/smWN.html

Spierenburg, Pieter. *A History of Murder*. Cambridge: Polity, 2008.

'Statistics on obesity, physical activity and diet England, 2012'. Leeds: Health and Social Care Information Centre, 2012.

Steinhauer, Jennifer. 'A literary legend fights for a local library', *New York Times*, 19 June 2009.

Stubbs, Sheila. *Birthing the Easy Way*. Self-published, 2010.

Sundaram, Jomo Kwame. *The State of Food Insecurity in the World: Economic Growth is Necessary But Not Sufficient to Accelerate Reduction of Hunger and Malnutrition*. Rome: Food and agriculture organization of the United nations (FAO), 2012.

Tacitus, *Annals*, trans. Alfred John Church and William Jackson Brodribb. Accessed 1 June 2013. Available at: http://classics.mit.edu/Tacitus/annals.html.

Taylor, A. J. P. *English History, 1914–1945*. Oxford: Oxford University Press, 1965.

Thomas, Alan and Harriet Pattison. *How Children Learn at Home*. London: Bloomsbury, 2008.

Thoreau, Henry David. *Civil Disobedience*, 1849. CreateSpace Independent Publishing Platform, 2010.

Thoreau, Henry David. *Walden*. Edinburgh: Magnetic North, 2009.

Thorpe, Lauren, Kimberley Trewhitt and James Zuccollo *Reform Ideas No 5 Must do better: spending on schools*. Reform, May 2013.

The Times. 'One million letters to taxman left unanswered', 28 January 2013.

Total military personnel and dependent end strength by service, regional area, and country. United States Department of Defense. November 27, 2012.

Tsu Lao, *Tao Te Ching,* (trans. Gia-fu Feng and Jane English). New York: Vintage Books, 1972.

Turk, James and John Rubino. *The Coming Collapse of the Dollar and How to Profit From It.* New York: Doubleday, 2004.

Tustain, Paul. 'Printing Money for Beginners (and Experts)'. Bullion Vault, December 2012. Accessed 1 June 2013. Available at: http://goldnews. bullionvault.com/files/PrintingMoney.pdf

Twain, Mark. *Pudd'nhead Wilson's New Calendar,* 1897. Clayton, DE: Prestwick House Inc. 2006.

Twain, Mark, and John Sutton Tuckey. *The Devil's Race-Track: Mark Twain's Great Dark Writings: The Best From 'Which was the dream?' and 'Fables of man'.* Berkeley: University of California Press, 1980.

Understanding Glasgow: *The Glasgow Indicators Project.* Accessed 1 June 2013. http://www.understandingglasgow.com/indicators/economic_ participation/overview

'Upwardly mobile', *The Economist,* 25 August 2012. Available at: http:// www.economist.com/node/21560912

Vasagar, Jeevan. 'Olympics 2012: third of Team GB medallists came from private schools', *Guardian,* 13 August 2012.

Walmsley, Roy. *World Prison Population List (Eighth Edition).* London: Home Office, 2009.

Webb, R. K. 'The Victorian reading public', in *From Dickens to Hardy.* London: Pelican Books. 1963.

Webb Young, James. *A Technique for Producing Ideas.* New York: McGraw Hill, 2003.

Weber, Chris. *Good as Gold? How We Lost Our Gold Reserves And Destroyed The Dollar.* Vancouver: George Edward Durell Foundation, 1988.

West, E. G. 'Literacy and the Industrial Revolution,' *Economic History Review 31* (3), August 1978.

West, E. G., James Tooley, and James Stanfield. *Government Failure: E.G. West on Education.* London: Institute of Economic Affairs, 2003.

Wheelan, Charles. *Naked Economics: Undressing the Dismal Science.* New York: W. W. Norton & Co., 2010.

White, Terence Hanbury, and Sylvia Townsend Warner. *The Once and Future King.* London: Voyager, 1996.Williams, Walter E. *Liberty Versus the Tyranny of Socialism: Controversial Essays.* Stanford: Hoover Press, 2008.Wilmot, John. *The Works of John Wilmot, Earl of Rochester* (ed. Harold Love). Oxford: Oxford University Press, 1999.

World Health Statistics 2013. Geneva: World Health Organization.

Wright, Oliver and Jeremy Laurance. 'NHS's darkest day: Five more hospitals under investigation for neglect as report blames "failings at every level" for 1,200 deaths at Stafford Hospital'. *The Independent,* 7 February 2013.

Yapp, Robin. 'Brazil's obesity rate could match US by 2022', *Daily Telegraph*, 15 December 2010.

Yardley, Jim. 'In One Slum, Misery, Work, Politics and Hope'. *New York Times*, 28 December 2011.

Zappa, Frank. Liner notes for the album *Freak Out!*, June 1966.

Young, Toby. 'Dickens and the profit motive,' *The Spectator*, 15 December 2012.

'2011 global study on homicide trends, contexts, data'. Vienna: United Nations Office on Drugs and Crime, 2011.

'2013 World Hunger and Poverty Facts and Statistics'. World Hunger Education Service. Accessed 1 June 2013. Available at: http://www.worldhunger.org/articles/Learn/world%20hunger%20facts%202002.htm

Notes

1 European Commission, *Eurostat*, news release, 31 May 2013.
2 World Hunger Education Service, '2013 World Hunger and Poverty Facts and Statistics' http://www.worldhunger.org/articles/Learn/ world%20hunger%20facts%202002.htm [accessed 1 June 2013].
3 Alex Callinicos, 'Anti-war protests do make a difference', *Socialist Worker*, 19 March 2005.
4 Chris S. Payne, 'Expenditure on Healthcare in the UK 2011', Office for National Statistics (ONS), 2012.
5 Oliver Wright and Jeremy Laurance, 'NHS's darkest day', *Independent*, 7 February 2013.
6 Lauren Thorpe, Kimberley Trewhitt and James Zuccolo, 'Reform Ideas No 5. Must do better: spending on schools', *Reform*, May 2013 http://www.reform.co.uk/resources/0000/0765/Must_do_better_ Spending_on_schools.pdf [accessed 1 June 2013].
7 BBC News. 'Literacy has stalled, Ofsted's chief inspector says', 15 March 2012 http://www.bbc.co.uk/news/education-17368311 [accessed 1 June 2013].
8 ONS, 'UK Public Sector Finances', February 2013.
9 Mark Knoller, 'National debt up $6 trillion since Obama took office', *CBS News*, 1 March 2013.
10 Milton Friedman, *Capitalism and Freedom*, 40th edn (Chicago: University of Chicago Press, 2002), xiv.
11 George Orwell, *All Art Is Propaganda* (Mariner Books: 2009), 168.
12 George Orwell, *Politics and the English Language and Other Essays* (Oxford: Benediction Classics, 2010), 18.
13 HousePriceCrash forum: http://www.housepricecrash.co.uk/forum/ [accessed 1 June 2013].
14 Friedrich Hayek, *The Denationalization of Money* (1976).
15 England and France were embroiled in as many as seven conflicts – directly or otherwise – during this period: 1688–97, 1702–13, 1744–8, 1749–54, 1755–63, 1779–83, 1792–1815.
16 Ian Donnachie, 'Industry and Technology', 2004. *The Glasgow Story* http://www.theglasgowstory.com/story.php?id=TGSDE03 [accessed 1 June 2013].
17 Ibid.

18   W. Hamish Fraser, 'Second City of the Empire', *The Glasgow Story*: http://www.theglasgowstory.com/storyd.php [accessed 1 June 2013].

19   John R. Hume, 'Industry and Technology, Vehicles and Locomotives', *The Glasgow Story* http://www.theglasgowstory.com/story.php?id=TGSDE09 [accessed 1 June 2013].

20   Glasgow Digital Library, 'The Singer Strike 1911' http://gdl.cdlr.strath.ac.uk/redclyde/redclyeve01.htm [accessed 1 June 2013].

21   Understanding Glasgow, 'Unemployment Rates Across Scottish Cities', (data from Annual Population Survey 2009) http://www.understandingglasgow.com/indicators/economic_participation/overview [accessed 1 June 2013].

22   P. Hanlon, D. Walsh and B. Whyte, *Let Glasgow Flourish* (Glasgow: Glasgow Centre for Population Health, 2006).

23   United Nations Office on Drugs and Crime, *Global Study on Homicide* (Vienna, 2011): http://www.unodc.org/documents/data-and-analysis/statistics/Homicide/Globa_study_on_homicide_2011_web.pdf [accessed 1 June 2013].

24   National Records of Scotland. 'Drug-related Deaths in Scotland in 2011', August 2012.

25   Centre for Social Justice. 'Breakthrough Glasgow', 5 February 2008 http://www.centreforsocialjustice.org.uk/UserStorage/pdf/Pdf%20reports/BreakthroughGlasgow.pdf [accessed 1 June 2013].

26   STV News. 'Glasgow Tops League Table of Unhealthy Cities' 31 October 2011 http://news.stv.tv/west-central/277062-glasgow-tops-league-table-of-unhealthy-cities/ [accessed 1 June 2013].

27   *The Times* (30 March 2008). This article is now off-line. *The Daily Record* has a shorter version of the same story. 'Shocking plight of jobs blackspot children revealed', 31 March 2008 http://www.dailyrecord.co.uk/news/scottish-news/shocking-plight-of-jobs-blackspot-children-972899 [accessed 1 June 2013].

28   Reform Scotland, 'Power for the Public', April 2008.

29   *The War Memoirs of David Lloyd George* (London: Nicholson and Watson,1933–1938), 28.

30   A. J. P. Taylor, *English History 1914–1945* (Oxford: Oxford University Press, 1965).

31   Frédéric Bastiat, *'Ce qu'on voit et ce qu'on ne voit pas'*, in *Essays On Political Economy* (1848), 25.

32   Ibid.

33   Walter E. Williams, *Liberty Versus the Tyranny of Socialism* (Stanford: Hoover Institution Press, 2008).

34   United States Bureau of Labor Statistics (BLS), 'A Century Of Family Budgets', *Monthly Labor Review* (May 2001).

35   Douglas Carswell, *The End of Politics and the Birth of iDemocracy* (Biteback Publishing, 2012).

Notes

36 Hannaford, Peter, ed. *The Quotable Ronald Reagan*. Washington: Regnery, 1998.

37 Albert Camus, *The Plague* (Penguin Modern Classics, 2002), 100.

38 Matt Ridley, *TED talk*, 'When Ideas Have Sex', Oxford, July 2010 http://blog.ted.com/2010/07/14/when_ideas_have/ [accessed 1 June 2013].

39 Matt Ridley, *The Rational Optimist* (Harper Collins, 2010), 7.

40 H. W. Turnbull, ed., *The Correspondence of Isaac Newton, vol. 1* (1959), 416.

41 Matt Ridley, *The Rational Optimist: How Prosperity Evolves*, (London: Fourth Estate, 31 March 2011), 72.

42 Quoted in Carl C. Gaither and Alma E. Cavazos-Gaither, eds, *Dictionary of Scientific Quotations* (New York: Springer, January 2012), 2nd edn, 2573.

43 Acton Institute, 'Interview with Jeane Kirkpatrick', *Religion and Liberty*, vol. 2, no. 2 March/April 1992.

44 Williams, *Liberty Versus the Tyranny of Socialism*, 101.

45 Anthony Ogus, 'Corruption and Regulatory Structures', *Law and Policy*, 26 (2004), 329–46.

46 E. C. Riegel, *The New Approach to Freedom* ed. by Spencer Heath MacCallum (California: The Heather Foundation, 1976) chapter 1.

47 Michael Rothschild, *Bionomics* (Owl Books,1995), xi.

48 Quoted in Philip S. Foner, ed., *The Basic Writings of Thomas Jefferson* (Wiley, 1944), 464.

49 Ridley, *The Rational Optimist*, 182.

50 John Kay, *Obliquity* (Profile Books, 2011), 173.

51 John Wilmot, *A Dialogue Between Strephon and Daphne* (1674).

52 Johnson, *Start It Up*.

53 Franklin D. Roosevelt, Second Inaugural Address, 20 January 1937.

54 Adam Smith, *The Wealth of Nations, book I, chapter II* (1776).

55 Johnson, *Start It Up*, 232.

56 Williams, *Liberty Versus the Tyranny of Socialism*, 284.

57 Riegel, *The New Approach to Freedom*.

58 Fyodor Dostoevsky, *Crime and Punishment* (London: Wordsworth Classics, September 2000), 129.

59 See Pieter Spierenburg, *A History of Murder* (Polity Press, 2008).

60 Indur M. Goklany, 'Death and Death Rates Due to Extreme Weather Events', International Policy Network, 2007 http://www.csccc.info/reports/report_23.pdf [accessed 1 June 2013].

61 Johnson, *Start It Up*, 232.

62 HousePriceCrash forum: http://www.housepricecrash.co.uk/forum/ [accessed 1 June 2013].

63 US Census Bureau, 2000 Census, *Average Number of Children per Family and per Family With Children*.

64 Office for National Statistics, 'Family Size in 2012', 25 March 2013.

65 US Department of Agriculture, Center for Nutrition Policy and Promotion report, 'Expenditures on Children by Families, June 2012'.

66 Maria Iacovou and Richard Berthoud, 'The Economic Position of Large Families' (Leeds: Department for Work and Pensions, 2006).

67 Department of Work and Pensions reported by Gerri Peev, '200 Families Claiming Housing Benefit Have 10 or More Children as Taxpayers face £150 million bill for "benefit broods"', *Daily Mail*, 31 December 2012.

68 *Daily Mail*, '£95,000-a-year Benefits Family of 12 Re-homed in a £1,000-a-week House ... After They Trashed the Last One', 5 September 2010.

69 John Adams, letter to Thomas Jefferson, 25 August 1787.

70 Jeremy Grantham, 'People Now See It Is a System for the Rich Only', GMO quarterly letter to the *Financial Times*, 5 February 2012.

71 Ellen Freilich, 'JP Morgan Houston Janitor Wants Jamie Dimon to Walk in Her Shoes', *Reuters*, 20 June 2012.

72 Interview for MTV, recorded August 1992. Never aired. http://www.youtube.com/watch?v=In2TRDEbmZ0 [accessed 1 June 2013].

73 Charles Wheelan, *Naked Economics* (W. W. Norton & Co., 2010), 228.

74 The widely watched 'Money As Debt' video by Paul Grignon is an excellent introduction to this subject. It's one of the places I started.

75 See David Graeber, *Debt* (Melville House Publishing, 2013).

76 Jaromir Benes and Michael Kumhof, 'The Chicago Plan Revisited', IMF Working Paper, August 2012, 14.

77 Rustichello da Pisa, *The Travels of Marco Polo*, (Google ebook) 353–5 [accessed 1 September 2013].

78 Friedrich Hayek, from an address entitled 'International Money', delivered to the Geneva Gold and Monetary Conference on 25 September 1975 at Lausanne, Switzerland.

79 Paul Tustain, 'Printing Money for Beginners (and Experts)', December 2012, 8.: http://goldnews.bullionvault.com/files/PrintingMoney.pdf [accessed 1 June 2013].

80 Thomas Paterson, 'For the UK to Return to the Gold Standard Today', *Gold Made Simple News*, July 2011: http://www.goldmadesimplenews.com/gold/for-the-uk-to-return-to-the-gold-standard-today-the-price-of-gold-would-be-23388-4605/ [accessed 1 June 2013].

81 Ayn Rand, *Atlas Shrugged* (London: Penguin Classics, 2007), 410.

82 Reuters, 'U.N. to let Iraq sell oil for euros, not dollars', 30 October 2000.

83 Positive Money, 'Positive Money Reforms In Plain English', 1 March 2013, 26.: http://www.positivemoney.org/2013/03/the-positive-money-system-in-plain-english/ [accessed 1 June 2013].

84 Bank of England statistical release for Notes & Coin, Central Bank Reserves, and M4.

85 John Maynard Keynes, *The Economic Consequences of Peace* (Sterling, 2007), 134.

86 Data published on the Bank of England and Federal Reserve of St Louis websites: http://www.bankofengland.co.uk and http://www.stlouisfed.org/ [accessed 1 June 2013].

87 Keynes, *The Economic Consequences of Peace*, 134.

88 BBC Radio 4, 'What is Money?', BBC, 26 March 2012.

89 The transfer of interest from the public to the banks every year is between £108–£250 billion (on Bank of England figures). This is about double what it would be if they were just intermediaries rather than money creators. So they benefit by a minimum of £50 billion a year. The seigniorage to the state on the creation of paper money in normal years is around £2 billion. If you wanted to add the reduction in the real value of the national debt, that might be about £20 billion a year in value. Banks are benefiting twice as much as the state, plus the state now has the cost of supporting the banking system.

90 Governor Ben S. Bernanke, 'Deflation: Making Sure It Doesn't Happen Here', remarks made before the National Economists Club, Washington DC, 21 November 2002.

91 Wikipedia, 'List of wars by death toll': http://en.wikipedia.org/wiki/List_of_wars_by_death_toll [accessed 1 June 2013]. This article is well researched, but there is no real way of assessing this numbers with total accuracy. If you want to delve deeper, try: S. Pinker, *The Better Angels of Our Nature*; C. McEvedy, *Atlas of World Population History*; H. Ramon Myers and Yeh-Chien Wang, 'Economic developments, 1644–1800', in Willard J. Peterson, ed., *The Cambridge History of China, vol. 9, part 1: The Ch'ing Empire to 1800*, (Cambridge University Press); J. Keegan, *The Second World War*; J. Ellis and M. Cox, *The World War I Databook* and J. J. Saunders, *The History of the Mongol Conquests*.

92 Riegel, *The New Approach to Freedom*, chapter 3.

93 Evgeny A. Preobrazhensky, *Bumazhnyeden'gi v epokhu Proletarskoi dictatury* [translation: *Paper Money During the Proletarian Dictatorship* (Moscow: State Publishing House, 1920), 4.

94 Alan Greenspan, 'Gold and Economic Freedom', published in Ayn Rand's 'Objectivist' newsletter in 1966 and in *Capitalism: The Unknown Ideal* (New American Library, 1967).

95 Chris Powell, 'Gold Is Limited Government, Which Is More "Civilized" Than The Alternative', *GATA* (6 May 2012): http://gata.org/node/11330 [accessed 1 June 2013].

96 Walter E. Spahr, *The Real Culprit*, Monetary Notes, volumes 19–23, Economists' National Committee on Monetary Policy, 1 July 1959.

97   *Guardian*, 'The Cost of Living: 1971 v. Today', 18 June 2011.

98   Data from sharelynx.com.

99   This quote was attributed to Mark Twain in *The Autobiography of John Hays Hammond* (Farrar & Rinehart, 1935), 97. Although Hammond knew Twain personally, there is no other authentic record that Twain made this statement.

100 Dominic Frisby, 'Smash the System', *The Idler*, issue 42, June 2009.

101 George Bernard Shaw, *The Intelligent Woman's Guide to Socialism and Capitalism* (Transaction Publishers, 1928), 263.

102 Professor Tom Fisher, 'The *Approximity* Gold Price Model', October 2009: http://gold.approximity.com/gold_price_model.html [accessed 1 June 2013].

103 Riegel, *The New Approach to Freedom*, chapter 3.

104 E. C. Riegel, Spencer Heath MacCallum and George Morton, eds, *Flight From Inflation: The Monetary Alternative* (The Heather Foundation): http://www.newapproachtofreedom.info/ffi/ [accessed 1 June 2013].

105 Ron Paul, 'Legalize Competing Currencies', Texas Straight Talk, 13 August 2012.

106 Douglas Carswell speech in the House of Commons, on the Currency and Banknotes Bill, 7 September 2011.

107 Douglas Carswell speech in the House of Commons, on the Financial Services Bill, 15 September 2010.

108 Quoted in Roman Frydman, Kenneth Murphy and Andrzej Rapaczyński, eds, *Capitalism With a Comrade's Face* (Central European University Press,1998), 356.

109 Milton Friedman, interview by John Hawkins, 16 September 2003.

110 George Bernard Shaw, *Everybody's Political What's What?* (Constable and Co., 1944) chapter 30.

111 Thomas Jefferson, draft of the Virginia Act for Establishing Religious Freedom (1779): http://religiousfreedom.lib.virginia.edu/sacred/vaact_draft_1779.html [accessed 1 June 2013].

112 John Stuart Mill, *Principles of Political Economy* (Oxford: Oxford Paperbacks, 2008), 174.

113 *New York Times*, 'Tax Form Baffles Even Prof. Einstein' (Associated Press article) 11 March 1944.

114 Figure applies to 2009. It has since become even longer.

115 *The Times*, 'One Million Letters to Taxman Left Unanswered', 28 January 2013.

116 See Charles Adams, *Fight, Flight, Fraud* (Euro-Dutch Publishers, 1982).

117 This is actually a misquote by Charles Adams in his book *For Good and Evil* (Madison Books, 1992), 257. The correct quote is: 'Whoever thinks a faultless piece to see, Thinks what ne'er was, nor is, nor e'er

shall be.' From *An Essay on Criticism*, 1709, (The Floating Press, 2010).

118   Tim La, 'A flat rate income tax system – just wishful thinking?', *MoneyWeek* magazine, 6 August 2006.

119   Quoted in Evan Esar, ed., *20,000 Quips & Quotes* (Barnes & Noble Books, 1995), 882.

120   Kevin Cahill, *Who Owns Britain* (Canongate Books Ltd, 2002).

121   Ibid.

122   Ibid.

123   Ibid.

124   Henry George, *Progress and Poverty, 1879* (Cosimo Inc., 2006), 299.

125   Mill, *Principles of Political Economy,* 174.

126   Kevin Cahill, 'The Great Property Swindle', *The New Statesman*, 11 March 2011.

127   Henry Law, 'What Is LVT?' Land Value Tax Campaign: http://www. landvaluetax.org/what-is-lvt/ [accessed 1 June 2013].

128   'In my opinion the least bad tax is the property tax on the unimproved value of land, the Henry George argument of many, many years ago.' Milton Friedman speaking in an interview with *The Times Herald*, Norristown, Pennsylvania, 1 December 1978.

129   Professor Klaus Schwab and Professor Xavier Sala-i-Martin, 'The Global Competitiveness Report, 2012–3', World Economic Forum: http://www3.weforum.org/docs/WEF_GCR_Report_2011-12.pdf [accessed 1 June 2013].

130   World Economic Outlook Database, International Monetary Fund: http://www.imf.org/external/ns/cs.aspx?id=28 [accessed 20 April 2013]; World Development Indicators Database, World Bank: http:// data.worldbank.org/data-catalog/world-development-indicators [accessed 18 April 2013].

131   Theodore Dalrymple, speaking at the Property and Freedom Society, Bodrum, Turkey, September, 2012.

132   *Daily Telegraph*, 'NHS Is Fifth Biggest Employer in World', 20 March 2012.

133   Ruth Alexander, 'Which Is The World's Biggest Employer?', *BBC News,* 20 March 2012; ONS data, reported in the *Daily Telegraph*, 'UK employment hits all-time high', 17 October 2012.

134   Great Britain, HM Treasury, *The National Programme for IT in the NHS* (London: The Stationery Office, 16 June 2006), 4 [retrieved 16 October 2011].

135   Laura Donnelly, 'Patients Starve and Die of Thirst on Hospital Wards', *Daily Telegraph,* 6 October 2012.

136   Office of National Statistics, Historical mortality rates: http://www. statistics.gov.uk/hub/population/deaths/mortality-rates [accessed 1 June 2013].

137 Payne, Chris S. 'Expenditure on healthcare in the UK: 2011'. ONS, 8 May 2013.

138 Rebecca Clancy, 'UK Employment Hits All-time High', *Daily Telegraph*, 17 October 2012.

139 Rachael Harker, 'NHS Funding and Expenditure', Social and General Statistics, House of Commons Library (2012).

140 P. J. O'Rourke, 'The Liberty Manifesto', a speech at the Cato Institute, 6 May 1993.

141 Malcolm Gladwell, *The Tipping Point* (Little Brown, 2000).

142 C. L. 'Butch' Otter, News Release, 17 March 2010.

143 World Health Organization, *World Health Statistics 2013*. Geneva.

144 US Government Spending: http://www.usgovernmentspending.com/current_spending [accessed 1 June 2013].

145 CIA, 'The World Factbook': https://www.cia.gov/library/publications/the-world-factbook/ [accessed 1 June 2013].

146 Robert Pear, 'Health Official Takes Parting Shot at "Waste"', *New York Times*, 3 December 2011.

147 Ron Paul, *The Revolution* (Grand Central Publishing, 2009).

148 Aneurin Bevan, *In Place of Fear* (Quartet Books, 1978), 100.

149 In this next section on the Friendly Societies in the UK, I am indebted in particular to two blog entries. The first is from Toby Baxendale of the Cobden Centre, entitled 'Working-Class Patients and the Medical Establishment'. The other on the blog *Devil's Kitchen* entitled 'New from Old: A Friendly Society', by Chris Mounsey.

150 David Green, *Working-class Patients and the Medical Establishment* (Gower, 1985).

151 Gosden, P. H. J. H. *Self-Help: Voluntary Associations in Nineteenth Century Britain*. London: B.T. Batsford Ltd, 1973. p. 91

152 Baxendale, 'Working-class Patients': http://www.cobdencentre.org/2010/08/working-class-patients-and-the-medical-establishment/ [accessed 1 June 2013].

153 Ibid.

154 Green, *Working-class Patients and the Medical Establishment*.

155 Blair, Tony, MP, speech to the IEA. 24 May 1994.

156 Kevin Alan Lee, *The Split Mind* (Nottingham University Press, 2011), 312.

157 Quoted in Daniel Hannan, 'Whom Do We Trust on the NHS: Elected Ministers or Trade Unions?', *Daily Telegraph*, 17 January 2011.

158 Quote from Suzanne Arms, author. I am extremely grateful in this chapter to the many mums that have contributed to chatboards across the net discussing their birth experiences.

159 Tina Cassidy, *Birth* (New York: Atlantic Monthly Press, 2006), 54–5.

160 *Guardian*, 'Home Birth: What the Hell Was I Thinking?',16 April 2011.

161 American Congress of Obstetricians and Gynecologists (ACOG), 'ACOG Statement on Home Births'. 20 July 2010. http://www. medscape.com/viewarticle/725383 [Accessed 1 June 2013].

162 National Collaborating Centre for Women's and Children's Health, *Final Draft of Guideline on Intrapartum Care* (London: Royal College of Obstetricians and Gynaecologists, 22 March 2007).

163 See J. M. Morse and C. Park, 'Home Birth and Hospital Deliveries', *Research in Nursing and Health,* 11, 3 (1988): 175–81.

164 Sheila Stubbs, *Birthing the Easy Way* (Privately published, 2005).

165 Morse and Park, 'Home Birth and Hospital Deliveries', 175–81.

166 G. Chamberlain and A. Wraight, eds, *Home Births* (Informa Healthcare, 1997).

167 Margaret Jowitt, *Childbirth Unmasked* (Self Publishing Association, March 1993).

168 Judith Goldsmith, *Childbirth Wisdom from the World's Oldest Societies* (East West Health Books, 1990).

169 Joseph Chilton Pearce, *Magical Child* (Bantam Books, 1980), 63.

170 See Jock Doubleday, *Spontaneous Creation*, vol. 2, chapter 74: http:// www.whale.to/a/doubleday.html [accessed 1 June 2013].

171 Quoted in Laura Kaplan, 'Unassisted Childbirth', *Scientific American*, 77 (1969), 31.

172 Wilma Pérez, 'Con el bono bajó la desnutrición y subió la cobertura institucional', *La Razón* (H/T Otto Rock, 25 May 2013).

173 Quoted in Edward Shorter, *Women's Bodies* (Transaction Publishers, 1982), 156.

174 National Perinatal Epidemiology Unit, 'Birthplace in England' (Oxford, November 2011). 'These figures include all NHS costs associated with the birth itself – for example midwifery care during labour and immediately after the birth, the cost of any medical care and procedures needed in hospital, and the cost of any stay in hospital, midwifery unit, or neonatal unit immediately after the birth either by the mother or the baby. The costs for planned home and midwifery unit births take account of interventions and treatment that a woman may receive if she is transferred into hospital during labour or after the birth. The costs do not include any longer-term costs of care'.

175 G. K. Chesterton, 'The Superstition of School' (1923): http:// grammar.about.com/od/classicessays/a/supschoolessay.htm [accessed 1 June 2013].

176 Lloyds Banking Group press release, 'Private school fees rise nearly twice as fast as inflation in the last decade', 27 August 2012.

177 The data site www.ukpublicspending.co.uk (compiled by Christopher

Chantrill) uses HM Treasury data and is excellent on all public spending numbers. Also see Paul Bolton, 'Education Spending in the UK', *House of Commons Library* (July 2012).

178 Department of Education (DoE) data: http://www.education.gov.uk/researchandstatistics and DoE 2012 Census; Independent Schools Council, 2012 census.

179 Independent School Fees Advice: http://www.schoolfeesadvice.org/home/key_facts/private_school_fees.aspx [accessed 1 June 2013].

180 Department of Education (DoE) data: http://www.education.gov.uk/researchandstatistics and DoE 2012 Census; Independent Schools Council, 2012 census.

181 Paula Rothermel, 'Home-Education: Aims, Practices and Outcomes (University of Durham, 2002). Paper presented at the Annual Conference of the British Educational Research Association, University of Exeter, England, 12–14 September 2002.

182 Graeme Paton, 'Third of GCSEs Taken at Private Schools Graded A*', *Daily Telegraph*, 3 September 2011; Graeme Paton, 'A-level Results 2012: Private Schools Dominate Top Grades', *Daily Telegraph*, 18 October 2012.

183 Jeevan Vasagar, 'Olympics 2012: Third of Team GB Medallists Came from Private Schools', *Guardian*, 13 August 2012.

184 Ibid.

185 S. Rashid and G. Brooks, *The Levels of Attainment in Literacy and Numeracy of 13- to 19-year-olds in England, 1948–2009*. London: National Research and Development Centre for Adult Literacy and Numeracy, 2010.

186 BBC news, 'Literacy Progress Has Stalled, Ofsted's Chief Inspector Says', 15 March 2012. http://www.bbc.co.uk/news/education-17368311 [accessed 1 June 2013].

187 Dr John Newton, 'Coalition "should introduce independent school voucher system"', *The Telegraph*, 31 January 2012.

188 Andrew J. Coulson, 'Markets vs. Monopolies in Education', Cato Institute, 10 September 2008: www.cato.org/pubs/pas/pa620.pdf [accessed 1 June 2013].

189 Mark Twain, *Following the Equator* (1897), 453.

190 Organisation for Economic Co-operation and Development (OECD), data via 'Class Size, Teacher's Pay and Spending: Which Countries Spend the Most and Pay the Least in Education?' *Guardian datablog*: http://www.guardian.co.uk/news/datablog/2012/sep/11/education-compared-oecd-country-pisa [accessed 1 June 2013].

191 Thorpe, Trewhitt and Zuccollo, 'Must Do Better: Spending on Schools'.

192 *Daily Telegraph*, 'More Teachers Quitting the Classroom over

Indiscipline', 26 February 2012.

193 Mark Harrison, 'The Seven Deadly Sins of Government-funded Schools', Cato Institute, 14 August 2005.

194 Claus Moser, 'Schools Inquiry plea to halt "Salt into Ignorance"', *Daily Telegraph,* 21 August 1990.

195 DoE data, 2010–11 via BBC News, 'What Does the Schools Spending Data Show?', 12 January 2011: http://www.bbc.co.uk/news/education-12175480 [accessed 1 June 2012].

196 See Bolton, 'Education Spending in the UK', and Thorpe, Trewhitt and Zuccollo, 'Must do better: Spending on schools'.

197 Ibid.

198 Quoted in Jennifer Steinhauer, 'A Literary Legend Fights for a Local Library', *New York Times,* 19 June 2009.

199 R. K. Webb, 'The Victorian Reading Public,' in *From Dickens to Hardy* (London: Pelican Books, 1963), 149.

200 *The Royal Commission on the State of Popular Education in England,* Parliamentary Papers, 1861, XXI, pp. 293–328; quoted in G. M. Young and W. D. Hancock, eds, *English Historical Documents,* XII, 1 (London: Eyre and Spottiswode, 1956), 891.

201 Ibid.

202 E. G. West, 'Literacy and the Industrial Revolution', *Economic History Review* 31, 3 August 1978.

203 G. Brooks and S. Rashid, *The Levels of Attainment in Literacy and Numeracy of 13- to 19-Year-olds in England, 1948–2009* (London: National Research and Development Centre for Adult Literacy and Numeracy, 2010).

204 E. G. West, 'Literacy and the Industrial Revolution'.

205 Quoted in James Tooley and James Standfield, eds, *Government Failure: E. G. West on Education* (IEA, 2003), 32.

206 Ibid., 90.

207 Quoted in Gene D. Phillips, *Stanley Kubrick* (Warner Books, 1975), 12.

208 Quoted in C. N. Douglas, ed., *Forty Thousand Quotations* (1917).

209 Ibid.

210 Quoted in Paul Schilpp, ed., Albert Einstein, *Autobiographical Notes* (1951), pp. 17–19.

211 T. H. White, *The Once and Future King* (Harper Voyager, 1996),194.

212 Leonardo Da Vinci, Notebooks, chapter XIX Morals, 1.2.1 What Is Life? (1162–1163), No.1175: http://en.wikisource.org/wiki/The_Notebooks_of_Leonardo_Da_Vinci/XIX [accessed 1 June 2013].

213 Plato, *The Republic,* 158.

214 Frank Zappa, liner notes for the album *Freak Out!* (27 June 1966).

215 Charles Dickens, *David Copperfield* (London: Wordsworth Editions, 1992), 139, 140.

Notes

216 Julius Caesar, *Commentarii de Bello Civili* [Commentaries on the Civil War], reprinted by William Mann, ed. (Thomas, Cowperthwait & Company, 1838), 169.

217 John Keats, 'The Vale of Soul-Making', in a letter to George and Georgiana Keats, 14 February 1819.

218 Quoted in *The Literary Works of Leonardo Da Vinci*, vol. 1, part 1 (S. Low, Marston, Searle & Rivington, 1883), 15.

219 Albert Einstein, *On the Method of Theoretical Physics*: the Herbert Spencer lecture, delivered at Oxford 10 June 1933. *Philosophy of Science*, vol. 1, no. 2 (April 1934), 163–9.

220 Fran Lebowitz, 'Tips for Teens': http://www.bizbag.com/Tips%20 for%20Teens/Tips%20for%20Teens.htm [accessed 1 June 2013].

221 Ken Robinson, 'TED Talk: Schools Kill Creativity', February 2006: http://www.ted.com/talks/ken_robinson_says_schools_kill_creativity. html [accessed 1 June 2013].

222 Ibid.

223 Jessica Shepherd, 'Student Debt Nears £60,000 for 2012 University Freshers', *Guardian*, 12 August 2011.

224 Ken Robinson, 'TED Talk', 2006.

225 Quoted in Linda Lear, *Beatrix Potter* (Penguin, 2008), 42.

226 John Stuart Mill, 'On Liberty', 1859 (Cosimo Classics reprint, 2005), 129.

227 Isabel Patterson, *The God of the Machine* (New York: Mises Institute, 2007), 258.

228 Noam Chomsky, *Understanding Power* (Vintage, 2003), 111.

229 Doris Lessing, *The Golden Notebook* (Fourth Estate, 2013), 16.

230 Ezra Pound, *ABC of Reading* (New Directions Publishing, 2011), 84.

231 Marcus Aurelius Antoninus, *Meditations, book I, verse 4*, AD 167.

232 Professor Stephen Arons. *Compelling Belief* (New York: McGraw-Hill, 1983), 88.

233 Ernest Dimnet, *The Art of Thinking* (Fawcett, 1956), 57.

234 Henry David Thoreau, *Walden, vol. 1* (Houghton, Mifflin and company, 1882), 115.

235 Paula Rothermel, 'Home-Education: Aims, Practices and Outcomes' (University of Durham, 2002). Paper presented at the Annual Conference of the British Educational Research Association, University of Exeter, England, 12–14 September 2002.

236 Alan Thomas and Harriet Pattison, *How Children Learn at Home* (Bloomsbury, 2008), 2.

237 Ibid.

238 Paula Rothermel, 'Home-Education: Aims, Practices and Outcomes'.

239 Andrew J. Coulson, 'The Real Cost of Public Schools' (Cato Institute, 2008), http://www.cato.org/blog/real-cost-public-schools.

240 Mill, *Principles of Political Economy*, 580.

241 Mill, 'On Liberty', 129.

242 Tacitus, *Annals, book III,* 27 (*c.* AD 69).

243 Statistics from LibDem home office spokesman Chris Huhne and reported in the *Daily Telegraph* and *Daily Mail,* January 22/23, 2010.

244 Mike Shedlock, 'EU takes Britain to Court over Garlic', *Global Economic Analysis,* entry posted 25 June 2013: http://globaleconomicanalysis.blogspot.co.uk/2012/06/eu-takes-great-britain-to-court-over.html [accessed 1 June 2013].

245 R. Roberts, *The Invisible Heart* (MIT Press, 2002), 26.

246 Bill Hicks, *Shock and Awe,* recorded 1992, B000096FOC, 2009, compact disc.

247 BBC News, 'Heroin use among young "rising"' http://news.bbc.co.uk/1/hi/wales/south_west/7358152.stm [accessed 1 June 2013].

248 Tim Leighton, 'Are Specialists Really Necessary?', Royal College of Psychiatrists: Faculty of Addictions Conference, Cardiff (May 2012).

249 Peter Reuter and Alex Stevens, 'An Analysis of UK Drug Policy', UK Drug Policy Commission. April 2007.

250 Quoted in Terry Crowdy, *French Soldier in Egypt 1798–1801* (Osprey, 2003), 21.

251 Reuter and Stevens, 'An Analysis of UK Drug Policy'.

252 International Centre for Prison Studies (ICPS). 'Prison Brief – Highest to Lowest Rates' (London: King's College London School of Law, 2010).

253 Roy Walmsley, *World Prison Population List.* 8th edn (London: International Centre for Prison Studies, King's College 2009).

254 (ICPS) 'Prison Brief – Highest to Lowest Rates'; Michelle Alexander, *The New Jim Crow* (New York: The New Press, 2010), 59.

255 Cited in American Civil Liberties Union, 'Words From Prison – Did You Know . . . ?', posted 12 June 12, 2006: http://www.aclu.org/womens-rights/words-prison-did-you-know [accessed 1 June 2013].

256 Alexander, *The New Jim Crow,* 59.

257 Edwin Mora, *CNS News,* '47,515 Drug-War Murders in Mexico in Just 5 Years', 12 January 2012.

258 Quoted in John S. Tuckey, ed., *The Devil's Race-track* (University of California Press, 1980), 337.

259 Indur M. Goklany, 'Modern Agriculture: The Pros and Cons of Modern Farming', *Property and Environment Research Center Report,* vol. 19, no.1 (2001), 12.

260 See Matthew R. Simmons, *Twilight in the Desert* (Wiley, 2005).

261 William J. Boyes and Michael Melvin, *Macroeconomics* (South-Western College Publishing, 2012), 31.

262 Edward Abbey, *The Journey Home* (Plume, 1991), 183.

263 Research by charity Empty Homes, based on Council Tax data: http://www.emptyhomes.com/statistics-2/empty-homes-

statistice-201112/ [accessed 1 June 2013].

264　Institution of Mechanical Engineers, 'Global Food; Waste Not, Want Not' (January 2013): http://www.imeche.org/knowledge/themes/environment/global-food [accessed 1 June 2013].

265　US. Food and Agriculture Organization of the United Nations (FAO), 'The State of Food Insecurity in the World', 2012: http://www.fao.org/publications/sofi/en/ [accessed 1 June 2013].

266　Great Britain, Department of Health Policy. 'Reducing Obesity and Improving Diet', 25 March 2013; NHS Information Centre, 'Statistics on Obesity, Physical Activity and Diet', 2012.

267　Robin Yapp, 'Brazil's Obesity Rate Could Match US by 2022', *Daily Telegraph*, 15 December 2010.

268　World Hunger Education Service, '2013 World Hunger and Poverty Facts and Statistics'.

269　Dambisa Moyo, *Dead Aid* (Penguin, 2010), 46–7.

270　Hernando de Soto, *The Mystery of Capital* (Black Swan, 2001), 20.

271　Institute of Liberty and Democracy (ILD). 'What We Believe': http://www.ild.org.pe/about-us/what-we-believe [accessed 1 June 2013].

272　*The Economist*, 'Upwardly Mobile', 25 August 2012.

273　Milton Friedman, *Irish Voice* interview with Sean O'Driscoll, 1 March 2006.

274　Jim Yardley, 'In One Slum, Misery, Work, Politics and Hope', *New York Times*, 28 December 2011.

275　*Slumming It*, Channel 4 television broadcast, January 2010.

276　Ibid.

277　Yardley, 'In One Slum, Misery, Work, Politics and Hope'.

278　Ibid.

279　Ibid.

280　*Slumming It*, Channel 4.

281　Ibid.

282　Milton Friedman, *Why Government Is the Problem* (Hoover Press, 1993), 18.

283　John Kay, 'London's Rise from Sewer to Spectacle', *Financial Times*, 16 January 2013.

284　Shane MacGowan, *Irish Voice* interview with Sean O'Driscoll, 1 March 2006.

285　Angus Maddison, 'World Economics, the West and the Rest in the World Economy', *World Economics*, vol. 9, no. 4 (2008), 76.

286　Douglas Carswell, *The End of Politics*.

287　See E. F. Schumacher, *Small Is Beautiful* (Blond & Briggs, 1973).

288　*The Spectator*, 'Dickens and the Profit Motive', 15 December 2012. NB Profit-making companies have been providing state education in Sweden since 1992, but attempts to do something similar with private providers in the UK have not always been successful. The most famous failure is Southern Cross Healthcare, which operated over 750 care homes and went bust in 2011. On the other hand, in January 2013, Hinchingbrooke hospital A&E, having been one of the worst in the region in 2011, was crowned best in the country in 2012, after private company Circle took over the running.

289 Reported by Isabel Oakeshott and John Harlow in *Sunday Times*, 'PM's Aide Exposes Impotent No. 10', 13 January 2013.

290 Address to the Disarmament Conference of 1932, reprinted in Albert Einstein, *Ideas And Opinions* (Broadway Books, 1995), 95–6.

291 Leon MacLaren, *The Nature of Society* (School of Economic Science, 1997), chapter 1.

292 Milton Friedman, *Capitalism and Freedom* (University of Chicago Press, 1962).

293 United States Department of Defense, 'Total Military Personnel and Dependent End Strength by Service, Regional Area, and Country', 27 November 2012.

294 HousePriceCrash forum: http://www.housepricecrash.co.uk/forum [accessed 1 June 2013].

295 Institute for Truth in Accounting: http://www.truthinaccounting.org [accessed 1 June 2013].

296 Quoted in Henrik Ibsen and Bjornstjerne Bjornson, eds, *Critical Studies, George Brandes* (Kessinger Publishing, 2004), 59.

Acknowledgements

This book is very much a product of the open source movement that is the internet. It could never have happened without all the knowledge, ideas, opinions, discussion and research that are so generously shared and so instantly available. I have drawn on it all with abandon – from highbrow academic work and detailed research reports right through to anonymous comments made on chatboards and at the end of newspaper articles. I've tried wherever possible to credit all sources, but there are so many, there are bound to be occasions when I have failed to do this. If so, I apologize now. But the first people I would like to thank are those of you that share your thoughts, experience, knowledge and opinion online. I am so very grateful.

Next, I would like to thank that other group of generous souls without whom this book would never have happened – those of you that pledged your support. My patrons – thank you for showing faith in me, and thank you for your patience in what has been too long a time getting this book to you. In particular, I'd like to mention Robert Pocock and Brian Cartmell for their generosity.

Subjects in this book range from our monetary systems to the way we give birth. I cannot possibly be an expert on all these subjects and I am not. I would like to thank all those experts who have helped me: Theodore Dalrymple (aka Dr Anthony Daniels), Ben Dyson of Positive Money, Toby Baxendale and Tim Evans of the Cobden Centre, Eliot Watkins, Jeff Tucker of Laissez Faire Books, Addison Wiggin of Agora, Henry Law of the Land Value Tax Campaign and Stephan Kinsella.

I'd like to thank the people at Unbound – and if it wasn't for Tom Hodgkinson of *The Idler* I never would have met them: Dan Kieran for his relentless positivity and enthusiasm – and for the title of this book; John Mitchinson for his calmness and wisdom; editor Isobel Frankish for her eye for detail, patience, never-ending encouragement and good humour; Cathy Hurren for being so bossy and for refusing to take any crap; Kris McManus for the video; Justin Pollard, Caitlin Harvey, Emily Bryce-Perkins, Jane Beaton and Xander Cansell. A special thank you has to be reserved for Emily Brand for her exacting insistence on precision while working under great pressure.

I would also like to thank the good people at *MoneyWeek*. Merryn Somerset Webb, the best financial writer of them all, for asking me to write for them. Merryn – you got me writing again. Editor, John Stepek, for his boundless patience and flexibility. And *especially* MD Toby Bray, for his never-ending support at every stage of this book, and for his superlatively useful comments, even when we were in the middle of a full-blown row. Toby – thank you!

Thank you to the beautiful Tamsin Rickeard, for her constant encouragement and support throughout the whole of this book from pitch to publication.

Finally, thank you to my parents. My mum, Christine Doppelt, in whose eyes I can do no wrong, for her endless faith and praise. And a man whose support, time, effort and help has been without equal, not just with regard to this book, but to the whole of my life. He is the greatest playwright living in the world today – my dad, Terence Frisby.

Subscribers

Unbound is a new kind of publishing house. Our books are funded directly by readers. This was a very popular idea during the late eighteenth and early nineteenth centuries. Now we have revived it for the internet age. It allows authors to write the books they really want to write and readers to support the writing they would most like to see published.

The names listed below are of readers who have pledged their support and made this book happen. If you'd like to join them, visit: www.unbound.co.uk.

Anita Acavalos
Felix Adams
Paul Adams
William Adams
Richard Adamson
Frank Airey
Charles Aitchison
Charlie Aitken
Leon Aitken
Arthur Allison
Altus Strategies Ltd
Christopher Amott
George Amponsah
Ian Anderson
James Anderson
Chas Andrews
Stanislav
  Andryszewski
Anonymous
Anonymous
Anonymous
Dan Antopolski
Martin Archer

Christopher
  Armstrong
Eric Armstrong
Bennett Arron
Ben Ash
Marcus Ashworth
Dan Atkinson
Nigel Atkinson
Mark Attwood
Nicholas Avery
Nick Baile
Malcolm Baker
Steve Baker
Steven Baker
Maurizio Balestrieri
Bill Ball
Andrew Ballantine
Derek Bamford
Phil Barker
Peter Barnes
Ian Barrett
Simon Barry
Konrad Bartelski

John Bartlett
Nick Battrick
James Bayley
Danny Beaudoin
Michael Beaudrie
Nigel Beck
Marc Beder
Graham Benjamin
James Benson
Mark Benson
Knut Erik Berg-
  Hansen
Edwin Berry
Lewis Best
Christine Bhatt
Matthew Bibby
George Biddleston
Andrew Bird
Chris Birtles
Kevin Bischert
Duncan Black
Hubert Bland
Neville Blech

John Denman
Sean Dennien
Philip Denwood
Gerald DeSouza
Sheila Diamond
Louis-Philippe
    DiLauro
David Dillistone
Debbie Dillon
Jason Diluzio
Vaughan Dinsmore
Tomasz Dobek
Noel Doherty
Don't Tread On
    Meme
Kevin Donnellon
Christine Doppelt
James Dowdeswell
Gerard Doyle
Mark Drury
Joe D'Souza
David Dunn
Pascal Dunning
Ed Dupuis
Joe Durak
Tim Durham
Fjodor Duschek
James Eades
Brian Eagle
Michael Eck
David Edmonds
Anne Edwards
Malcolm Edwards
Lyn Egan
Margus Ehatamm
Wekkel Ekkel
Ilicco Elia
Hope Elletson
David Elliott
John Elliott
Paul Ellis
Mark Elvin
Alan Ereira
Mark Estdale
Dan Evans
Michael Evans
Willie Evans
Bill Evetts
Michael Fabbri

Per Fagrell
Anthony Farrant
Noel Faulkner
Rudiger Feiler
Lee Feldman
Peter Ferguson
Mark Fergusson
Eamonn Ferrin
Robert Finnerty
Michael Fisher
Oliver Fisher
Murray Fisk
Andrew Fitts
Gerald Charles
    FitzGerald
Kurt Flamant
Michael Flanagan
Brian Fleming
Adrian Flitcroft
Stephen Flood
Liam Flynn
Peter Ford
Matt Forde
Derek Forrest
Peter Forsberg
Andrew Fothergill
John George
    Fothergill
Rob Fox
Rosie Frampton
Neil Francis
Neil M. Francis
Tom Francis
Isobel Frankish
Neil Fraser
Andrew French
Timothy French
Eliza Frisby
Samuel Frisby
Terence Frisby
Ferdinand Frisby
    Williams
Lola Frisby Williams
Michael Frizell
Richard Frost
Terry Frostick
Bernhard Frye
William Frye
Jonathan Fuller

Richard Furness
Stephen Gaastra
Mark Gahagan
Peter Gaines
Hilary Gallo
Andrew Gamble
Richard Ganley
Nati Garcia
Victor Garcia
Simon Garden
Gregory Gardner
Sandy Garfield
Mike Garside
Stephen Garvey
Simon Gates
Michel Geraissate
Jean Germain
Warren Gilchrist
Andrew Gill
Stephen Gill
Bruno Giversen
Andrew Gladstone
Pete Gold
GoldCore.com – Gold
    Bullion Dealers
Lisa Goldstein
Sophie Goodhart
Robert Goodman
George Gordon-
    Smith
Philip Gosling
Danny Gould
Grier Govorko
Nils Gran
Voula Grand
James Grant
John Gray
Anthony Green
Derek Green
Guy Green
Hugh Green
Paul Greenfield
Edmund Greening
Mark Greening
Suzanne Gregg
Matthew Grice
Darren Griffin
Colin Griffiths
Ground Figure

Rupert Gruen
Sacha Grut
Judith Gunton
Jahor Gupta
William Hackett-
 Jones
Paul Hadley
Magnus Haglund
D Haigh
Denis Haman
Alan Hamilton
Gordon Hamilton
Michael Hampton
Paul Handscombe
Kevin Hanley
Diane Hannon
Tom Harbert
Dominic Harcourt-
 Webster
James Harding
Chris Hardy
Nick Hardy
Ken Harris
Martin Harrison
Andrew Hart
Anne Hart
David Hartley
David Hartnett
Caitlin Harvey
David Harvey
Carl Hashim
Peter Haslam
Mark Haswell
Jon Hather
Peter Heaney
Adrian Hecker
Tim Hegarty
Robert Hegner
Mark Hellaby
Mark Helyer
Louis Hemmings
Gavin Henderson
Geoff Henderson
Stuart Henderson
Matt Hepburn
Bernard Hepplewhite
Ian Heywood
Lee Higgs
Nick Hildred

Doug Hill
W. David Hill
Guy Hills
Chris Hoare
Richard Hoblyn
William Hockenhull
Frank Hodder
Derek Hodge
Tom Hodgkinson
Ross Hoffman
Paul Hoffmeister
Ann Hogarth
Andrew Holder
James Holland
Mike Hollings
Pierre Hollins
Barry Holmes
James Hoontrakul
Christian Hooper
George Hornby
Diana Horner
Vic Hough
Anthony Howard
Ben Howard
Carrie Howes
Craig Howie
Nick Howle
Alex Hubbard
Michael Hudson
Bill Hughes
Joe Hughes
Paul Hughes
Damian Humphreys
Phil Humphreys
Philip Hunter
Tor Inge Husby
Shabbir Hussain
Syahril Hussin
Andrew McAllister
 Hutchinson
Robert Hyatt
Daniel Isaacs
Majeed Jabbar
Chris Jackson
Daren Jacobs
Peter Jadinge
John Jakeways
Alastair James
Laurence James

Paul James
Toby James
Mike Jay
Richard Jefferies
Peter Jenkins
Giles Jerrit
Nathan Jewell
Andrew Johnson
Chris Johnson
James Johnson
Paul Johnson
Alan Johnston
Claire Jones
Colin Jones
Howard Jones
Michael Jones
Nick Jones
Spencer Jones
John Jordan
Mark Jose
Adam Kafka
Petri Kajander
Jalil Kamaruddin
Ashish Kamdar
Gary Kavanagh
Edward Kelly
Paul Kelly
Will Kendall
Will Kenning
Stuart Kenworthy
Malcolm Ketteridge
Dan Kieran
Stirling Kimkeran
Alistair King
Jonathan Kingan
Laszlo Kiralyfi
Stephen Knapp
Katie Knight
Nicola Knight
Robert Knight
Tony Knight
Paul Knott
Aaron Koenig
Deborah Kohn
Peter Kosut
Daniel Krauss
Bronislaw Kruk
Mr Peter Krupa
Paul Kullich

Oliver Kunze
Archavir Kurktchian
Adam Lackie
Virinder Lail
Kwee ying Lam
Dave Lamb
Daniel Lamont
Joness Lang
Valerie Langfield
Mats Larsson
Roger Latham
Ronald Laures
Malcolm Lawrence
Geoff Leach
Jimmy Leach
Sam Leadsom
Richard Lee
Anthony Leese
Robert Leitao
Wojciech Lesniak
Simon Levene
William Lewis
Andy Liao
Alistair Lindsay
Peter Liney
James Lloyd-Davies
Martin Lofgren
William Long
Connie Lopes
Tim Lorimer
Don Lowery
David Lowton
Frank Lucas
Michael Lucey
Deborah Lyons
Franky Ma
Colin Mcandry
David McCabe
Iain Maccallum
Brian McCluggage
Michael McConville
Colum McCoole
Grant McCormack
Alasdair Macdonald
Jamie Macdonald
Ross Mcdonald
McGill Family
Jeremy Mcgivern
Paul McGuinness

Harry MacInnes
Robert McIntosh
Magnus Macintyre
Edward J. Mack Jr.
Dennis McKay
Michael McKay
Ian Mackenzie
James MacKenzie
Steve McLoughlin
Sarah McManus
Clinton Madgwick
Neil Maedel
Wallace Magee
Carlo Maggi
Yogesh Mahajan
Markus Maresch
Alexandros Markesinis
David Marney
Tom Marsden
Joanne Martin
Robert Masding
Peter Masters
Matandu Matandu
John Mathisen
Ronald Matsushige
Catherine Matthews
Larry Matthews
Roger Matthews
Tim Matthews
William Matthews
Ioannis
   Mavrogiannakis
David Maxwell-Lyte
Sally Maybury
Daz Meena
Amjad Mehdi
Mark Mellett
Sean Melody
Naran Mepani
Andy Merritt
Tony Michael
Andrea Michelli
Peter Milburn
Alan Miller
June Millward
Peter Milne
Anna Minton
Sacha Mirzoeff
Ian Scott Mitchell

R. Scott Mitchell
John Mitchinson
Greg Moffitt
Stephen Mold
Silviu Moldovan
Richard Montagu
Robert Monti
Andrew Moon
Paul Moone
David Moore
Michael Moore
Sarah Moore
Ben Moorhead
C. Moretti
Chris Morgan
David Morgan
Paul Morgan
Robert Moriarty
Charles Morris
Geoff Morris
Les Morton
Alan Moss
Elizabeth Moss
Russ Mould
Nick Moult
Waldemar Mrozinski
Dirk Mueller
Orlagh Mullan
Matthias Müller
John Munro
Ben Murphy
Denis Murphy
Gavin S. Murray
   Threipland
Paul Musgrove
Laurence Myers
Rajiv Naik
Pradeep Nalluri
Colin Napier
Eirik Narjord
Hugh Nash
Mohammed Nazir
Unia Ndhlovu
Ben Neale
Ghassan Nehaili
David Neill
Fraser Neilson
Philip Nelson
Keith Neumeyer

Charles Newall
Andrew Newman
Bernard Newman
Peter Newman
Richard Newton
Kim Nguyen
Colin Nicholson
Ian Nicholson
Nigel & Ruth
Malin Nilsson
njs njs
James Noble
Keith Noble
Padraic Noonan
Ross Norman
Andrew David Norris
Sam North
Darren Northall
Matthew Noyes
Ruairi O'Brien
Graham O'Connor
Kevin O'Donovan
Edward O'Hara
Brendan O'Keeffe
John Oliver
Bryan O'Mahony
David O'Reilly
John O'Reilly
Mike O'Reilly
Ian Ormiston
Steven Osborn
James Osborne
Kieran Osborne
Peter Osborne
Lavinia Osbourne
Brian O'Sullivan
Stephen Owens
Dylan P.
Jim Page
Jonathan Paisner
Chris Pallister
John Paoli
Richard Park
Helen Parker
Thomas Parker
Adam Parkin
Tony Parkin
Nigel Parkinson
James Parry

Andrew Parsons
Shailen Patel
Greg Patterson
Martyn Pearce
Paul Pearson
Ian Peckett
Tony Pekarik
Christopher Perry
Larry. Pesavento
Tracy Pettengell
John Pettit
Gregory Petts
Jon Pfaff
Brian Phillips
Peter Phillips
Phill Piddell
Marco Pieters
Robert Pinto-
   Fernandes
Nigel Pitchford
P Brian Pitzel
Duane Poliquin
Morgan Poliquin
Justin Pollard
Jonathan Poole
Roman Pope
Steven Poulton
Mandi Pour
   Rafsendjani
John Power
Patrick Power
Eugenio Pozzo
Prana Capital LLP
Walter Pretorius
Tim Price
Jeff Pritchard
Ken Procter
Nigel Punter
Huan Quayle
Pedro Quelhas
Ann Ralles
Steve Ramsden
Alexander
   Randarevich
Mike Rathmell
Mircea Rau
Peregrine Rawlins
Steve Reay
Nicholas Redfern

Alex Redgrave
James Regan
Omar Rehman
Bill Reid
Douglas Reid
Jason Reid
Lisa Reid
Andy Rendle
David Rhodes
Nicholas Rice
Graham Richards
Alastair Richardson
John Richardson
Jon Richardson
Fred Rickaby
Tamsin Rickeard
Bernard Riley
Sean Ring
David Roberts
Ian Roberts
Jamie Roberts
Samuel Roberts
Wyn Roberts
Antonia Robertson
Ian Robertson
Tim Robertson
Neil Robinson
Eric Robitaille –
   HonestMoney.org
Peter Rockell
Barbara Roddam
Óscar Rodríguez
Dafydd Rogers
Kouros Roshanzamir
Charles Rother
Graham Rowan
Peter Rowe
Chris Roy
Christopher Thomas
   Ruane
John Rubino
Linda Rumble
Leo Ruscillo
Stephen Rush
Nick Russell
Sally Ryder
Patrice Sabatie
Christoph Sander
Bryon Sanders

Justin Sanders
George Satlas
Iain Satterthwaite
Kevin Savage
Steven Saville
Paul Saxby
Eamonn Scanlon
James Scanlon
Detlev Schlichter
Bob Schofield
Reinhard Schu
Toby Schumacher
Max Scianna
Andrew Scott
David Seton
Robert Seward
Bill Shacklock
Richard Shapley
Jeremy Shaw
Kevin Shears
John Shirlaw
John Shore
Paul Simpson
Matthew Skellern
Paul Skinner
John Slind
Adam Smith
Andrew Smith
Chris Smith
David Smith
Graham Smith
Richard Smith
Steve Smith
Tony Smith
Kellie Smitheman
Campbell Smyth
Tony Smyth
Andy Solyom
Richard Soundy
Adrian Spencer
Michael Staedler
Mark Standley
Larry Staples
Mark Staples
John Mark Staude
Adrian J.A. Stead
Alan Stevens
David Stevens
Guy Stevens

Ian Stevens
Peter Stevenson
Tony Stroud
J. Stunt
Dr James H. Sturgeon
Charlie Styr
Frank Sullivan
Udo Sutterlüty
Geoff Sutton
Cecil Swampillai
Stephen Swan
Damian Sweeney
Geoff Swettenham
Will Swift
Jamie Swinton
Amy Sylvis
Christopher Tait
Graham Tanker
Norman Taralrud-Bay
Emma Taylor
James Taylor
Jay Taylor
Ken Taylor
Roger Taylor
Darren Theakstone
Ulf V Thoene
Lee Trevelyan Thomas
Philipp Thomas
Piers Thomas
Richard Thomas
Dave Thompson
David Thompson
John Thompson
Roderick Thompson
Daniel Thorley
Robert Tilly
Frank Tinney
Michael Todd
Ricardo Tomás
Ian Tootill
Ray Toots
Tony Tornquist
Sion Touhig
Evgenia Toulinov
Richard Tregear
Chris Tripoli
Wai Hong Tsang
William Tuke
Fionn Turnbull

Mark Turner
Shaun Turner
Mark Tweedie
Kevin Tyrrell
Jeremy Tyzack
Jag Uarpaw
Paul Vahur
Mike Valiant
Udo van den Heuvel
Heiko van der Linden
Gert van der Neut
Knut Vatneström
Nerina Vaughan
Mark Vent
Mike Vessey
Chris Vezey
Brian Vickery
Lisa Vidergauz
James Vincent
Jose Vizcaino
Jennifer Volk
Charles Vollum
Alan von Altendorf
Andrew Vout
Ted Wainman
Cosmo Wales
Adam Walker
Antony Walker
Graham Walker
Keith Walmsley
Richard Walton
ChiChi Wang
Antony Ward
Martin Ward
Adam Warn
Mark Waterfield
Gerard Waters
Malcolm Waters
Stuart Watkin
Eliot Watkins
Chris Watling
Ian Watson
Mathew Watson
Nigel Watson
Clive Watts
Stephen Watts
William Waugh
David Webb
Jonathan Webb

Aaron Webber
Edward Wells
Jesper Wetterbrandt
Jody Wetton
Chris Wharton-Hood
Paul Whelan
John Whitaker
Andy White
Brian White
Graham White
Mark White
Matthew White
Samuel R White
Trevor White
John Whiten
Andrew Whittaker
John S Whittaker
Barnaby Wiener
Niall Wijetunge
Joss Wilbraham
Brian Wilding

Robert Wiles
Alastair Wilkie
Peter Wilkins
Steve Wilkinson
Lindsay Williams
Tom Williams
Will Williams
Lee Willis
Martin Willitts
David Wilson
Rich Wilson
Steve Wilson
Tom Wilson
Neil Winters
Royston Wise
John Withers
Stefan Woehl
Stephen Wolff
John Wolstencroft
Alice Wong
Anthony Wood

Ian Wood
Ultan Woods
Nick Woolard
Ian Woolley
Michael, Hannah and
    Joe Woolley
Adrian Woolmore
Julian Wooster
Peter Wraith
Felicity Wren
Christopher John
    Lloyd Wright
Paul Wyatt
Roger Yeomans
Mathew Youkee
Andrew Young
James Young
Tony Young
Steve Zoltowski

A note about the typeface

The main text of *Life After the State* is set in Adobe Caslon Pro, a modified version of an older, eponymous typeface designed by William Caslon around 1725. Hailed as both practical and elegant, Caslon drew on seventeenth-century Dutch designs, and the type is said to be a nod towards the earlier (and equally popular) Garamond typeface created in the sixteenth century. The first printings of the American Declaration of Independence were set in Caslon in 1778; in 1931 George Bernard Shaw declared to his printer, 'I'll stick to Caslon until I die'; and Simon Garfield praised its 'vaguely piratical cragginess' in his book *Just My Type*.

American calligrapher and type designer Carol Twombly updated Adobe Caslon Pro while she was working at Adobe Systems between 1988 and 1999. In 1994, she won the prestigious Prix Charles Peignot, awarded by the Association Typographic Internationale to a promising typeface designer under the age of 35. She was the first woman to do so since the prize's inception in 1982.

The headings are set in a modern form of Franklin Gothic, one of the most popular serif types in existence. The original Franklin Gothic was designed by Morris Fuller Benton in 1903 for American Type Founders, a manufacturer of metal type and a business formed in 1892 by the merger of 23 type foundries, between them representing about 85% of all metal type manufactured in the US. In the late twentieth century, a type designer called Vic Caruso began to work on different thicknesses of Franklin Gothic – one of which has been used in this book – for the International Typeface Corporation, founded in 1970 and, ironically, one of the world's first type foundries to have absolutely no historical connection to metal type.